ALL AT SEA

Ensign Louis R. Harlan, January 1945. Photo by Reeves, Atlanta.

All at Sea

COMING OF AGE IN WORLD WAR II

Louis R. Harlan

University of Illinois Press

URBANA AND CHICAGO

This book is printed on acid-free paper.

Library of Congress Cataloging-in-Publication Data

Harlan, Louis R.
    All at sea : coming of age in World War II / Louis R. Harlan.
      p.   cm.
    ISBN 0-252-02232-7 (cloth : alk. paper)
    1. Harlan, Louis R. 2. World War, 1939–1945—Personal narratives,
American. 3. World War, 1939–1945—Naval operations, American.
4. World War, 1939–1945—Campaigns—France—Normandy. 5. Normandy
(France)—History, Military. 6. Seamen—United States—Biography.
7. United States. Navy—Biography. I. Title.
D773.H37   1996
940.54'2142'092—dc20
[B]   95-32515
                                            CIP

To the memory of
Harold W. "Cotton" Clark

Contents

Preface

The writing of this book has been on my mind for many years. World War II haunted my generation of Americans, chiefly because it coincided with our coming of age. The war also released us Americans from the static grip of the Great Depression and set us in motion toward what seemed a noble mission, rescuing Europe and Asia from aggressive tyranny and by the same bold stroke establishing our land of liberty as the leader of a free world. These were distinct goals, but at the time and in the circumstances they blended together in our thought and feeling. It is now more than fifty years since I joined the United States Navy during World War II and took part in D Day, the climactic event of that war, the Normandy invasion of June 6, 1944. Fifty years later we know much more about the events of that time than we knew then, at least in a factual sense. We also know better now how it all turned out, in an imperfect world mission for the United States in the era of the cold war. Historians too young to have stood on the beach at Normandy have been diligently sifting through the documents of several national archives and have interviewed many of the participants. Through their writings we now know which generals' plans went awry, what unexpected developments greeted the first paratroopers, frogmen, and initial assault squads, and sometimes even where the bodies were buried. But for every gain in knowledge of those stirring times, something has also been lost. The public celebration of the fiftieth anniversary of D Day, for example, was an unrelenting glorification of heroism, largely in terms of death. The heroes of Normandy were the dead, and vice versa. Even the survivors who participated in the ceremonies were caught up in this view of the celebration. They the living were not the heroes; their importance derived from their remembrance of fallen comrades. We missed an opportunity in 1994 to learn from the experiences of survivors.

I was one of tens of thousands of young Americans and Brits and Canadians who played a part in the global drama of D Day. Mine was by no means a starring role, but I have some standing to expound on how it really was, at least on my ship on my particular sector of sand on Omaha Beach. I recall bravery but also fear, seasickness, and wanton destruction on that day of wrath. The heroism and self-sacrifice of war is, indeed, worthy of celebration, but darker threads are also woven into the tapestry of even the one "good war" of recent memory. War has hardly proven to be an adequate solution of the problems of the twentieth century. Just as World War I had led directly toward World War II, in its turn World War II led directly into the travails and moral jungles of the cold war. Neither the A-bomb nor the collapse of the Soviet Union brought about an "end of history."

With the optimism of youth I embraced World War II at the time, but I have not felt that any war since then was worthy of my engagement. Both the Korean and the Vietnam Wars seemed to me betrayals of what we had fought for. Though I thoroughly approved of World War II at the time and joined in it wholeheartedly, I also was conscious of the less than heroic way my shipmates and I fought the good fight. Oh, we were generally of stout enough heart, but we were also self-serving, amateur warriors, and capable of thoughtless cruelty to those not part of our group. We hadn't a clue as to where the war was leading us. We were babes in the woods, adolescents awkwardly moving toward manhood. It would be an understatement to say that we made mistakes.

Because World War II strongly influenced my decision to become a professional historian, it is appropriate that I return the favor, applying the skills of the historical craft, if not always history's objectivity, to the problems of memory that plague any writer recounting long-past events. My own memory of the war is strongly colored by the war stories I have told friends and relatives over the years. The memories

I repeated were firmly fixed; those I did not repeat faded into oblivion. The seeming clarity of remembrance has been achieved by repetition. A selective memory unconsciously retains what advances the story, to the neglect of less functional details. I noticed in my recent interviews of my shipmates that they often had forgotten episodes in which I was involved, but remembered, more clearly than I, occasions when they were at the center of the action. There is also another plague of memoirists, the conscious or unconscious desire to appear in a good light, to justify one's course of action and have the last word. Since many of my war stories poke fun at pretensions, including my own, I believe I have usually avoided the pitfalls of self-serving memory. But the reader should remain on guard against my possible lapses.

As a check on the distortions of unaided memory over such a long span of time, I have gathered in the past ten years a considerable amount of documentation. This began in 1984. When I was very sick in a hospital, newspapers all over the country announced that I had won the Pulitzer prize for a biography of Booker T. Washington. My book had also won other prizes, but because the Pulitzer involves journalists the media always give it much more attention than other prizes. My health, naturally, took an immediate turn for the better. More to the point, while I lay in my hospital bed my girlfriend of World War II days, the Diana of my story, read about the Pulitzer and called me long distance. I hadn't heard from her in decades, but fleeting fame has a power to rekindle even very old embers. "Did you save the letters I wrote you during the war?" I asked her. She did. They were in a shoe box in her closet, and she agreed to send them to me. Later she found an additional shoe box. I now have photocopies of all these letters, and have liberally quoted from them in this recounting of my wartime experiences. Unfortunately, I had long before burned her letters to me.

Harold W. "Cotton" Clark, the executive officer of my ship during the first year of my story, and then the skipper throughout the following year, secretly kept a diary of the first year. Because it naturally reflected his own viewpoint rather than mine, it offers a rich counterpoint to my own memories and letters of the same period. Regrettably, at the end of our European sojourn, soon after Clark became skipper, his new rank brought an increased sense of responsibility, and he stopped making entries in his diary because that would violate *Navy Regulations*. My letters to Diana continued, however. They were soon supplemented by other letters from Sylvia, my California love, that cast a strange reflected light on my year in the Pacific. Curiously, I have all or most of my letters to Diana but only two from her that somehow escaped the bonfire in my backyard after the war. I have all of Sylvia's letters to me, but only one of mine to her, and after 1946 I completely lost touch with her.

Other sources supplement the letters and diary. For the entire period from commissioning to decommissioning of LCI(L) 555, the ship's log is preserved in the National Archives. The log is a rather dry record of technical data—the location and movements of the ship each day, the weather, and so on—but it is helpful in fixing the exact time of key events. The National Archives also has official reports of the battles we took part in. In 1991 I taped extensive interviews with Harold W. Clark and Russell Tye, fellow officers aboard the 555. They also recalled many of our common experiences, often from a different perspective, and brought back to mind things I had completely forgotten. I have in my possession tapes and transcripts of these interviews.

The illustrations presented a special problem. I did not own a camera at the time, and what few photographs others gave me I kept for fifty years in a Christmas card box. Russell Tye and Gloria Clark have supplemented them with others in their possession. Remarkably, none of us had any photographs of Jack Flinn, the ship's first skipper. Not only did he not like to be photographed but none of us wanted his photograph, or wanted to keep it. I must leave his appearance, therefore, to the imagination of the reader.

As this manuscript emerged from the chrysalis of my war stories, a number of friends were burdened with the reading of various drafts. The most long-suffering of the readers was my wife Sadie, who heard all of the war stories more than once and read every draft, even my account of wartime romances. She deserves a service ribbon if not a medal. Ray Smock, for many years my co-editor of the Booker T. Washington Papers, also helped me edit the present manuscript and made many helpful suggestions. My fellow historian Otto H. Olsen provided counterpoint by virtue of his own experience as a merchant seaman and officer in many of the same waters. Russell Tye, my ship-mate, corrected my memory of many shared experiences. Mary Giunta directed my attention to photographs in the National Archives. Teresa Hruzd and Darlene King saved me from several disasters in this, my first book written on a word processor. I thank the copyeditor, Patricia Hollahan, for good advice, a sharp eye for errors, and even improving my French.

ONE

Ninety-Day Wanderer

The bus transporting me to my ship was no Greyhound but a broken-down school bus commandeered into wartime service. It rattled its way through a cold rain in early March 1944, leaving at midnight from the Navy Yard in Washington toward the naval amphibious base at Solomons, Maryland. I sat there on the hard seat in my unbelievably heavy officer's greatcoat, its shiny new epaulettes emphatically proclaiming me "ensign" (or was it "insane"?) in the United States Naval Reserve. I had just taken my place in the hierarchy of the wartime military, with a secure status at last after three humiliating months of midshipman training, and was on my way to my first assignment. The Navy ranked me above the many in their bell-bottoms and peacoats, but at the very bottom of the few. I was an officer on the outside, but at heart still a midshipman, said to be the lowest form of naval life. My overcoat was the biggest thing about me, reaching below my knees, but even it was not enough to keep out the chill that crept through the door and window cracks of the ancient bus, a chill that was of a piece with all of my Navy experience thus far. I hadn't been warm since the Navy had snatched me the previous fall from the warm cocoon of my southern college and taken me north to New York City.

During the long night ride, I tired of what little I could see in the rain and darkness of the coastal plain outside, and inside the bus was a similar monotony of peajackets and close-cropped heads. As I alternated between light sleep and bare awakening, my mind flashed backward to the ego-bruising experience of midshipmen's school. I had been a

stranger in a strange land, beginning as an adolescent and ending not
quite matured into the shape and spirit of manhood. If I had had the
gravitas of a fatter man, I wondered, instead of being a lean 140 pounds,
would I have cut a more impressive figure in close-order drill? If only
I had a larger head and impassive face instead of a thin visage swallowed up by my visor hat and outsize ears! If only my face were a mask
instead of a mirror of my feelings. I combined incongruously the intellectual and physical self-confidence of a college Phi Bete athlete with
the insecurity of one who graduated in the bottom half of my midshipmen's school class, baffled by its technological view of the world. Occasionally my mind wandered forward to my vague, uncertain future,
to the unknown ship I was traveling to meet and the cold, gray sea I
would sail upon for the first time. It seemed to me that the one great
fault of midshipmen's school was that it taught us nothing about the
sea.

In a sense the Navy and I had been fellow travelers toward a rendezvous for two years. For me, as for many other young men of my
generation, the war seemed part and parcel with my passage from adolescence to manhood. War and manhood merged into one in the rite
of passage. Drills and inspections and uniforms were all part of the
ritual. Hence our scorn of the 4Fs and the feather merchants who were
excluded from the rites. War was our generational destiny, and we could
only dimly imagine the peacetime ahead when war would no longer
be central to our lives. Hence the nostalgia the forties generation would
later feel for "the good war." They would perceive it not only as good
in purpose but good in its effect on their lives. To the forties generation, war had a central place similar to antiwar in the lives of the six-
ties generation. The whole world was ablaze with war, and its cycles
dated and punctuated the stages of our lives. I could still remember the
tears of gratitude in my mother's eyes when Chamberlain returned
from the Munich Conference proclaiming "peace in our time." But the
war came anyhow with a seeming inevitability. France fell the week I
graduated from high school in the class of 1940. My generation, at least
in the South, was totally committed to the Allied side. I heard only one
person express sympathy with the Nazis. She was a voice student who
hung around with German-born opera singers. News of the Japanese

attack on Pearl Harbor found me at college, in the middle of a Sunday afternoon touch football game. I was then a sophomore at Emory University, commuting to classes by bicycle and working half-time to pay my college expenses and fraternity dues. Though painfully shy, I found in college the honor and status that I had been denied in high school as the brother of the school's "bad boy." I worked my way through college in the dean's office, the university print shop, and the library, later as a National Youth Administration coach in an elementary school, and finally as a lifeguard at the university indoor pool. I found my true home in the Emory library and on the university swimming team.

After many false starts and brief encounters, I found a steady girl, Diana, whom I planned to marry as soon as we both grew up and the war ended. I was far surer of my own feelings than of hers. Girls were by definition a mystery, after all, and Diana the huntress kept her own counsel in matters of the heart. I gradually learned that she was torn between her own warm heart and the code of Atlanta sub-debs known as "pinks." I first met Diana at a swimming party in a lake, the ideal setting for me to show off my physique and swimming prowess. Or did I win her over by the whimsy of my conversational style as I played Lil Abner to her Daisy Mae? The bad news was that she was from out of town and was only visiting her aunt in Atlanta for the summer. Our relationship was largely epistolary almost from the beginning. Diana had just graduated from high school and was on her way at summer's end to a girls' college in Virginia. Almost as tall as I, she had a good figure, broom sedge blonde hair, dreamy hazel eyes above an uptilted nose, and the most kissable rosebud lips I had ever seen. A face that would launch at least one ship, and a figure of generous proportions. Her outspoken grandmother once described her succinctly as "big tits, big butt, and stubborn as a mule." My infatuation with Diana for the moment replaced even world war, the great romance of our time. Later, when war came closer, the motive behind any derring-do I dreamed of would be to shine in her eyes.

In 1942, not embarrassingly long after Pearl Harbor and before being eligible for the draft, I volunteered one morning to be sworn into the Navy, along with several dozen other sheepish youths at an empty movie theater in downtown Atlanta. Though held hostage overnight at a collection point near the Atlanta airport, I was considered officer material on account of my college status and was placed on inactive duty in the Navy's V-1 program until such time as I graduated from college or Uncle Sam needed me, whichever came first. So my oath of allegiance was not without "purpose of evasion." Though I never heard the matter plainly stated, the Navy then had all the officer candidates it had training schools for, or ships to assign them to.

I returned to college after my induction only nominally a serviceman, without uniform, with only an identity card to distinguish me from draft-dodgers and 4Fs who were everywhere reviled. Being in the Navy made little immediate change in my life except in two particulars. Instead of working every summer I now attended summer sessions in hope of graduating before the Navy took me. And I added science courses, including an entire year of physics, in the expectation that its abstractions would somehow be transmogrified into useful knowledge when I became a naval officer. In fact, I never found any use whatever for physics in the Navy. Perhaps I needed more physics, or perhaps more quantum theory that was then coming into vogue.

The Navy arrived on campus in a rush in the spring of 1943, beginning the V-12 program. The university continued to operate with its faculty and classes intact, but changed its academic schedule to a trimester system. The Navy enlistees on campus, however, and others brought in from other colleges, were now put into uniform—bell-bottom trousers, dinky shirts (blouses!), and coats of navy blue, topped by the ludicrous round caps that only tradition could justify. Large contingents were transferred from the University of Georgia and other schools as far away as Kentucky to fill the dormitories commandeered by the Navy. After nearly three years of commuting to college, I found myself living in a dormitory room with four other Navy gobs, none of whom I had ever seen before. We soon established a rough camaraderie, marred only by the obvious effeminacy of one of the roomies. He made a valiant effort not to stand out as different, but between dark and dawn he indulged in pirouettes and other ballet steps, and he consorted with other enlistees of suspect sexual preference. The rest of us tried to ignore it.

The naval officers assigned to our campus studiously avoided inter-
ference with our classes, confining themselves to indoctrination by
calisthenics at the crack of dawn, marching us to and from the dining
hall, and occasional afternoon assemblies. At one of these assemblies
the commanding officer of our unit, a rough customer from Texas,
shouted in a threatening manner what was intended to be a reassurance. "Don't be afraid of me," he said, "I shit out of a meat ass-hole
just like the rest of you." There were a few guffaws from the audience,
but most of us were shocked by the crude language of our leader. It
was my first introduction to the sustained foul language of men among
men, as distinguished from the less steady stream of dirty words of
adolescents. We heard later that the commander was upbraided by
college officials who found his language inappropriate on a liberal arts
campus, particularly a Methodist one. It remained, however, the most
memorable learning experience of that trimester, in class or out. The
university bent a little to adjust to the new circumstances. Up until
then, in appeasement of Southern Methodist leaders, the school had
outlawed dancing on campus except at the privately owned fraternity
houses. Now, under Navy auspices, there were dances every weekend
in the mess hall, complete with jitterbugs as well as us ordinary danc-
ers. By taking six courses I managed to graduate with full credits in
that first and only trimester, and in late October along with two of my
roommates and many others I "shipped out" to midshipmen's school.
I learned later that seniors called into service a few courses short were
given their degrees, but that was unnecessary in my case.

As a child of the Great Depression I had had little chance to travel.
The train ride to midshipmen's school at Columbia University and my
three months' training there were the farthest distance and the longest time I had ever been away from home and family. At twenty-one I
was too old to cry, but homesickness was no respecter of age. Its agony was even worse for being tearless and so long delayed, and it did
not pass for the entire three months of fall and winter in that northern clime. Furthermore, the winter of 1943–44 was severe. Cold rain,
whistling wind, and more snow than in all my previous years didn't
help my homesickness. My memory of those months is a smear of
dirty snow, muddy shoes, and bone chill.

When our troop train pulled into Penn Station, my former room-mates and I dashed for a few minutes aboveground to gawk at the canyons of midtown Manhattan before descending again to the subway for our ride to Columbia University. We did not know it then, but we wouldn't see the bright lights of midtown again for three weeks. The subway was another new experience. Not yet made garish by spray-paint graffiti, the subway was grimy from forty years of shuffling feet, but the tilework at the subway stops was impressive. We poured out of the 116th Street station in a state of high anticipation. Our orders were to report to John Jay Hall to begin our lives in the sixteenth class of the United States Naval Reserve Midshipmen's School.

Begun by presidential proclamation in June 1940 and disgorging half-trained ensigns every three months since, the midshipmen's school at Columbia had grown from 200 in the first class to our class of 2,500 cadets, taking over more and more of the university as its civilian student body dwindled on account of the war and the draft. That every midshipman was white did not strike me then as either unusual or inequitable, so conditioned to segregation had I become. After all, my public school and college and V-12 program had also been all white. The city of New York was equally segregated residentially and occupationally. My only contact with black people while there was when I went to swim at a YMCA pool near the Columbia campus in south Harlem, or when I watched the black future tennis star Althea Gibson practicing on the campus courts near our drill field, one of the few places she could find a tennis court available to her.

Arriving at John Jay Hall, my home for the next sixteen weeks, I found that I had been assigned to a room on the tenth deck. Those on the decks above ten were allowed to ride the building's only elevator; those on deck ten and below were expected to run double-time up and down stairs. Being on deck ten, I had the maximum number of stairs to run. We had only a short while to contemplate the luxuriousness of our quarters, a ten-by-ten room with a double bunk—naturally I had the upper. We were soon escorted to a haberdashery at Broadway and 112th Street, where I acquired 25.6 pounds of shoes, shirts, socks, suits, and other clothing, carefully selected of course by expert tailors.

Indoctrination occupied our full attention for the first three weeks, at the end of which came the dreaded bilge list. We discovered that those ubiquitous officers, who so thoughtfully inquired our names as they checked our getting up and our going to bed and everything in between, were actually compiling dossiers on each of us, attesting to our fitness to be officers. The routines were endless: standing out in the cold for morning roll call, calisthenics, close-order drill, standing watch, double-timing up and down stairs several times a day. Was it all necessary, we often asked ourselves, and didn't it interfere with our classes and study, which were surely more important than the little, niggling things they hounded us about? We soon learned that the way to stay off report was to avoid the attention of officers whenever possible.

After the three weeks of screening were over, miraculously I was still alive. The officers apparently did not know my unfitness for monotony as well as I did. That weekend we received our first liberty. Some newfound friends and I celebrated our survival by walking down Broadway to 42nd Street, stopping at every oyster bar we passed to have a dozen on the half shell. We did what servicemen did everywhere—went to the movies, hit the USO, and gradually found where the nightclubs were.

On weeknights, we were too busy doing homework to get liberty in town, and it wasn't allowed even if we had had free time. Weekends also often involved guard duty, though exactly what we were guarding so carefully I never understood. Guard duty was just another of the things "they" did to "us" to grind us down, one of the "thousand natural shocks" that Shakespeare spoke of. I do remember, however, a few free Saturdays. On one of these, my former V-12 roommate Mitch received a visit from his fiancée. She brought a friend, and I was chosen to double-date at the movies, dinner, and Tony Pastor's nightclub. Another time, a group of young women from across the Hudson in Elizabeth, New Jersey, did their part for the war effort by inviting midshipmen to a weekend house party in the suburbs. I attended and was assigned an attractive date, but I was miserable because I could not measure up to her idea of manly prowess. A pond in the yard had been frozen into a skating rink, and I had never seen an ice skate before. Though I made a valiant effort to stand up to this latest challenge of Yankeeland, I never mastered the art of standing. I spent the afternoon as the sore butt of cruel laughter. Feeling that my date was ashamed of me made it a very long weekend, and I was glad when it was time to return to my billet and nurse my bruised ego. On another weekend, I escaped from greater New York entirely by a train trip to Elizabeth. June, a friend from high school days who had somehow learned my address, invited me down there to a dance given by fellow workers in a war plant. Years earlier, she used to follow me home from high school and gradually overcame my shyness. She had become a nurse after high school, but a long assignment at a mental hospital was so disagreeable that she abandoned nursing to work in a war plant. She was a "Rosie the riveter," but I cannot recall quite what it was they riveted in Elizabeth. Many of her fellow workers were of East European origin, and the polka was their dance of choice. The fitness program of midshipmen's school had prepared me physically if not culturally, and dozens of dances taught me the polka in a hurry. I have avoided it ever since. June, on the other hand, I would see again just after the war at the Brooklyn Navy Yard, where she had returned to nursing duty in the Navy.

I recall little about my classes every day in navigation, seamanship, ordnance, damage control, and Navy regulations, except that my liberal arts skills seemed inadequate to unlock this endless new world of the practical and technical. How could a man who had never been to sea really understand seamanship, or navigate accurately by stars he couldn't distinguish from each other? Oh, I got a smattering of this and that by rote, as did others around me, but our hurry-up midshipmen's school was not Annapolis. Our class in seamanship spent only one morning tying knots under the eye of an impatient chief petty officer at the USS *Prairie State,* an obsolete battleship converted into a training ship. A week later those knots were all untied again in my mind. Plane recognition was only a blur on the screen to begin with, and soon became even blurrier as the number of planes mounted.

At the time I lacked perspective on my difficulties as an officer trainee. I accepted the rationale that underlay the program and blamed myself for my inability to meet its standards of what knowledge was most valuable. In retrospect, I believe the Navy mistakenly tried to train us rather than educate us. Close-order drill, for example, designed to train us to unthinking obedience, would be virtually useless aboard a ship. Our classes crammed our rote memory but neglected to challenge our skeptical intelligence, curiosity, or spirit of intellectual play, the very qualities for which we college men were presumably being recruited. All work and no play made Jack—this Jack, anyhow—a dull midshipman.

Though half-educated at best, we were thoroughly drilled, for midshipmen's school was administered like a boot camp. We marched everywhere—to chow, to classes, to the parade ground, even to church, for religion was part of our duty. There may have been some undiscovered atheists in foxholes during that war, but none were recognized at midshipmen's school. You were either a Protestant, a Catholic, or a Jew. At first, I marched unprotestingly with the Protestants to the nondenominational Riverside Church a few blocks from the campus, a magnificent structure under the leadership of the Reverend Harry Emerson Fosdick. We only heard Fosdick once, however. A Navy chaplain presided over our regular services and droned a commonplace sermon best suited to robots. After a month or so of this, I expressed a preference for Catholicism because it allowed me to fall out of ranks and walk, not march, with a smaller crowd to, believe it or not, a less formal service. I was not Catholic, but it was my preference.

The drill instructor of my company was a bullnecked, barrel-chested brute, Ensign T. E. Pounds, a former chief petty officer who had accepted a commission apparently for the pure pleasure of bullying us future officers. It seemed to be his duty to humble our spirits. He murdered the English language in a very loud voice, but we didn't dare tell him so. In fact, we were terrified of him and trembled in his presence. With him, it seemed, there could be no appeal to reason. Our communications with him consisted entirely of yes sir, no sir, and no excuse sir. Probably deep in his heart this raging bull was insecure, but he could not have been more insecure than those under his command. War has a way of throwing authoritarian personalities to the top, and Ensign Pounds would not be the last one I would meet. His favorite expression was "I shoulda joined t'Army." It doesn't sound so bad on paper, at a distance of fifty years, but the key to its effectiveness was delivery, and the power of office.

9

Midway through the training program, one Saturday with three or four friends I took a ferryboat ride to the Statue of Liberty. Hardly had the ferry got underway when it swung into the wind. The wind lifted my midshipman's hat and sailed it like a kite for several seconds before it landed in the water. I stood bareheaded watching my hat float astern and gradually sink, hardly realizing it was mine. The crowd laughed and cheered. Even my friends joined in, making light of this disaster, but my heart sank as I began to realize my predicament. Nobody on earth is more vulnerable than a midshipman without his hat. I finally laughed with the others, but all afternoon I scurried from pillar to post hiding from officers, who seemed to appear everywhere "not single spies but in battalions." On the way back the subway station was crawling with officers. My friends, now that they had had their laugh, stood watch for me while I hid behind the massive pillars of the subway station. At the last second I made a dash for the subway car, and while riding northward we plotted our strategy. We got off one stop south of the Columbia University station at 112th Street, and I skulked below while my friends scouted for officers aboveground. On their all-clear signal, I ran as fast as I could out of the station, hoping I would only be a blur to passers-by, or that my speed rather than my hat would be the most noticeable thing about me. Luckily the Saks clothing store a block up Broadway from the station was still open, and I could charge a hat there. I found one that actually fit, unlike my previous one that had sailed so easily off my head, and I strolled out as the cock of the walk. This was one of the few moments of mastery I experienced during midshipmen's school.

With the exception of that ferry ride, the only experience we midshipmen had of going down to the sea in ships was on one bitterly cold January day. Before dawn we went by Navy bus to a dock in the wasteland of Flushing Flats and boarded a YP or a PY, I am not sure which. It was a harbor craft converted into a training ship by the installation of guns and other Navy equipment. We donned foul-weather gear that gave us the look of "men from Mars" but was not warm enough to keep out the chill as we cruised Long Island Sound in midwinter, practiced our signals and boat drills, and pretended to fire the guns. We rotated from one watch station to another under the close attention of instructors and crew, and stole what time we could below decks to thaw our aching hands and feet. At noon we dropped anchor at Cold Spring Harbor and eagerly devoured the box lunches that had been the butt of early morning jokes. After chow, our final test of seamanship was to weigh anchor and bring our ship safely back to the dock.

Christmas far from home provided leisure enough only for loneliness and self-doubt. Our constant anxiety about possible failure subsided somewhat in January, when the final bilge list was posted. "Needless to say, I was not on it," I wrote Diana, hiding my great relief. "One of the boys in V-12 with me bilged out today. I wish I knew of something that would be of some comfort to him, but I just can't think of anything. The worst part of it is that although he is a stupid egg, he thinks he's a genius or something like that and all this failure is a surprise to him." In characterizing him, I could have been describing myself, except that by some miracle I still survived.

We midshipmen continued, however, to live in terror of some careless slip that would end our brief careers. "Here I am on watch again," I wrote Diana. "Nothing has happened so far since I relieved, but I'm looking for an officer to pop up any minute and ask me what my Air Raid and Fire drill duties are. I know them too, by damn, and also that the fire-bucket is aft by the hoist and that when a member of the off section of the watch, I lay below and stand by to evacuate the ship's records from the disbursing office—in other words when I'm not on duty I run down and tote the filing cabinets out." While I was standing watch and was in the middle of writing this very letter an officer did appear, sat down in my chair, and chatted with me. "They stand outside in the stairway and write an aptitude slip on me after they leave," I wrote. "I don't think I got a very good one. I wish I could hold my tongue. Just as he was about to leave he asked me what condition the windows are in an Air Raid drill. Like a rash fool I popped up with 'They are called ports, sir, but they are closed.' He turned red with either embarrassment or anger, mumbled a few words and left. I am really worried."

An omen of my probable survival, however, was that the administrative officers of the school inquired what sort of duty assignment I wanted. As I wrote to Diana, "Any time you feel like feelin proud of me you can go right ahead. Cause I'm right proud of myself too." We had adopted a mock-southern spelling in imitation of our cultural hero, Lil Abner, and would continue it for the remainder of the war. "I've just volunteered for duty in the amphibious forces (landing craft for tanks and infantry). I'm pretty sure I'll be able to get it too, because the government is building more of them than all other craft put together. I applied for Atlantic Fleet too and may get there in time for the invasion of Southern France." Not only was I sure what kind of ship I wanted without ever actually having seen a landing craft, but I even thought I knew where the long-awaited assault on Fortress Europa would occur.

Figuring large in my calculations was that two of the Navy's three amphibious bases were along the East Coast, one at Solomons, Maryland, and the other at Little Creek, Virginia. "We have no maps in here," I wrote Diana, "so how about measuring off the mileage, & customarily traveled routes" between these bases and her college town. "Don't you wish you were going to France?" I asked. "I bet you're jealous. I hope you are jealous of French women. . . . I just feel so exhilarated tonight that even so far away from you I can't be sad."

"I still feel happier than a June-bug with you loving me and other things going so well," I wrote Diana soon afterward. As a member of the midshipmen's school swimming team I had won two races and anchored the winning relay in a meet against Brooklyn College. Though my ego had otherwise been badly bruised, I could still take pride in my athletic prowess. I was full of plans to visit Diana as soon as I graduated and got the customary week's leave. "Some say Amphibs are good duty and some say they aren't," I wrote. "But they sound like a lot of good sport to me. Our job will be to carry men, supplies, and tanks to the beaches of an island we are invading in small ships, make a landing, unload them, and go back for another load."

Landing craft were much on my mind in the final days of midshipmen's school. "Speaking of Amphibs," I wrote Diana, apropos of nothing, "we get 12 weeks training in most cases here in the U. S. and then are carried across to one of the battle zones, probably to the Mediterranean if I get Atlantic Fleet. The Isle of Capri and gay Paree are over that way, aren't they? An old-timer friend of mine told me right after

I got in the Navy 'If you get within walking distance of France, start walking, for it will be well worth your while.' I hope you are jealous-er than hell. Seriously, though, we are going to be the boys who will win the war. The big ships have largely done their job of defense. Now that the tide of the war has changed invasion is the battle-cry, and I aim to be right in the thick of it."

Diana must have encouraged my obsession with landing craft, for I wrote a few days later, "I'm glad you like the idea of amphibs. At a time like this I believe that's the only branch of the naval service to get in. So you know something about LCT's, huh? I want an LCI for transporting infantry and making a beachhead but of course I'll have to take what they give me." "I may flunk out yet," I added. "My easiest course, Navigation, suddenly got into a hard part, celestial navigation, while I sat back in comfort till suddenly I discovered I didn't know where first base was. Now I'm scared to death."

My romantic fixation on the LCI (Landing Craft, Infantry) continued, though I had never seen one except in photographs. "That picture you sent was of an LST—" I wrote Diana, "the largest of the landing craft, which are of various shapes and sizes depending on their use. They all look more like river tugs than anything else. The LCI only is a pretty ship [I drew its silhouette] with a clipper bow and graceful lines. It carries infantry troops. Then the LCV carries jeeps, peeps, artillery vehicles, etc. The LCP is a small personnel boat, the LCVPs carry both. Etc. Etc. But I'm hoping for LCI duty. . . . I ought to be in the Mediterranean or Pacific war zone by May. Then again I might get DE [Destroyer Escort] School with 4 months training. You never can tell after you've once joined the Navy."

It soon became clear that I would graduate slightly below the middle of the class. "You know, it feels mighty good in a way to be getting right into this big war after watching it from the sidelines for so long," I wrote Diana. "It's just like admiring the job another person's doing and feeling all the time that you ought to be doing more than standing around admiring it. And Midshipman Harlan now sweeping his billet day by day will soon be sweeping the seas."

We arose early on February 24, 1944, polished our shoes to a high shine, and marched to the graduation ceremony of the Sixteenth Class of Reserve Midshipmen. In a separate ceremony, we were sworn in as ensigns. I was now, miraculously but almost irrevocably, a naval officer, with all the responsibilities and insecurities thereunto appertaining. I threw my hat in the air with the others, but I had dark forebodings. I had learned the hard way that my kind of verbal intelligence was not highly prized in the gruff and stumble of the drill field. I felt ill-suited and ill-prepared to deal with the practical problems of a ship at sea. The war seemed to be rushing me into manhood before I was quite ready for it. In this siege of self-doubt I was surely not alone, though I felt alone. The war would be a transforming experience for an entire generation of Americans, who would later remember it with a nostalgia not justified by the evidence.

"My orders have come," I wrote Diana on graduation day. "I report February 28th to the Commandant of 3rd Naval District here in New York City." My anticipated week's leave had shrunk to just three and a half days, too short a time to return home and visit my parents, but time enough for a weekend with Diana at her college in Virginia. "I guess I was a fool to count on a week or so," I wrote. "It's disappointing as heck, and I've been wishing I had somebody's shoulder to cry on, namely yours." Sea duty, I reflected, did not mean necessarily that I would go directly to a war zone. It probably meant a training base in England or somewhere else outside the continental United States. Sea duty also meant that I would get my first month's pay in advance, plenty of money to enjoy liberty every night until the Navy made up its mind where to send me.

I took a hurried train ride to Diana's college, staying in the college guesthouse and facing down the suspicious harpies who guarded the virtue of young ladies in the dorm. Diana and I escaped to the local movie theater one night, and to a play the next, and when we were alone for a moment in the closely chaperoned drawing room of the dormitory, I planted a daring kiss in the cleavage between her breasts. She gave a reassuring gasp. I hoped that that signified a passionate nature, but I did not press my luck any further. After all, I was a virgin myself.

Standing in a train aisle all the way back to New York to the tune of a sailor's guitar, I arrived in the big town about dawn, got my first barbershop shave in the station, grabbed a cup of coffee, and lurched with my seabags toward the naval district headquarters on Church Street. I dropped my orders into a waiting hand, flopped into a conveniently positioned chair, and fell instantly asleep. The next thing I knew was a loud voice thundering in my ear, "You are to report to Norfolk Naval Operating Base in the morning." Someone thrust a transportation request into my hand and shoved me back toward Pennsylvania Station. There I managed to get a Pullman reservation on a train leaving at midnight. I had all day on my hands, if I could stay awake to enjoy it.

Leaving my seabags in a locker, I walked to the Hotel Commodore and bought a third-row ticket to see Paul Robeson play Othello that night at the Shubert Theatre. I chose it over "Oklahoma!" and other hit plays in that heyday of Broadway theater, and I like to think that it was because, almost unconsciously, I was ready for a shock to my received southern attitudes about black people. I sat transfixed and not the least bit sleepy during the three-hour performance. Uta Hagen was Desdemona and José Ferrer played Iago, but it was Robeson I had come to see and Robeson I would remember. He filled the stage with his magnificent presence. I may have turned a corner in my life that night. I would like to think that from then on I began to judge black people as individuals. Alas, that memory is contradicted by evidence in my wartime letters. I remained a racist, but this and other wartime racial encounters with black people and white liberals set me on a path that diverged from my southern heritage.

Boarding the Pullman, I slept until eleven o'clock the next morning. The Pullman porter had to drag me bodily from the berth, and I lay inert in the aisle, still largely asleep. Since my body blocked traffic, the porter stuffed me back in the lower berth, and I finally awakened. We still had not reached Norfolk, wartime train service being what it was. When we finally did reach our destination, I had to catch one bus after another to reach the base, then was routed from one building to another, meanwhile without food or drink. At last I leapt the last hurdle of this unique commando course and stood like a hound dog, beaten almost to my knees, before the appropriate lieutenant (j.g.). Lifting a finger, he spelled my doom: "Report immediately to Amphibious Training Base, Solomons, Maryland, for transportation to your ship." Why had my superiors in their wisdom sent me all the way to Norfolk instead of directly to Solomons? Mine not to reason why.

Taking two more city buses to reach downtown Norfolk, I got a room at the Navy YMCA where I could leave my bags while buying my train ticket. As I put down my bags, however, an irresistible force dragged me to the bed, and before I knew anything else I awakened the next morning, fourteen hours later. According to my orders, I had to be out of town by noon, and it was too late to go by train. I stood up on the bus all the way to Washington, only to find that I had yet more time to kill, as the next bus to Solomons left at midnight. There must have been an aura of newly minted ensign about me, because for the first time in my life I was picked up by three women, ditching each of them in turn for a less attractive one until the last was so homely that my only escape was to take the Navy bus to Solomons. At least, that was the story I told Diana. Four hours' sleep and six hours of pacing the floor at the Solomons naval base finally brought me to my ship. This four-day odyssey of misdirection foreshadowed my wanderings aboard ship for the next two years, but fortunately I could not know that at the time. I was eager for the adventure that beckoned ahead.

TWO

Shakedown

In the early morning of March 2, 1944, after a sleepless night, I waited at the Solomons amphibious training base to report to my ship. LCI(L) 555 was out cruising in the Chesapeake Bay, but word finally came that it had returned to port. I grabbed my gear and hurried toward the dock. There it was in the morning light, a gray-blue, angular mass of welded steel, 159 feet long and 23⅔ feet wide, moored at the dock alongside three other LCIs. None of them had names, as more traditional naval vessels did. I wondered whether its number was significant. Was it the 555th LCI constructed, or was the number just arbitrarily assigned? I was kept as much in the dark as the enemy on that question. As I edged toward my destined ship, I wracked my memory of *Navy Regulations* for the proper greeting as one reported aboard for duty. As I recalled, as I stepped aboard I was to face aft, salute the ensign (flag), and request the watch officer's permission to come aboard. But there was no watch officer at the ship's gangway! An enlisted man lounged there, sloppily dressed in dungarees and with a three-day growth of beard. A gun strapped to his waist was his badge of authority. Oh, well, I thought, this isn't a textbook war. I propelled myself forward and stepped upon the narrow, rickety gangplank, dragging my two seabags. Facing aft, I let go of the seabag in my right hand to smartly salute the ensign, and barked loudly the unaccustomed words, "Request permission to come aboard, sir."

At that moment the seabag I had let go fell from the gangplank into the oily water below. Barely concealing a smirk, the enlisted man reached out to help me aboard. Then he coolly grabbed a gaffhook, lifted my dripping seabag to the deck, and said, "Wait here." My first order, delivered by an enlisted man. This was my introduction to "Rusty" Rost, the bosun's mate, a burly ruffian in charge of the deck crew whom I would learn to respect as a skillful improviser and one of our ablest crew members. He had gained his know-how the hard way, quitting high school to work for several years on ore boats in the Great Lakes.

Rost returned with the ship's executive officer, Ensign Harold W. "Cotton" Clark, the only officer then aboard. Clark was a friendly, freshly scrubbed young man who looked like Joe College himself. I was reassured to find that he was a fellow southerner. I liked him the minute I saw him, and I soon learned that everyone else did. "Call me Cotton" were among his first words. Not Ishmael but Cotton. My formal reporting to the skipper, the commanding officer, would have to await his return from shore. Meanwhile, I learned that Clark had recently graduated from Vanderbilt University into the midshipmen's school class that preceded mine. He thus had a couple of months' seniority over me, and had been trained in the amphibious training base at Little Creek, Virginia, before joining the 555 when it was commissioned in February in Barber, New York. Clark was tall and athletic-looking, with fair skin, brown-yellow hair, and blue eyes in a round, chubby face. I would be the fourth officer, he said rather cryptically. I soon learned that the fourth officer ranked below the skipper, the exec, and the engineer and was something of a fifth wheel. I would be Lord High Everything Else, with all the miscellaneous duties. "I haven't done much so far," I wrote Diana that night, "but will right away have a chance. It's 12 now and I just got through with a petty and tedious job such as the youngest officer always gets."

The ship had two officers' cabins, each with an upper and a lower bunk. In other words, the naval architect had provided four beds for the four officers. Since the skipper insisted on occupying the captain's quarters in lonely splendor, however, and the exec and engineer occupied the other cabin, as fourth officer I would have to bunk in the troop officers' quarters, a forward compartment where Army officers would be quartered on the way to the beach. This was my first knowledge of the skipper's obsessive avoidance of personal intimacy even with his fellow officers. I was well enough pleased with this billet for the time being. Though it cut me off from companionship with the other officers, that did not seem so bad after the crowded conditions of midshipmen's school. The chief fault of my new quarters was lack of wardrobe storage, so I had to dress out of my oil-stained seabag until a footlocker was furnished. My sack was of stretched canvas laced around an oblong steel tube fixed to the bulkhead, rather than having the springs and mattress of the bunks in the officers' cabins, but I found that in heavy seas canvas rode the waves with less jiggling than springs. I would discover also, however, that being so far forward in the ship, my quarters took more of a pounding in heavy weather when the bow heaved out of the water and smacked its flat bottom on the surface. The washtub design of an LCI had been invisible in the photographs I had seen in midshipmen's school, because its flat bottom was below the waterline. It may have had a clipper bow, but it surely didn't have a clipper keel. It rode the waves like a bucking horse.

As I settled into my quarters that first night aboard, I thought I could hear Rost outside in the crew's mess hall, saying in a stage whisper, "Look what nine o'clock brought." He must have told the whole story of my seabag mishap and my addressing an enlisted man as "sir" in requesting permission to come aboard. I heard muffled guffaws, and remarks that sounded at least in my imagination like "They get greener every day."

That first morning I also met the engineering officer, Myron E. Davis, known as Curly, a stocky, swarthy, hairy man with a mop of dark curly hair and a permanent five o'clock shadow. Several years older than I, twenty-five if he was a day, Davis gave me a gruff but friendly hello in a midwestern accent and stuck out a hand stained with black diesel oil. As I got better acquainted with him over the following months, I noticed that he always made much of being one of the boys, disdaining the privileges of rank. He worked in a short-sleeved skivvy shirt or rolled-up sleeves alongside his men in the engine compartment and treated them as equals. As long as I knew Davis, he looked more like a grease monkey than a naval officer, and he preferred it that way. Davis had studied engineering at Ohio State and returned to the family dairy farm in southern Ohio until called into the service. He trained at the engineering midshipmen's school aboard the USS *Prairie State,* the battleship converted into a training ship anchored in the Hudson River near Columbia University. Davis had reported to the ship at the time of its commissioning two weeks earlier in New York and therefore was senior to me.

Curly Davis seemed affable and happy enough on first acquaintance, but I soon learned about the darker angels of his nature. He brooded deeply over the fate that was inexorably taking him overseas. He was married and about to become father to a child he would not see until it was many months old. He had been a Republican isolationist, and he not only hated the war but resented the government that took him away from home and family and from the dairy he regarded as essential enough to warrant his exemption from military service. He also hated Roosevelt as the warmonger Democrat who had tricked us into war. He considered the war and his part in it a personal conspiracy against him. One had to sympathize with Davis's homesickness as he faced the prospect of going overseas before he could even see his first-born son. I came to resent, however, his paranoid politics and his midwestern rural prejudices that seemed to me somehow worse and more illogical than my southern ones.

The skipper did not return to the ship until around midnight, and I met him only briefly then. I would have a better chance to size him up, to frame his "fearful symmetry," the next morning. We got underway around dawn for a day of beaching and retracting drill on a nearby strand. Lieutenant (j.g.) Jack Flinn, one rank above the rest of us, was a long drink of water, so tall that his pants were too short, ending an inch above his shoes. The first impression was of a Lincolnesque height and homeliness, with a sallow complexion, thinning hair, and deep lines etched in his face. Though actually only about six feet three, he gave the impression of greater height because of his thinness, scarecrow arms, and permanent stoop. Unlike the rest of us, he had to stoop to clear the hatches and the overhead. He was considerably older than the junior officers, perhaps thirty-six, and seemed even older than he was. We junior officers never discovered any Lincolnian wisdom in Jack Flinn, but he certainly looked the part, with a saturnine expression and an aloofness and melancholy that required months for us to fathom. It was clear from the beginning, however, that he was not a man to "mess around with." He was always ready to find fault and assume the worst in others.

Flinn remained apart in his own cabin, and even in the officers' wardroom he held us at a distance by his sardonic, sneering smile and inscrutability. He was unsociable and had no small talk. The crew jokingly called him "Smilin' Jack," though never to his face and almost never in the presence of officers. We junior officers assumed that his behavior stemmed from a feeling of superiority to us young greenhorns. Or, we speculated, perhaps it was because he was the only Jew aboard the ship and expected the worst from us Gentiles. When I first heard Flinn's name I assumed he was Irish-American, but Cotton Clark whispered ominously, "He's Jewish," as though that connoted a conspiracy of the elders of Zion. Flinn was pointedly a secular Jew, not an observant one. He lived by the cynical, irreverent code of the legal profession rather than by any religious precepts, as far as we could tell, but he was clearly set apart from Gentiles in an American society that was deeply anti-Semitic, despite our public claims to be fighting the war on behalf of European Jews and other victims of Hitler's tyranny. Whatever the reasons, the skipper kept at a vertical, horizontal, and psychic distance from everyone else aboard, cloaking himself in an aura of myth and mystery. He didn't even have in common with the other officers the experience of midshipmen's school. He had secured his commission as a lieutenant (j.g.) directly out of civilian life. We knew he had been a San Francisco lawyer, but we never learned what law school he had attended or anything about his practice, and were afraid to ask. We automatically assumed the worst about him, that he had been a shyster, an ambulance chaser.

My first impression of Flinn, however, was of a hard taskmaster, hard on himself as well as others. "The captain works himself to death and tries to do all the work," I wrote Diana after a few days aboard. "He stands watch all the time we're underway. We all work day and night. The crew hasn't had liberty but one night since the 19th of February when they came aboard the ship."

Then only about two weeks old, our ship was on the shakedown cruise that all newly commissioned ships had to go through, to test for any possible structural or functional weaknesses and to train its officers and crew until they became an efficient team. For us this shakedown was particularly appropriate, for only one enlisted man, a gunner's mate named Moyle, and none of the officers had ever been to sea before. The skipper once claimed in a rare moment of wardroom conversation that as a youth he had once sailed on a banana boat to Central America, but we didn't believe him. Just as he never praised us, we resisted belief in anything good about him.

On my second day aboard ship, we left the base at Solomons as part of a flotilla of LCIs, and practiced beaching our craft as though landing troops ashore. It was the standard practice of LCIs to head straight toward a beach at slow speed, drop the stern anchor about fifty yards offshore, and continue moving forward while paying out the anchor cable until the bow touched dry land or, as was usually the case, until the bow scraped bottom in about three feet of water. To lower the ramps on either side of the ship, on which troops would disembark, we swung out a pair of metal arms to which cables were attached, and used a winch housed in the bow compartment to pull the heavy metal ramps forward and lower their front ends into the water. The theoretical soldier who would walk off the ends of these ramps would touch bottom waist deep or even shoulder deep in the water and struggle with all his gear toward dry land. It was clear to all of us from the beginning that these LCIs were only barely serviceable as a way to put troops ashore. The naval architect who designed the ramps had badly miscalculated. At their lowest point, the ramps hung three feet or more above the sandy bottom. Retraction of the ramps required, in addition to the winch, several deckhands pulling them back into their housing. Then we retracted the ship from the beach simply by turning the winch on the fantail that drew in the anchor cable and thus pulled us backward.

Beaching was easy to accomplish in the relatively calm water of Chesapeake Bay, but it would prove much more difficult in the surf of ocean beaches and in high winds. The theory of beaching was simple, but in practice many things could go wrong, even in the Chesapeake. Sometimes we failed to drop anchor at precisely the right distance from shore. On other occasions, the anchor dragged in the soft sand or mud so that, after retracting, our bow had barely cleared the bottom when the stern anchor came out of the water. At other times, the wind would cause us to drift sideways into the beach, or into other LCIs beaching beside us, when we would narrowly escape damage by putting rope fenders over the side at the point of impact.

During all these exercises and during cruises in formation with our flotilla, we junior officers took turns standing watch in the conn, as we called the conning tower of the ship. The skipper was always present in these maneuvers, however, and always in personal charge, barking his commands through a tube to the quartermaster on watch in the pilot house—the glassed-in space below the conn. The quartermaster adjusted the ship's rudder or steered on a compass point according to the captain's order. He transmitted the captain's order as to speed down to the engine room by means of the engine-order telegraph, a circular gadget that rang a bell and set the engine speed anywhere from all ahead flank to all back full. Variations for maneuverability were possible through, for example, going ahead with the starboard engine and at the same time going back with the port engine, which would pull the ship to port. These were all necessary from time to time, because, unlike a car, a ship had no brakes.

The skipper left nothing to chance or to junior officers in handling the ship during the shakedown cruise. We and the signalman stood in silence behind the skipper in the crowded little conn, studying charts of the bay, trying to look wise, and awaiting our turn to take the captain's place in guiding the ship, a turn that never came. The skipper did it all, throughout the shakedown cruise. Not once did a junior officer stand watch underway in the true sense of the term. We never directed the ship's course or speed, never got the feel of the ship or the feel of command. Evidently the skipper had such a low view of our capabilities that he was afraid to hand over the ship to us even for an instant. We began to internalize the feeling of incompetence that the skipper's distrust implied. Soon we were all thumbs and elbows, incoherent and not always alert. Often our minds were wandering when rarely, out of the blue, the skipper called on us for a response. We confirmed his low expectations of us at every turn. A week after my arrival, the shakedown cruise was completed. The junior officers by then were more thoroughly shaken down than the ship was.

Throughout the shakedown, a full lieutenant named Starkus was aboard ship as an observer, but he did precious little observing. He got out of the sack at 1100, had his breakfast at noon, and spent most of the remaining time in the officers' wardroom reading cowboy stories, drinking coffee, and complaining about our cooking. According to scuttlebutt, Starkus was an old Naval Academy man gone wrong, who had been farmed out to this sinecure. We guessed that he must have been involved in some scandal that had blighted his naval career. Officers and crew alike held him in contempt, calling him behind his back a chow-hound, a sack-hog, or just "that damn Starkus." For a while a communications officer from the Solomons base came aboard to instruct me in my duties. He, too, seemed to be a misfit, with little more knowledge than I had of codes, ciphers, and records, and caring considerably less.

My quarters held eight canvas bunks, and at first I slept on one of them and piled my personal gear on the other seven. The Navy abhorred a vacuum, however, and soon moved to fill it. The two observer officers were also assigned to my quarters during the shakedown, and then the ship acquired additional crew members, including Walter Jones, pharmacist's mate second class, who set up his sick bay at one end of my spacious quarters. After a while the observers left, but Jones stayed on. He bunked with the rest of the crew, however, and used the sick bay only during work hours. He was an old Navy hand, having joined the Navy in the mid-thirties after "graduating" from the Civilian Conservation Corps. This was his first sea duty, however. He planned to stay in the Navy after the war, out of fear of unemployment in the postwar depression we all assumed would occur.

"My job as fourth officer is communications and supply," I wrote Diana after the first week, "though I've had very little chance to do much in this so far." My duties also included supervision of the ship's store, which sold cigarettes at cost, without tax. It also did a brisk trade in candy and condoms. I was more than a seagoing storekeeper, however. I was a fighting line officer who took his turn on watch in the conn and, whenever the moment of danger should come, had a battle station at the starboard gun turret. My early favorable impression of the LCI as a class of ship still held up under closer scrutiny, but that was partly because we had not yet been out to the real ocean or into a storm. "By the way," I wrote Diana, "this is a mighty nice ship, the best type in landing craft. We're the fastest, the least crowded, and the best-looking ship."

On the last night of his stay as observer, Starkus inveigled the ship's officers into a game of poker as we lay at anchor. We had heard his bragging for days that he had cleaned out every poker game from Nome to Point Lookout, from Quoddy Head to Biloxi. When we actually settled down to card-playing, however, he lost for twenty-seven consecutive hands, and I won as steadily as he lost. I had no claim to expertise at poker, and it was probably beginner's luck, but I also savored my victory as revenge for all the quiet people of the world against blowhards such as Starkus. I silenced Starkus for the next eight hours, until he woke up next day at noon and went ashore. That was the last we ever saw of him.

In company with other LCIs, the 555 proceeded down the Chesapeake Bay and out its mouth to the amphibious base at Little Creek, Virginia, a few miles from Norfolk. We continued to practice beach landings along the way, at Point Lookout, where the Potomac and Patuxent rivers met the bay, and at Virginia Beach, where ocean surf made beaching harder and more like what we would probably experience in a combat situation. We talked excitedly of the possibility of German U-boats lurking nearby, but we saw none.

Clearly something was afoot when officers and crew got three-day passes, though the captain was as uncommunicative as ever. As fourth officer I had to wait my turn and got only a 48–hour leave. That was just time enough to go home to Atlanta for the first time since I had left for midshipmen's school six months earlier. I had only from 6 P.M. Sunday evening until 1 P.M. Monday at home, but that was worth the journey. My mother sent me back to the ship with a huge box of cake, homemade baking powder biscuits, and fried chicken, my first home-cooked food in a long time and my last for a long time to come. I decided to hoard this treasure until I was a thousand miles from land, when it would remind me of home if it hadn't gone rotten. She also gave me a cookbook for the ship's cook, to teach him how to make bread.

In my heart I knew by then that we were headed overseas, though I didn't know when or where. Why else would everyone aboard get leave? Unless we were going somewhere exotic, why would we be storing so many supplies? As supply and commissary officer, in charge of both food and supplies, it was my duty to inspect all goods as they came aboard. The toilet paper problem was not only a omen of our future but a microcosm of the problem of naval supply. We ordered 2500 rolls of toilet paper, deemed to be a six-month supply, but for unexplained reasons each day a caravan of trucks arrived at the dock to satisfy what the supply depot believed to be our outlandish demands. We soon had some 6000 rolls. If the 555 placed its rolls of toilet paper end to end, I calculated, it could encircle the globe. This experience proved that not all red tape was red.

"This is a lot of fun so far," I wrote cockily to Diana. "I'm still searching for some little part of the ship to send you that nobody would miss. I wish I could send you me for a short while, only somebody would miss me." Excitement at the prospect of sea duty mounted day by day. We put ashore a steward's mate who had proven unsatisfactory in his week of service in the officer's mess, and received aboard his replacement, C. R. Richardson, who would be with us for a year. Richardson was a middle-aged black man from Virginia who had previously worked on a railroad section gang. Though he had had little education and apparently no training in his duties, Richardson made up for these shortcomings by diligent efforts to please and to do his duty. A lifetime of segregation had taught Richardson to wear the mask, to dissemble in the presence of white people, to keep his feelings to himself. I would never have come to understand him except for the fact that, as the fourth officer, I also had the duty of censoring the enlisted men's mail to make certain they wouldn't reveal our whereabouts or plans in case the letters fell into the hands of the enemy. It was clear from reading his letters that there was no danger of that from Richardson. His education in geography was so deficient that he had no idea where he was or where he was going. He had an exaggerated fear of that ultimate white man, Mr. Hitler. I also learned from Richardson's letters that, as the only black man aboard, he cast a shrewdly critical private eye on the behavior of whites. In censoring the mail, I saw race relations in a new perspective.

As our departure date approached, one day I picked up a packet of secret and confidential Navy publications at the Norfolk naval base, looking much like a mailman in my Navy grays, a recent change from the khaki work uniforms sported by older officers. The likelihood of overseas duty became a certainty on April Fools' Day, though we junior officers presumed that the skipper had known all about it for some time. The pharmacist's mate lined us up for inoculations and vaccinations on the eve of departure overseas.

We came to accept the fact of leaving shore, but we were less certain we were ready for the briny deep. Was our shakedown thorough enough? Were we ready yet to look death in the face? Our last Chesapeake cruise gave us a chance to find out. The inexperienced or lunatic commander of our LCI flotilla ordered us out of port in a fog so thick, as a crew member put it, that you could play football on it. Our ships huddled close together and crept through the narrow Norfolk ship channel only as fast as we could dig our way through the fog. While we were in the middle of the channel, the gigantic New York ferry suddenly loomed out of the fog at great speed and pounced on us like a beast of prey. It was about the size of a battleship and brightly lit, but the fog was so dense that we saw it only seconds before it was on us, speeding at about eighteen knots as only a drunk driver would do in an automobile, now making a lot of racket. Immediately the skipper ordered, "All engines stop, right ten degrees rudder." We could only wait and pray. First seen only about a hundred yards away, for seemingly endless seconds it maintained course and speed, directly toward us. If it hit us, we would sink like a rowboat cut in two. Then it sighted us, veered to starboard, and passed us with only six inches to spare. We could hear voices above the roar of its engines and see the faces of its passengers. By that time collision drill had sounded, half our crew were struggling into life jackets, and on the ferry we saw men hopping up and down like grasshoppers, women scurrying like ants. Then, as soon as the ferry passed us, the fog swallowed it up as though it had been but a dream. The entire incident lasted about a minute of clock time. Chattering in relief at our narrow escape, we dubbed the incident the Battle of the New York Ferry and designed an imaginary service ribbon to commemorate the occasion, snow white with green edges.

On the night before sailing, I wrote Diana: "Final inspection for lashings, condition of the ship, etc. by Commander Brown was supposed to be yesterday. We were ready. Today we were still ready. At evening chow we decided to relax, the crew took off their shirts as usual, captain and exec went ashore, and suddenly out of the night with only me and the engineering officer aboard, in walks the commander with his newly wedded wife ready to inspect. So I caught hell instead of the captain while the Commander's wife drank our coffee in the wardroom." To make matters worse, it was shirtless hell I caught, as I had followed the crew's example and peeled down to my skivvy shirt.

By then I had said good-bye to Diana so many times that it must have begun to bore her, but lovesickness and homesickness know no restraint. It suddenly seemed unfair that we would be off to sea at the very moment that the winter of our discontent was ending, but regret gave way to the spirit of adventure. Minutes before sailing I sent Diana one final note. "After five hours in conference with Commander [M. B.] Brown," I wrote somewhat exaggeratedly, "I discovered this isn't duck soup we're sailing into but winter and rough weather and all the wiles of a crafty foe. It'll be as exciting as hell, though. . . . The worst thing about leaving is being unable to get your letters and not being able to write you. The only thing left is to pour my heart into these grape-ade bottles and cast them into the sea every night at dusk. Maybe next summer you'll see a soft drink bottle bobbing in the surf at Myrtle Beach." To underscore my juvenile fantasy, I drew a little boat on the waves, a setting sun behind it, and a pop bottle bobbing in the water. Still unsatisfied, I added another metaphor for good measure. "Couldn't you wrap yourself in a bandana handkerchief marked 'Bundles for Britain' and addressed to LCI(L) 555? Your roommate Betty would be able to put you up on the parcel post counter and I know a perfect place on the ship for a stowaway. It is a little compartment called Echo Sound, a beautiful name."

THREE

A Funny Thing Happened on the Way to the Azores

Reveille sounded at 0500 on the rainy morning of April 3, 1944. At 0751 we cast off all lines, backed out of our pier in Norfolk, and headed out of Hampton Roads on our ocean voyage. The men stood on deck and took a last long look at land, not quite knowing what an ocean voyage would be like, but fully aware that many a stormy wind would blow ere they'd come home again. We moved out to join the convoy. Passing through the defense nets at the mouth of the Chesapeake Bay, we could see ships of many sizes and shapes heading in the same direction. They would be other units of our convoy. Our nearly brand-new ship was in good condition as LCIs went, but it was one of the Navy's smallest oceangoing vessels, and men and officers alike were skeptical of its seaworthiness.

Our ship was part of Convoy UGS 38, comprising about sixty ships and rumored to be the largest convoy ever to cross the Atlantic. It was part of the buildup for the long-awaited D Day landings somewhere on the coast of Europe. Our ship took its assigned place behind LCI(L) 537 in the right rear of the convoy, the very last ship in the sixth column. Leaving the last channel buoy behind and setting off into the vasty deep, Jack Flinn sighed with relief that his long shakedown ordeal was over. With hardly a word, inscrutable as ever, he turned the conn over to the junior officers, the very officers he had so deeply distrusted that he had never allowed us to take charge underway in the relatively safe waters of the Chesapeake. Now, suddenly, he put us in full charge and disappeared into his cabin. Each junior officer would serve four hours on watch and eight hours off, then rotation would put us on watch again. The skipper did not stand watch at all.

Cotton Clark was the first to take over the conn, in the late afternoon and early evening, and he described his experience later in his private diary: "I followed the YMS [a small mine sweeper], per instruction by Captain only to be severely reprimanded by him later for falling too far behind our column and the 554—about which he told me nothing. We fell in behind an LCI and took our bearings for the night off this ship and another freighter off our port bow. Hit the sack about 2200—left word to be called at 0330 for watch. Slept approximately 2 hours. The ship rolled and pitched severely—one time tossing me completely out of my bunk. Ship would crack and pop like a whip. Most every man was seasick. Davis was a pitiful sight—couldn't eat a bite. I offered to stand his watch but he wouldn't hear to it. I ate but one meal this day—at times felt very badly but at this date hadn't 'put the bird.'" Clark's diary was secret because it was illegal. Fearful that a private record might fall into enemy hands and reveal ship movements even though the log and other records be destroyed by specific order, the Navy forbade anyone to keep a diary or journal. It made no systematic effort to enforce this prohibition, however.

Curly Davis stood the second watch, and it seemed pitch dark when I arrived to relieve him for the midwatch. Our ship and all the others were completely darkened at night. Not even a match could be struck topside to light a cigarette. In a few minutes, however, my eyes adjusted to the darkness. The night sky was clear, the moon cast a wide belt of light on the water, and the stars were more brilliant than I had ever seen them. The sky did not lack visibility, but the convoy was so huge that it stretched over the horizon and could not be taken in at a glance even during daytime. We could see nearby ships, however, and could judge our distance from them by the white water splashing at their bows, by their wake astern, and by the sound of their churning engines. Perhaps because of seasickness, Davis had strayed even farther out of position than Clark had. I spent most of my watch wandering from column to column searching in vain for our ship's proper station. I became well acquainted with our entire convoy of tankers, freighters, large and small minesweepers, and LCIs, guarded by eight destroyer escorts stationed on our flanks to guard against submarine attack. An air attack, however, seemed to be the chief anticipated threat, even though enemy planes could not cross the Atlantic without refueling. Navy blimps patrolled overhead all the first day but disappeared sometime in the night, and there was no air protection whatever after that until we approached the English coast many days later.

As I stood watch there under the everlasting stars, I was conscious of having left behind everything that was familiar. I was on unknown waters, headed for an unknown land. Midshipmen's school had cured my homesickness, however, and I was eager for the great adventure ahead. I was both thrilled and unnerved by the fact that, for the first time, control of the ship was in my hands, without the skipper breathing down my neck. At that moment, astray in the convoy, I would have welcomed a little attention from the skipper. After Davis left, I stared through the binoculars trying to ascertain our position. Suddenly I felt a need to be fortified against scurvy during the long voyage ahead. I sent Paul Hoylo, the signalman who stood watch with me in the conn, down to the fantail where crates of fresh grapefruit were stored in a food locker. He came back with a whole grapefruit, and I proceeded to peel and eat it section by section. Though it protected me against a largely imaginary scurvy, the grapefruit was actually the worst thing I could have eaten. My digestive tract responded to the massive intake of grapefruit pulp by giving me my first and only case of seasickness. I leaned over the side of the conn and disgorged all my stomach's contents in one violent retch. My head cleared, I continued my watch without further mishap but without regaining station. Mine was not the worst case of seasickness that night. Davis was as sick as a dog, and no sea dog at that. Maybe the captain was also seasick during this stretch of rough weather, but if so he never let us know it. He kept his own counsel in this as in everything else, and remained an enigma to officers and crew alike. We knew, however, that he spent much of his time in the sack.

When Clark relieved me at four in the morning, I made my way over slippery decks to the chaos below. Practically every man aboard was sick. Smells of vomit and fuel oil smote the nostrils in a deadly combination. I slid and staggered to my bunk but had hardly crawled in when general quarters sounded and everyone hurried to his battle station. It was only a drill, but it also brought the captain topside. He immediately found much to criticize. Dawn made it clear that we were badly out of station, in the middle of the convoy instead of on its right flank. Under the lash of the captain's tongue, Clark maneuvered to rejoin our column. Once secured from general quarters, we might have expected breakfast, but the cook did not stir from his bunk. He was among the sickest of all. Kitchen odors only caused him to revisit his seasickness. It did not matter, because appetites were scaled down to the size of individual snacks. A few iron-stomached fellows played poker, but most were comatose between watches. "This damn ship is not as seaworthy as I had talked myself into believing," I wrote Diana at the beginning of a long letter I would mail when we reached port. "I'm feeling pretty good now but not at all salty. If you can't read this very well it's because the ship pitches or rolls about once to every word."

Rain came down in buckets the second day out, and on the third day came fog so thick that we lost the convoy entirely for a while. Our destroyer escorts herded us back like a flock of sheep. I tried to describe those first three gruesome days in my ongoing letter: "It's like being a punch-drunk boxer with somebody you can't see always hitting you in the face, in the body, behind your back, and whenever you strike back your opponent isn't there. Confusin but not amusin." Showers were out of the question, not only because we had to conserve fresh water but because we would have bounced from wall to wall in the seawater shower stalls. We slept in our uniforms, too tired to change into night clothes. The only living thing aboard who was well during the first three days was Salty, a speckled white cat that Rost, the bosun's mate, had smuggled in just before we sailed as the ship's mascot. On the other hand the cat was not yet shipbroken, and nobody could figure out how to begin the process. We couldn't put him out of the house. The cat's mess had to be accepted as simply part of the general mess and disorder.

As we passed Bermuda on the fourth day, fifty miles to our south and too far away to see, the weather suddenly moderated—it was spring after all. The sun came out. The wave pattern changed from deep troughs to long, low swells, and the water changed color from grayish green to deep blue. We slowly returned to life. We shaved, took bucket baths, and changed clothes. A cleaning crew made the decks shipshape again, and the entire crew aired bedding in the sun. Soon the weather was so warm that we stripped down to shorts and cut our Navy-issue work shoes into sandals. Red backs in the late afternoon were a dime a dozen.

We were Smilin' Jack and his pirate crew, or at least we looked the part. But the skipper's nickname, based on a character in a popular comic strip, was intended to be ironical. He actually never smiled if he could help it. On rare occasions a sardonic half-sneer appeared on his dour countenance but never a sunny smile and certainly never a giggle or a belly laugh. I noticed that when we stripped down in the warm weather the skipper kept his shirt on and his skinny legs inside his pants. Was this because of embarrassment or his obsession to maintain a distance between himself and the rest of us? We never asked.

I tanned my body by day and began to enjoy my night watch, brightened as it was by a full moon. Our ship's wake gleamed like silver as it stirred the microscopic, phosphorescent plankton. Flying fishes played at our bow. It was "like a Dorothy Lamour movie only better," I wrote Diana. "Looks like land is still out of sight, but I'm so comfortable I could drift like this for weeks, basking in the sun, watching the waves ripple and curve." Though the cook still looked as though he had lost his best friend, he now dragged himself to the kitchen and began to cook regular meals. We no longer had to eat canned turkey from the can. Life returned to as normal as it could be aboard a ship. When Cotton Clark tried his hand at cutting my hair, I emerged from the ordeal like a chick from its egg. I couldn't see what he was doing at the time, but I thought later that he must have used his scalping knife. "Gave Louis Harlan a haircut to-day," Clark wrote in his journal. "Can safely say I would starve to death at this profession—his head blended in very wonderfully with the sea—both wavy."

"The rest of our pirate crew think very romantic thoughts about your three pictures I have in my quarters," I wrote Diana. "The enlisted men seem to admire most the honey-coloured hair of the [studio photograph]. Cotton Clark appreciates the twinkle in your eye in the white-dress-with-flowers-around-the-neck-and-roguish-smile picture. The motor-macs concentrate their interest on the bathing-suit-on-the-golden-sands-of-Myrtle-Beach photograph. I, simple soul that I am, dote upon all three." The motor-macs referred to were the motor machinist's mates who operated and repaired the ship's diesel engines.

The good weather allowed me the leisure to study our crew. Because of the small size of our ship there were only about twenty-five enlisted men. In addition to the six motor-macs in the engine crew and about ten seamen who made up the deck crew, the ship had one of each kind of petty officer or else a "striker," a seaman who had received special training in some branch of naval lore but who did not yet have the experience to be a petty officer. There was one cook, one quartermaster, one steward's mate, one pharmacist's mate, three signalmen, one for each watch, a boatswain's mate (or bosun), an electrician, a radioman, and a number of seamen, first class. Strikers far outnumbered petty officers in our inexperienced crew.

The ethnic diversity of our crew amazed me as a southerner accustomed only to a differentiation into whites and blacks. Louis Yealdhall of Baltimore, the quartermaster, was probably of English descent, but there was Starkey the Irishman, Smigielski the Pole, Pisaneschi the Italian, Hoylo the Norwegian, who eternally quarreled with Peterson the Swede, Richardson the black steward's mate, Rost the Teuton, Champagne the Louisiana cajun, in short, once each of many ethnic groups. They all spoke English, of course, and were at least second- or third-generation Americans, but they were very conscious and proud of their ethnic distinctiveness. Even those Mediterranean people I had heard derided down South as inferior to "real" white people took pride in their ethnic origins, and each seemed to have a rival or enemy ethnic group against which to measure itself. We were a small, floating United Nations. If we could only tolerate our diversity and work well together, I thought, maybe there was hope for a better postwar era.

An important part of our differentness, however, was hierarchical and hegemonic. Officers and crew were set apart into the haves and the have nots, in different uniforms, as though in the service of separate nations. Officers came from college—that was the crucial difference—and enlisted men straight out of high school or from blue-collar work.

That may seem a small distinction in the present day of nearly universal access to higher education, but in the 1940s and in earlier decades back as far as memory served, college was only for the favored few, for those whose parents could afford to send them or help them through. To graduate from college, or even to have been there, put one immediately on a higher status plateau. The Navy's hierarchical structure, its ranks and orders, challenged the democratic political credo of American society but also reflected in high relief America's hierarchical social reality. In our ship's crew, the marginal figure was the signalman Paul Hoylo, who identified with the officers and had had a year of college. Though he had chosen to enlist rather than seek a deferment through the V-12 program, by the time he reached our ship Hoylo had probably regretted his decision. At any rate, he kept aloof from the other enlisted men and preferred the company and conversation of the officers, and because of his sharp intelligence and what we would today call a preppy manner he could hold his own in intellectual conversations with the officers during long watches in the conn. "A good talk with Paul Hoylo, the Signalman who stands watch with me," Clark wrote in his diary early in the voyage. "A swell fellow from Montana. Happens to be a SX [Sigma Chi] pledge, and the best 3rd Class Signalman in the business." The other junior officers echoed these sentiments, though what the skipper thought of Hoylo remained the usual mystery.

The seventh day out was Easter Sunday. The Jewish skipper either ordered or allowed his Gentile executive officer to conduct religious exercises. Clark noted in his diary: "Some of the fellows requested it so I took the Prayer Book Mother had given me and together with her favorite poems which were inclosed, and a Bible, I worked out the following program in hopes of giving the fellows a few thoughts on this rather unique Easter:

1. Call to Worship (Poem)
2. Silent Prayer, followed by Lord's Prayer
3. Apostle Creed—in unison
4. Scripture Reading   Matt:28
                        Luke 24: 1–12 (Bill Stine)

5. Poem (Paul Hoylo)
6. Remarks
7. Dismissal Prayer by Davis"

In my lengthening letter to Diana I described the scene less reverently: "We convened in sundry places on the gun deck while Bro. Cotton Clark led us in a word of prayer. It was very impressive, but I resisted the temptation to shake the preacher's hand after services. We said the Lord's Prayer, the Apostles' Creed and a few po'ms of the Edgar Guest style."

Easter Sunday's weather was perfect for an Easter parade, if there were only an avenue. The weather reminded Clark of other rites of spring back home. "The sun was really high and a day which was strictly 'baseball all over.' Almost made you glad you were alive—but better still, back home loosening the ol' wing. Kept thinking of all the wonderful times I've had on days such as this—and what playing sports really meant to me."

The improved weather also gave us a chance to do the normal things that the storm had made impossible. I chose *Moby Dick* and *My Sister Eileen* from the ship's small paperback library, while Cotton read *The Robe.* Conversation was also possible in the good weather. We learned that Davis was expecting a son, due about July 15, and of course he could hardly wait for the news. The steward's mate, C. B. Richardson, became a figure of fun for the white officers. I described his comical remarks to Diana in a poor imitation of his dialect: "Uncle Sam sho am a powerful fellow. Give you somp'n to eat, a pillow for yo' head and kivvers to kivver you up, and somp'n even to ride in, just like a automobile. Just gives you a ride around everywhere. Yeah, Uncle Sam sho a pow'ful fellow." In a similar vein of condescension in his diary, Cotton Clark gave his impressions of Richardson: "Our steward's mate is a scream. A big-eyed negro, about 35 years old, who takes everything most serious. He had been at Solomons for only two weeks and without any foreword as to going across, was sent to our ship. His wife and family do not know his whereabouts. He swears that when the 'shooting' starts he's going to high tail it for the lowest deck. Seems to be a very trustworthy fellow and sincerely believes in the Supreme

Being. Keeps me laughing constantly and what a sight he is in life jacket and helmet!" We were not even aware that our racial attitudes were derived from white stereotypes reinforced by the Hollywood movies. We saw this fellow human only as a joke.

We junior officers were preoccupied with the captain's constant public criticism, which rankled worse with every passing day. If he had to upbraid us, we thought, why couldn't he call us aside and give us private hell, instead of embarrassing us in front of the men and thus undermining our authority as officers? Cotton Clark felt the indignities with particular keenness because he sought constantly to be the best officer possible, and because as executive officer he had direct charge over the crew and therefore more dignity to maintain. On one dark and rainy night watch when the ships ahead were barely visible, Clark saw another LCI about to run us down and sheered sharply out of the column, later rectifying our position. "As visibility became worse and with the sight of a white and red light off our bow, called captain," Clark wrote in his journal. "As usual he gave me plenty of hell about everything in general without first asking of the circumstances causing our position out of column. So happened that as he came to the conn the visibility improved somewhat (by virtue of the moon being astern of us coming through the clouds slightly) so he saw no reason why we weren't in perfect station. The twelve hours of watch standing this day was beginning to best my even temper and I could hardly hold back telling him what I thought. However, Davis relieved me soon and I hurried down below—all too disgusted to sleep."

Coming on watch two days later, Clark found the ship again somewhat out of station but soon brought it back in column. "Was now beginning to have a little self-confidence in my ship handling and without the 'help' of the captain could get by fairly well." Years later, Clark confided to me that at some point, perhaps this early, he privately confronted Flinn about his practice of public reprimand and asked him in future to do his reprimanding in private, for the good of the ship. The captain respected him for his forthrightness, said Clark, and after that accorded him more respect. Davis and I should have done the same thing, Clark suggested, and thus avoided continued humiliation. Clark attributed Flinn's behavior to the fact that he was Jewish and said that in his postwar work as a stockbroker he had had many dealings with Jews and had learned that he had to deal with them forthrightly and toughly from the outset or they would run all over him. Clark was apparently unaware that he was employing a classic anti-Semitic cliché. I cannot recall attributing Flinn's worst faults to his Jewishness, but I conceded that Clark was right about the way we should have handled Flinn's bullying.

While I stood watch at three in the morning on the seventh day out, the rudder indicator suddenly blinked out and the ship went careening to starboard, heading toward ships in the next column. As the officer in charge, I had to act fast. I got the engines backing full and we shuddered to a halt just in time to avoid ramming another LCI. The convoy moved ahead while we lay dead in the water, and soon we were straggling nearly out of sight. Down below the skipper was pulling on his pants, for the sudden halt awakened everyone on the ship. The skipper reached the conn and took over, while I stood by as the watch officer. The rudder problem, however, was in the hands of Davis and his motor-macs down in the engine room. Finally, after more than an hour of helpless drifting, the engine crew got the rudder repaired, and we speeded up to regain the convoy some ten miles ahead.

The idyllic weather lasted for about a week as we proceeded slowly across the Atlantic. Occasional reports of possible U-boats from our convoying warships added an extra fillip of perceived danger. At this stage of the war the likelihood of submarine attack was actually rather remote, particularly for a ship as small as ours and with such a shallow draft that torpedoes would pass harmlessly under us. Of course, a surfaced submarine would have more firepower than we had. We knew, however, that loose lips this far from land couldn't sink ships, so we freely compared notes on what we would do if confronted by U-boats.

Our circumstances abruptly changed on April 13, when we reached a point due south of the Azores. The main part of the convoy continued on course toward the Strait of Gibraltar, while Task Group 66.9, consisting entirely of LCIs, veered northward on a course of 017 degrees toward Horta, a port on Fayal Island in the Azores, part of neutral Portugal. Just as we swung to this new course a rain squall turned into a raging storm, with torrential rain, lightning, and fog. A high wind whipped up the waves, and the ship rolled and pitched, creaked and groaned. As Richardson, the steward's mate, described our situation, "You look out one time and she looks like she's headed for heaven—another time and she's going to the bad place for good." The weather pattern we were experiencing was characteristic of that region of the Atlantic, where the Gulf Stream current chilled by its northern circuit met the relatively warm Mediterranean water and climate and caused turbulence of both air and water. Our ship struggled to maintain station in our small convoy. Though disconcerted by this sudden change of weather, we little suspected the embarrassment and possible disaster that lay ahead.

When I climbed to the conn to relieve Curly Davis at 2000, dusk was turning into night. Seasick as usual, Davis was steering the ship through the semi-obscurity without any clear knowledge of his position. Our official speed was nine and a half knots, but I noticed that other LCIs were passing us half-hidden in the rain and darkness. Was one of them the ship we were assigned to follow, or were we in the wrong column? For the first time since I had begun standing watch underway, I refused to allow Davis to turn over his watch to me, because if I did his straying from station would be attributed to me. Davis, exhausted and nauseous, angrily insisted on my relieving him then and there, but I stood my ground and called for the skipper to settle the dispute. The skipper on arrival began immediately to upbraid me equally with Davis for being out of station. I coolly explained that I could not be held accountable, since I had just arrived and had refused to relieve Davis until the ship was in proper station. I also reported that other ships had passed near us at greater speed.

Flinn remained in the conn in charge of the ship's course and speed for an hour or more. "All ahead full," he ordered the quartermaster, increasing the speed from about 9.5 knots to about 12 knots. He searched in vain for other ships in the gathering dark, and finally turned the ship over to me. Going down to the pilot house just below the conn, he made a handwritten entry in the ship's log, "Maintain present course and speed all night," signed it "Jack Flinn, Lt. (j.g.) USNR," and informed me of his order. "But, captain . . . ," I called to him through the voice tube, but he cut me off. "My order stands," he said sharply. "Don't call me unless absolutely necessary."

I was acutely aware of the blunder Flinn was committing. He had increased the speed to full, forgotten that he had done so, and ordered that speed to be maintained all night, compounding the error by refusing to listen to my protest. If we were then in the general vicinity of the rest of the convoy, by morning we would be out of sight ahead of it. The predicament brought on by the weather and Davis's seasickness was now aggravated by the captain's arrogance. I have often wondered since whether I was also at fault. Perhaps I should have insisted further on making him aware of his lapse of memory, despite his squelching refusal to listen. With another captain more tolerant of disagreement I might have been more insistent, but this captain had built a wall around himself. He had created his own disaster by keeping us junior officers at arm's length and encouraging us to believe ourselves incompetent. It was a Navy dictum that the captain was always right.

Many years later I returned to the ship's log, now deposited with those of other ships in the National Archives in Washington, fully expecting to find my memory of the incident confirmed by the skipper's order written and signed into the record. But there was no mention of the order. I was disconcerted for a moment, and then remembered back to those days aboard ship. At the end of every month the handwritten log was typed up in a "smooth" version, signed by the captain and executive officer, and sent to the office of the Chief of Naval Operations in Washington. The captain had conveniently removed his order from the log in order to protect his reputation, and after transcription the handwritten original as usual was destroyed. Here was a rare case in which the historical record distorted and even erased what had actually happened.

When Cotton Clark relieved me at darkest midnight, we were completely lost from the convoy, the sea was rougher than ever, and the ship was taking a bad beating, heaving itself half out of the water at the crest of each wave and crashing flat-bottomed into the trough below. "We kept steaming at 12.5 knots on base course," Clark wrote in his diary after his watch. He had no more relish than I for awakening the skipper. "Kept sharp lookout entire watch but sighted nothing whatsoever. At dawn there was still no ships in sight—definite now that we were lost and entirely on our own. We had no protection—kept on base course. I was under the impression that we were ahead of the convoy considerable for we had made a goodly speed during the night—running on all seven engines." The eighth engine had been disabled for some time.

Making my way below, I shed my wet clothes, crawled into the sack, and slept as well as I could with the ship pitching and creaking and the engines intensifying their roar whenever the screws broke the surface at the peak of a wave. Though I didn't get seasick, I got little sleep, and next morning I looked out of my quarters on a scene of chaos from stem to stern. Relieving Davis at 8 in the morning, I found that Clark and Davis also had followed the skipper's order to the letter and steamed at full speed all night. The rain had ended, but the waves were still high and the sun was completely obscured by heavy clouds. No other ship was in sight. Once again I refused to take over the watch, and this again triggered Davis's anger and frustration. His scowl was even fiercer than before because of a heavier growth of black stubble beard. One didn't dare shave in rough weather. I again summoned the skipper. Confronted with the predicament his arrogance had caused the night before, the skipper was ready to blame me again as well as Davis, but I pointed out to him that we had simply followed his explicit and signed order. He muttered something about expecting us to show common sense, but he was trapped by his own words. I took a little satisfaction in the captain's discomfort, but the fact was that we were now lost at sea, and in submarine-infested waters.

The skipper ordered a return to standard speed and disappeared below, looking forlorn but still keeping his own counsel. Just before noon he appeared on the gun deck with a sextant to try to get a fix on the sun. Mariners had known for five hundred years that one could determine one's latitude by the angle of the sun from the horizon at noon. On this day, however, this ancient lore was of no use, because the sun was hidden by the clouds. As the day wore on there was no sight of either ships or land. "Ran into a school of porpus fish," Clark wrote in his diary. "Saw a few sea-gulls and flying-fish. This gave us a bit of hope—kept on base course, just hoping & praying that soon we would pick up a ship & that she wouldn't be a submarine! Almost gave up hope of reaching land to-day. Sea still extremely rough—at times we were at capsizing angles." The entire crew was seasick. There had been no hot meals for three days, and the galley smells were almost unbearable. Clutter was everywhere, and there was no will to clean it up.

Near dusk of that long day, while on the gun deck waiting for my turn to go on watch, I sighted an ominous cloud ahead, almost black against the sky, reaching to the horizon as I imagined a tornado would. It had a funnel, but the funnel was at the top instead of the bottom of the cloud. I pointed it out to Davis, who was on watch, and then to the skipper. The skipper agreed that the cloud certainly looked threatening. By then the whole crew was out on deck looking, talking, gesticulating at the cloud, which grew darker by the minute. Finally the gunner's mate, Moyle, the only one aboard who had been to sea before, said, "That's land." The sighs were audible.

Our dark cloud was Mount Pico, a volcano rising majestically from the sea to a lofty peak about a mile and a half high. Its sharply pointed peak still smoldered, or was it simply haloed by a cloud? Pico was on the island adjacent to Fayal and our port of Horta. The only land the rest of us had ever seen from the sea had been the east coast of the United States, which is so flat it hardly appears above the horizon. Sailors have always honored the lookouts who first sight land, but could I take credit for it? I saw land first, but didn't know it when I saw it. That was my naval career in a nutshell. And little honor would redound to any of us from this sorry episode. It was of some comfort to us stragglers that, though lost from our convoy, we had at least managed to steer a straight course to our destination by dead reckoning, without help from celestial navigation.

But all was not well that ended well, for fate had one more spin of the roulette wheel against us. It was nearly dusk as we approached the dark cloud that was land, too late to try the harbor's narrow, tricky entrance before nightfall. The skipper hurried below to study the charts in the radio shack that doubled as a chartroom. All of these volcanic islands rose abruptly from the sea floor, and there was no shallow water for an anchorage overnight. The skipper concluded that the only thing to do was to mark time until dawn would allow us to steer through narrow Fayal Channel and enter port. Perhaps he hoped that the rest of the convoy would have arrived by then, so we would attract less attention. Who knew what thoughts and emotions churned inside of him? How could he explain? Whom could he blame? Just as I went on watch, the skipper ordered us to sail back and forth on reciprocal courses all night in front of the harbor entrance, in a holding pattern. Fortunately, the wind died down in the lee of the islands and, as Clark noted in his diary, "the sight of land cured most cases of seasickness." Those not on watch slept well that night. We later heard that forces ashore had observed our movements in front of the harbor and assumed that we were a German U-boat lurking offshore in hope of a kill. Whether this was true or only a rumor, our ship's profile above the water line did indeed have an uncanny resemblance to the silhouette of a surfaced submarine.

When dawn arrived we were still alone, and our ship entered Horta harbor on Clark's watch but with the skipper in the conn giving the orders. A pilot arrived by boat to guide us to our anchorage, where we tied up alongside the British ship *Crane*. The pilot gave Flinn orders to report to the harbormaster ashore. He and Clark, as executive officer, went ashore, while the rest of us were barred from liberty and had to content ourselves with gazing at our exotic surroundings. We had hardly tied up when a dozen small boats manned by small boys and old barefoot men came alongside selling baskets, bananas, and trinkets. Meanwhile, the skipper reached shore looking jaunty enough, but on his return he looked decidedly crestfallen. As usual, however, he was uncommunicative, and we never learned what the authorities ashore said to him about our ship's early arrival. About noon the other LCIs of our convoy arrived and tied up alongside us or anchored nearby.

In his diary Clark described his brief sojourn ashore: "Took a quick 'bucket bath' and the Captain & I went to see the American Consul. Walked down the main street—brushing aside oxen driven carts, barefooted citizens & Portugal soldiers. Streets were narrow and of cobble stone. Consul was a very inconsiderate fellow who tried to give the impression of a big dealer. A small, dried up fellow who wore a tweed suit which looked as though it hadn't been pressed for months. We drove down to a British Ship in order to get instructions. This ship had been torpedoed in the stern and was to be used permanently at Horta. British officers treated us swell—had two beers which almost knocked me for a row of pins. After getting instructions, walked back to town. Purchased some gift at a small shop but as we started to pay American money was [un]acceptable. Came back to ship—all disgusted because we couldn't get liberty."

Meanwhile, those of us barred from shore made full use of eyes and binoculars in studying the paradise around us. The water was an impossible thin-milk blue, unlike any water we had ever seen before. Horta, a town of about 10,000 inhabitants, lay before us, the pastel colors of the buildings and their tile roofs making a contrast with the blankness of the open ocean we had viewed for the previous fortnight. To our right was the cone of Pico overshadowing the harbor, terraced farmland like giant steps up its slopes almost out of sight, toward its cloud-surrounded, snow-covered peak. This was our first foreign land, and it looked as if straight out of a storybook. Through our binoculars we saw shady doorways of the dockside stores, oxcarts bringing farm produce to market, dark women in shawls with large urns balanced on their heads. The hills around us, cultivated to the last square inch, spread like a lush green patchwork quilt. We could see one man, said to be the American consul, dashing about looking busy while the rest of the place dozed in siesta. When I told the skipper how beautiful I thought the country was, he said it was nothing compared to California.

Unwashed Portuguese workers came aboard to unload a transshipment of stores from our ship to the United States government facilities at Horta. They worked from dawn to midnight of our second day in port, a Sunday, for what was said to be a dollar in American money or 25 "skuts" [escudos] in theirs. The bumboats continued to come alongside. The principal medium of exchange being cigarettes, the ship's store in my charge did a land-office business in cigarette cartons sold to crew members as trade goods. I myself used cigarettes to buy a juicy, sun-ripened pineapple, and just as I had finished eating it word arrived that I had probably caught typhus or dysentery. Only time would tell, but the pharmacist's mate took time by the forelock and hastily inoculated us all against typhus. The boats also bootlegged a strong drink, said to have caused a Britisher to die and a number of others to go blind or insane. The flotilla commander gave a summary court martial to one motor-mac on another ship for bringing a drink of this hooch aboard ship.

We tightened our own security by stationing two men instead of one on gangway watch and loading the .45s they wore at their hips. "Fifth column activities were a known fact in this place," Clark noted in his diary. "The place itself was most conducive to German spies. It makes the whole program of censorship regulations, etc. seem futile, since it is probable indeed that the enemy knows exactly when we leave, how many ships, our escort protection, and possibly where we are going." If so, the enemy knew more about our destination than we did. We presumed it was England, but could only guess what port. The favorite guess was Plymouth, perhaps because its name was better known than others on the Channel coast.

Moving from the inner harbor to a new anchorage in Horta Bay, we remained for four days in sight of but out of touch with this paradise spiced with danger. Finally, the skipper gave us the word that we would get underway next morning, our destination Falmouth, in Cornwall, southwest England. A British officer named John Kennedy came aboard to ride with us to England. I had long conversations with him about England, as he shared my makeshift quarters. On April 19 we got underway with our convoy consisting of ten LCIs, twelve small mine-sweepers (YMS), two fleet minesweepers (AM), and many trepidations. The air protection we thought had been promised by the British was not apparent. Our course would carry us near the French coast held by the Germans and their French collaborators. We imagined the worst, a hazardous passage through enemy-infested waters, the AMs our only hope, numbers our only safety. To straggle might be disastrous. To the superstitious among us, bad matters were made worse by the fact that our convoy flag bore the number thirteen!

Actually, the five-day voyage was uneventful except for our own small errors, shortcomings, and fears. On the first two days a light wind was behind us, the sky sunny, and the sea calm. During the first day one of our sister LCIs broke down and had to return to port and join a later convoy. This time the LCIs were in the middle of the convoy, the AMs guarded us—one ahead and the other astern—and the YMSes were on both flanks searching for underwater craft. The only under-water "craft" we spotted was a whale, surfacing and blowing steam close by, almost close enough to touch. On the late afternoon of the third day a dense fog set in and the ships next to us became invisible. We had to keep a taut watch that strained our eyes from constant staring through binoculars. The convoy somehow managed to stay together that night, and the fog lifted in the morning on another good day.

The next night, however, visibility turned bad again. When Clark turned the watch over to Davis, thankful he didn't have to stare through binoculars any longer, all the ships were visible. When I relieved Davis, we were out of sight of the convoy again, but in company with three other ships. Davis claimed that the other ships had led him astray. I foolishly agreed this time to take over the watch and just hoped that in the early daylight I could get us back into place again before the captain was out of the sack. Daylight showed that we had strayed about eight miles to port of the convoy, and we quickened speed and regained our station by 0630, before the skipper was up. The skipper gave me and Davis a public tongue-lashing anyhow. Clark noted in his diary, "The Captain raised hell with all officers—particularly Davis, upon whose watch the incident occurred. However, Harlan took over at four, and he was as much or more to blame than Davis. Harlan is a very heavy sleeper and it takes him fully one or two hours to completely wake up." Clark's conclusion that I was equally at fault was contrary to the facts, went even beyond the skipper's general criticism, and can best be explained by the fact that Clark shared quarters with Davis and naturally heard his version. How could I have been responsible, when separation from the convoy occurred on Davis's watch? My only fault was in not refusing to relieve Davis this time, probably because I took pity on his forlorn state of seasickness. I did not know Clark's privately recorded opinion at the time, of course, but I sensed the need to protect myself not only against the captain's wrath but against other insecure junior officers who were only too willing to shift blame. By the end of our Atlantic voyage, the entire ship was quivering with insecurity.

Clark's diary entry was accurate, however, in its estimate of the morale among junior officers and crew. "The dislike for the Commanding Officer continues to grow and perhaps more in abundance," Clark wrote in his diary. "He has proven to be a most moody fellow, one to criticize constantly and as one of the men put it, 'a sea-going lawyer who is all out for himself.' The ship is disorganized considerable—the Captain playing the role of Exec, Eng. officer, Comm. Officer & Captain, all in one. While his knowledge of Engineering is certainly limited, Davis has taken a back seat in this Dept, but naturally gets all the blame for something wrong. The men have hit a new low in attitude toward work. Scarcely none are rated and they take their work haphazardly. As for himself, he hasn't spoken one word of praise or appreciation since I can remember. His criticisms are harsh, never constructive, and always seem to take place in front of the men—which is certain to decrease what confidence they have in me. His presence irritates me considerably and I try to steer clear of him. It is a relief to eat alone sometimes—tho the absence of conversation at regular chow time is sometimes embarrassing."

The next day, as we approached the Scilly Isles off the western tip of England, British planes appeared overhead, the first sign of the air cover we had been promised. As we passed the light at Bishop's Rock, we immediately felt the brisk, cold wind of the English Channel, choppy water, and the fear of submarines based only a hundred miles away on the shores of occupied France. Now seemingly at close quarters with an unseen enemy, we passed a tense night torn between fear of danger and eager anticipation of landfall. Many of the crew stayed up all night, and the junior officers felt that the skipper should have been present in the conn that night instead of in the sack.

General quarters sounded frequently the next morning, as one of our escort vessels made sonar contact with a submarine and dropped three depth charges. A German plane was shot down by a British one off our port bow, but after that we were again devoid of air cover on a sunny day conducive to air attack. The sight of land about midmorning accentuated the positive but did not eliminate the negative nor even Mister In Between. This time we at least knew land when we saw it. Within an hour we could discern what seemed to be castles along the Cornish cliffs that stretched above the water for miles. Countless blimps anchored to land dotted the coast as far as the eye could see. Through our binoculars we could pick out an air base, and overhead now were many planes, some of them evidently practicing dive-bombing. Three PT boats, cutting through our convoy at high speed, forced our officer on watch to stop all engines and put them into reverse to avoid these little gnats. He shouted a curse vainly into the wind.

As we swung into Falmouth harbor, we saw a game of rugby in progress on a field of vivid greenness near the water. Everywhere we looked ashore was unbelievably green, except where houses on the steep hillsides and their gardens offered splashes of other colors. Falmouth was a perfect picture of what Americans imagined England to be. The war had intruded itself on this peaceful scene, however. Nearly every bush along the shore was camouflage for an antiaircraft gun. A pilot arrived in a launch to guide us to our mooring with other LCIs at Flushing Trot. Liberty ashore began that very night for half of the crew and officers.

Our ship, on arrival at Falmouth, became part of an LCI flotilla that had been there for the past three months preparing for the invasion of France. The skipper donned his clean uniform and set out to report to his new flotilla commander. Then we junior officers, visiting our counterparts on the other LCIs, began to learn the secret our cryptic skipper had carefully concealed from us over the past two months. The 555 was not his first LCI but his second! After securing his commission as lieutenant (j.g.), Flinn had trained briefly at an amphibious base in Miami, and the previous fall he had taken command of an LCI at Solomons, Maryland, on its shakedown cruise. While he was away in Miami on unauthorized leave—chasing a "floozie," we were told—his executive officer rammed another LCI and put a substantial hole in it. A naval board of inquiry found Flinn guilty of neglect of duty and removed him from command. Flinn had tried to argue that the accident was not his fault, since he was not even aboard at the time, but the board concluded that that was no excuse, since a captain is always responsible for the conduct of his ship and Flinn's absence was unauthorized. Furthermore, Flinn was judged responsible for the incompetence of his subordinate, for he had been in charge of his training. And if his executive officer was incompetent, the board asked, why had Flinn sent in a favorable fitness report to the Bureau of Naval Personnel?

When Flinn was removed from command of his first ship, the flotilla commander thought he had seen the last of him. The Navy bureaucracy, however, in a fit of absence of mind, reassigned Flinn to command another LCI, the 555. We were then victimized by Flinn's earlier embarrassment. He had learned a lesson, but his learning had not ripened into wisdom. He learned not to repeat the mistakes that had led to his first loss of command, but his correction of earlier errors led him into new errors. By refusing to let us handle the ship, out of fear of another accident on the shakedown cruise, he had limited our training opportunities. His public browbeating and sarcasm toward the junior officers, his private aloofness, were also efforts to correct earlier errors. Even his decision not to share quarters with the executive officer, contrary to the original design of these quarters, was probably a "correction" of his fraternization on his earlier ship. Consciously or unconsciously—we never knew which—he succeeded in getting us junior officers to internalize the incompetence he charged us with, thus preparing us to accept the unfavorable fitness reports he would submit on us, which would exonerate him from any trouble our ship got into. This tortured reasoning had a logic all its own, but not one that would help us hapless junior officers. It would explain not only his concealment of his own dirty little secret but the terrorism that reduced Davis and me, and to some degree Clark, to the condition of bumbling idiots who obligingly lived up to the skipper's lowest expectations of us. It was a case of giving a dog a bad name. The arrogance that caused us to get lost at sea actually stemmed from a deep-seated and warranted insecurity.

Flinn now had to report to the same flotilla commander who had removed him from his first command. The commander was outraged that the same bad penny had turned up again, this time with a new instance of incompetence—our untimely arrival in the Azores. From our arrival at Falmouth until the Channel crossing two months later, whenever there was a dirty job to be done, or supplies to be picked up, the commander dispatched the 555, while those on other ships got three-day passes to London. From the perspective of fifty years, I can now feel a little compassion for Flinn as well as the officers under him, but the quality of mercy is strained a bit.

FOUR

Yank in the Streets

For two months after making port at Falmouth, we were often on the move between there and other small ports of the West Country, shuttling supplies and personnel from place to place. These errands were probably important to some larger plan of preparation for "the big one," the invasion of France, but we blamed our hapless skipper, who was in the flotilla commander's doghouse and thus drew all the disagreeable assignments nobody else wanted. Our resentment stayed at the boiling point, and his churlish temper did not improve a whit. It even got worse as he passed the commander's flak on to us. Navy lingo had a word for us. It was fubar—fucked up beyond all recognition.

We miraculously escaped any new misadventures for the time being, and tightened ship now that we were close to shore and subject to inspection. Under orders from the exec, the crew cleaned their quarters, picked up clutter on the decks, maintained a sharp gangway watch, and went back to basics in attire and conduct. There was once again a place for everything and everything in its place. Morale, however, remained in the pits.

The safety valve of our discontent was overnight liberty whenever we were in port, for half the crew and officers one night and for the other half the next. We rode at anchor with other LCIs in Flushing Trot, a body of water upstream about a mile from downtown Falmouth. Once every hour until midnight, a liberty boat manned by retired veterans of the Royal Navy plied between our anchorage and the Prince of Wales Pier in town. At the foot of narrow cobblestone streets leading steeply down from the residential hills was a tiny downtown, consisting of a few elegant small hotels such as the Prince of Wales, and a scattering of hole-in-the-wall pubs, bars, and cafés. In peacetime the town had made its living as a not very fashionable summer resort (nearby Torquay was nicer), with fishing and light shipping to supplement tourism, and it undoubtedly would return to these occupations after the war. For "the duration," however, it was servicemen—mostly Americans—who put money in the pockets and pocketbooks of Falmouthians. Only rarely did one see a civilian automobile, but many military vehicles were parked in front of shops and pubs.

The typical shop was built on the order of a house, dark and old, without the display window or flashy sign one would find in America. I found all this shabby understatement charming compared with the neon jungles of American nightlife. Some shops and taverns were closed for lack of goods to sell, but servicemen and their girls, young and not so young, crowded into those that were open. Some of the girls we met worked as waitresses in the pubs, but others were off duty and available. Even so, men far outnumbered women in this and other Channel ports. Yanks, as all Americans were called regardless of origin, outnumbered and outspent the Limeys, as we derisively termed all British servicemen. It was "the world turned upside down" again, American GIs having a monetary advantage in the competition for girls even in the Englishmen's own country. Young Englishmen were mostly somewhere else, in the service or in war industries, and American sailors held sway in the town except for competition from American soldiers at a nearby base and an occasional British serviceman on leave.

"The girls over here that I've met are pretty much like girls back home," I wrote Diana, "except that they talk so fast you can't understand them, and have big, bulging muscles in their legs from walking up and down the hills. They know all the American songs, though, and jitterbug as much as we do." That reference to bulging muscles was overstated. It was the sort of slander one felt free to utter against foreigners. Even Cotton Clark, usually scrupulously fair, indulged in this chauvinism. "The people are an odd lot," he told his diary, "congenial when talking to them but you could feel a strong resentment on their part of the Americans taking over their town."

The War and Navy departments tried to bridge the cultural gap with a thin paperback "Short Guide to Great Britain," for the use of military personnel only. I still have a copy, on the cover of which someone—not I—painted a crude swastika. It surely could not have been I—I was for Roosevelt, not Hitler. It was "Not to be republished, in whole or in part, without the consent of the War Department," but surely after this lapse of time a few passages are permissible. The British, according to this guide, were "reserved, not unfriendly. . . . The British dislike bragging and showing off." British landmarks were not bigger than ours, but were older. Don't tell Britishers that we had won the last war. "Don't play into Hitler's hands by mentioning war debts." Above all, "NEVER criticize the King or Queen." Or the food, beer, or cigarettes. And if invited to eat with a family, don't "eat up their weekly rations." Unfortunately, this good advice was honored more often in the breach than in the observance.

Falmouth had been bombed about two years earlier, but most of the bombs had fallen harmlessly in the harbor. A badly damaged church in the center of town, however, was silent evidence that not all the bombs had missed their targets. Falmouth was only twenty minutes "bombing time" from German bases on the far shore. One night while we were there, even that late in the air war, Falmouth had an air raid alert when German planes flew over, but they were either reconnaissance planes or in search of bigger game. The "all clear" sounded after only ten minutes, and I slept through the entire excitement. The only movie house in town, an ancient dark hole, was showing *Coney Island*. *North Star* and *Phantom of the Opera* (the Paul Muni version) were coming attractions—all American films. The theater had no counter for the candy and popcorn that were major elements of moviegoing in America.

Occasionally we had dinner in one of the cafés, but good food was scarce among civilians. A toasted cheese sandwich might be the most interesting thing on the menu, but it would be served with an old-world elegance unheard of in an American greasy spoon. Farther down the street was an English barbershop, where I treated myself to a non-GI haircut for a shilling and tuppence. The barber was as loquacious as his American counterpart, but there were subtle differences. The

English barber did not close-crop the hair on the sides and back, and he had an assistant to brush and comb the hair after the head barber finished—all this for the English equivalent of a quarter!

Our nightly entertainment was mostly in pubs, where there were no distinctions of rank and the drink was warm English beer. There were dances for officers only at the Falmouth Club—elite, sedate, chaperoned occasions where couples danced not cheek to cheek or even front to front. They danced to the side of each other to the music of a four-piece band. On a fast number, usually of American vintage, however, the feet of English couples flew at an amazing speed, comparable only to those of jitterbugs back home.

Falmouth is enshrined in memory as the town where I lost my virginity at the age of twenty-one. True, there had been a near-miss in the summer after I graduated from high school, when a friend of mine from out of town had learned the address of a whorehouse in Atlanta and felt the need of my company in approaching it on Sunday morning. He figured correctly that the trade would be light on a Sunday and the girls more open to turning a trick with adolescents. We entered the living room of a shabby house in the seedy part of town. The girl of my choice led me off to a room and disrobed before I could think what I was supposed to do next, and I was suddenly staring at forbidden fruit, nipples that looked back at me like the headlights of an oncoming car. I fumbled toward her and clumsily caressed her breast, and wondered what to do next. Sensing my inexperience, she did the rest, all of it. She helped me off with my clothes, pulled me toward the bed, furnished the condom, and helped me put it on. Ah, there was the rub! I had spent a feverish night anticipating this occasion and was so aroused that as she massaged my penis before inserting it I came in her hand. Blushing with embarrassment, I apologized profusely, paid her anyhow, and urged her not to mention this downstairs. She replied in a motherly tone, "Of course not. Accidents will happen in the best of families." Except for that borderline case, my virginity was still technically intact four years later and I ached to lose it in a proper manner. Falmouth, my first foreign town, was my opportunity.

Condoms were available to me without embarrassment because I was in charge of the ship's store. Why I had only one condom stowed in my wallet when I went ashore, I do not remember, but that was how it was. Wandering into a pub at night, I met some Army enlisted men who had planned to give some English girls an American-style hayride in the back of an Army truck. Getting permission to join their party, I bonded with one of the girls and rode with her through the moonlight for a couple of hours. In the aroma of the hay and the anonymity of the darkness I "made hay" with the winsome lass by hugs, kisses, and some exploration, and to my surprise she offered no resistance. About midnight, when the hayride ended, she invited me to walk her home. The last liberty boat was about to leave the pier, but I threw caution to the winds. I was thoroughly aroused, and armed with my single condom. This might be a night to remember.

Home turned out to be a large house filled with small bedrooms where she and other working girls in their late teens and twenties lived together away from home. At that late hour, the house was dark and everyone seemed asleep. She invited me in, shushed me into silence, and led me on tiptoe to her bedroom and her narrow single bed. As we lay there awkwardly but pleasurably, she bared a breast and let me kiss it but wouldn't shed her clothes. I groped at her underclothes and figured out why. I felt not the silk panties of fantasy but a single cotton undergarment that went from shoulder to crotch, the sort of underclothes only children wore in America. Was this because she was too young for what was about to happen, I wondered briefly, but her wandering hand gave reassurance of maturity. I pushed her underpants to one side and entered her as quietly as possible. In spite of the constant danger of falling out of bed, we had a lovely, or at least a lusty and satisfying, intercourse.

As we lay half in and half out of the narrow bed, she whispered compliments of my sexual prowess, comparing me favorably with other boys she had "done it" with. She made me promise, when I saw her again, to acknowledge her, not to pretend that I didn't know her. As we lay there in the afterglow, the urge came to both of us to make love again. But I had only the single condom. No problem, I thought, I'll use it again. It had slid away to one side, but I found it again in the dark and slid it back on. I could only hope that I had it on right side outmost. We made love again, this time at greater length, and fell apart exhausted. Whispering a promise to meet again, I crept silently out of bed and out of the house.

I coolly sauntered down to the pier. I had had my rite of passage, but I wondered then and later if my one-condom protection had been sufficient. I still wonder, for I never saw her again. I went the way of the sailor, as our ship left port before I got another liberty. What was her name? I cannot remember. This being my first offense, I lacked the perspective to understand the banality of sex without love. At least this particular girl was not a virgin, but I knew that only after the fact. Reaching the Prince of Wales Pier, I found a liberty boat just casting off its lines and jumped aboard in the nick of time, only to find that it was the wrong one, going to another anchorage. An hour later it brought me back to the pier, and I spent the night there contemplating the sex act until the early morning boat took me back to my ship.

We took advantage of the days in port not only to chase girls but to put our ship in order. Work crews came aboard to tune the engines and weld some stanchions that had given way during our ocean storms. The crew chipped and painted the ship from stem to stern, a work of many days, intended to build character and pride in the ship but falling short of the desired effect. In company with about a dozen other LCIs, American and British, we spent a day brushing up our beaching technique at a little shallow beach near Nare Head in Gerrans Bay, some ten miles from Falmouth. Flushing out our freshwater compartments below decks, we took on fresher water.

Once a week one of us officers rowed ashore from our anchorage to get our bread ration. A bread truck from the city brought the bread to a quonset hut and stacked it on the floor like cordwood, each heavy brown loaf weighing four pounds. The bread was just as it came from the oven, without basket or wrapper. It passed through four or five hands from oven to truck to storage to user, and thus was exposed to all the dirt of its surroundings. Despite this offense to American standards of hygiene, the English whole wheat bread was delicious and bore favorable comparison to American bakery bread. I was one of the few on my ship who properly appreciated it, however, because I had grown up with homemade bread. The men longed for what they were used to, the standard, air-inflated, tasteless American white bread.

One day in May we and the other LCIs "stripped ship," cutting our supplies down to the needs of thirty days, sending everything possible to be stored ashore. This lightened our ship to a draft of only four feet, seven inches, making it possible to get closer to shore in beaching. It was one of our early signs that we would soon be beaching on "the far shore." We took on a large supply of K rations for future troops. As supply officer I took the liberty of eating a sample of the rations as a between-meals snack, but found it disappointing, unfit for man or beast.

On May 15, at the crack of dawn, we got underway in company with five other LCIs. After a long day of rough weather, we entered Portland harbor. The two towns of Portland and Weymouth, with a combined population of about 35,000, were joined by a causeway from the mainland to the Bill of Portland. In peacetime they were summer resorts and still clung tenuously to a festive atmosphere. Hardly had we arrived, however, when an air raid alarm sounded. We thought we heard gunfire at a distance, and soon a smokescreen obscured everything. We saw beacons flashing in every direction but no planes, and after an hour we heard the all-clear signal. Perhaps it was a drill or a false alarm, but it raised our hackles. We seemed to be edging closer to the dogs of war. On Sunday I attended a church on the Bill of Portland and heard a pacifist sermon—not a policy-oriented one, but stressing the Christian virtues of loving one's enemy and seeking a common ground of humanity after the war. Some servicemen in the congregation were obviously upset by the sermon and went away muttering about treason, but it seemed to me a healthy antidote to the demonizing of the enemy during wartime, a sign that free speech was still alive in Britain.

Tempers aboard ship remained close to flash point. Discontent spread down the chain of command from the skipper to junior officers and on to the crew. We felt that not all our enemies were across the Channel. Cotton Clark spoke in his diary for all the junior officers: "For almost a week the Captain has ridden me continuously, at times questioning my truthfulness it seems. He never confides in me and what information as to operations, etc I gather from adjoining ships or strictly by the grapevine. The situation actually proves very embarrassing at times in the presence of other junior officers. It seems that his scheme is directed at breaking us three almost to depth of relying upon him solely and he means to do just that by destroying every bit of confidence we have. In my mind I feel superiority to him in every way almost but certainly his 'policy' has given me an unsure attitude of doing even the smallest task where he is concerned. He challenged my ability to handle a muster this morning, to count life jackets, and called me a procrastinator, accusing me [of] be[ing] afraid of the men in dealing out penalties and other things, which when all piled almost make you hate the guy with a purple passion. Certainly he isn't worth the time in which he predominates my thoughts—but after all I must eat and sleep on the same ship."

Davis and I were at least equally with Clark the butt of the skipper's sarcasm, but Clark's post as executive officer forced him into more frequent contact with the skipper and made him the nearest target. As fourth officer I could evade the skipper's attention, but I could not escape all the odd jobs that defined my position as "lord high everything else." During our time in port my duties made a combination of stevedore and clerk out of me. Hour after hour I supervised the loading of supplies, prepared all the ship's reports and requisitions, and as communications officer had to update constantly our codes and ciphers and destroy the outdated ones, and periodically had to keep the ship's store open. As the candy supply became depleted, I proclaimed a ration of five candy bars a week for each man, not all of them chocolate, at the price of 2.8 cents a bar. Baby Ruths and Hershey almond bars were the first to disappear. Over time, the supply was reduced to Walnettos, a chewy caramel nut confection that grew harder by the day. We never ran out of cigarettes, however. Somebody back in the States probably recognized them as our most effective trade goods, and maybe the cigarette lobby had something to do with their constant availability. After all, Lucky Strike green had gone to war. There were even a few cigarettes in the canned Army C rations.

I was proud of becoming an old salt, with my gold braid tinged with green by the salt air. I was delighted to be about to take part in "the big show," as we called the invasion of Europe before we learned its name was Overlord. But I hated the mundane shipboard chores. Poring over the ration record, the signal books, the typewriter (I was the only officer who could type), and the *Yeoman's Guide* was not my idea of winning the war. Furthermore, I was three thousand miles from my girl and the nearest Coke bottle. I sought one day to drown my troubles with a swim at the Weymouth beach. It looked inviting, but the water turned out to be so cold that I turned blue and didn't thaw out until the next day. No Channel swim for me, at least not in May.

The skipper ruled his ship by the principle of divide and conquer, setting officer against officer, officer against crew, and crew against officer, thus channeling some of our discontent away from himself and toward each other. I tried to make friends of my fellow officers, but Davis was absorbed in his own misery of homesickness and Clark sought escape from everyone on our ship, confining his friendships and confidences to officers on our sister ships. Seeking to correct what the skipper called his leniency toward the crew, Clark mildly and privately reprimanded Paul Hoylo, the signalman, whom he actually thought the outstanding man in the crew, for failure to stand a scheduled watch. To Clark's surprise, Hoylo responded by bitter resentment, insulting Clark behind his back. It became a vendetta. They had stood watch together in the conn for most of the Atlantic voyage, had shared life stories and value judgments and seemed to be good friends. Clark felt shocked and betrayed by Hoylo's sudden hostility at a time when the skipper was also riding him. As days passed, Hoylo maintained his resentful attitude, ignoring and avoiding Clark as much as possible. Falling back on tested methods of college fraternity camaraderie, Clark wrote Hoylo a short note, ending it with the statement that "most Sigma Chi would handle such affairs man-to-man." Clark was a good man, but he was young enough to think the complex problems of human relations could be solved by adherence to the fraternity man's code. Hoylo refused to be mollified for quite a while, and attached himself to me as his new confidant among the officers. I tried to mitigate this pointless quarrel, and Hoylo finally came around. He had a new wariness of officers, however.

The skipper, perhaps unconsciously, fomented and aggravated such quarrels among those under his command, and soon sowed the seeds of another quarrel, this time between Clark and me. While small stores that we needed, such as new shoes for the crew and candy and cigarettes, were sitting on the Weymouth dock ready for loading—goods that the skipper had told Clark to let me handle—the skipper got underway to move the few miles to Portland. Had the skipper waited fifteen minutes longer, or notified me that the goods were there on the dock, they could have been brought aboard. Soon afterward the skipper said to Clark in front of the crew, "You missed the boat on these items." This small incident failed to cause a quarrel between Clark and me, but it revealed the skipper, as Clark said privately in his diary, as "a sneaking, double crossing fellow with no thoughts whatsoever concerning the next man." Our days cooped up together were filled with such petty tensions. We needed some action to make us forget it all.

We sailed west to Dartmouth for a few days, and each of us in turn got a two-day leave. I planned to use my leave to take a train trip to London, where I would be able to spend a few hours sightseeing before returning to the ship. I thought, like Puss in Boots, I would at least be able to say I had been to London. As I rode the train toward London, however, I struck up an acquaintance with an attractive English girl about my own age or perhaps a few years younger, traveling in my compartment. I learned that she was on her way to join an agricultural program to aid the war effort. She and other girls would be trained on a country estate north of Exeter to grow food crops badly needed by the people in the cities. I soon came to believe that a date with her in rustic surroundings would be a greater adventure and a better way to "know the English" than a few hours gawking at the sights of London.

When I proposed to accompany this young woman to her new quarters, carrying some of her heavy luggage, she said she thought there would be no objection to a date, because she wouldn't yet have been assigned any work. I left the train with her and carried her bags for several miles out into the countryside. Surely, a date would be an appropriate reward for my labors. Finally, toward dark, we reached her destination, a handsome manor house, but as we went in the door we confronted a most formidable, skeptical, and regal personage—either the owner of the house or the woman in charge of the agricultural program. She was aquiver with disapproval of one of her girls arriving with a serviceman in tow.

That was a whole new perspective for me to consider. I put on my best southern manners and hoped my officer rank might melt her icy disapproval, but she ordered me out forthwith and ordered the girl to report somewhere in the bowels of the house. The girl whispered that she would send word to me if I would wait outside. I stepped out and waited in the growing darkness, until finally another girl came out with the message that she would not be coming, that all new arrivals were restricted to "barracks" for several days. Several other girls made offers of a date, but I took the view that if I couldn't have my chosen date I would have no date at all. I walked back to Exeter, spent the night in a hotel that had been commandeered by the USO, and made my way forlornly back to my ship next day, thinking that London might have been better after all.

On May 21 we left Weymouth-Portland for Plymouth. After a rough all-day trip we entered Plymouth harbor and were led up the quiet Tamar River to moor in a cove at Saltash, a little working-class suburb of Plymouth across the county line in Cornwall. Spring was far advanced now, and the countryside close around was verdant. Some Army personnel arrived in a motor launch to load 10–in-1 rations and Army blankets aboard our ship. Clearly, some action was in the offing. The Army left a sergeant aboard to guard these supplies.

Liberty was freely available during our ten days in Plymouth. I went into town and was shocked at the devastation. "The hell has been bombed out of the town," I wrote Diana, "and half the buildings are just heaps of concrete." On a Sunday afternoon Curly Davis and I went out to the beach, and the water looked so inviting I resolved to try another swim next time I got ashore. The sun was hot enough for a suntan. The temperature was over eighty. Davis and I went to the officers' club for drinks, to a show, a restaurant, and an open-air concert by the Royal Marine Band.

Plymouth had charms to soothe the savage breast. Artie Shaw's band came to town, and Clark's diary recorded the occasion simply as "Swell music but gals few and far between." He failed to capture the real drama of the occasion, as I described it to Diana from "Somewhere in England": "Night before last the Captain decided to take liberty on my night and Cotton Clark's, and since Artie Shaw's Navy band was playing for a dance ashore, we decided to leave anyhow and only the engineering officer was aboard. Well, we knew we would have to avoid the captain, because he doesn't have a conscience to trouble him. There are supposed to be two officers aboard and he would put the blame on us. So Cotton and I travelled alone. He went to the dance first and who should he see but the Captain, who was bewildered by the stealthy blow of gin but recognized Clark. So he says to Clark, 'I think I'll head back to the ———— dance for the last few pieces.' So who should I see in the train station but the captain. He didn't see me, and I got on the next car. I went to the dance just as he went out the door and Clark was there too. Meanwhile a message had come three hours before to the ship to send an officer messenger and two men ashore *at once*. Davis, the engineering officer, didn't know what to do. If he went it would be a court-martial offense. So he sent two men to look for me. They went to every pub and every dance in town, paged me, and in general raised hell. Finally, after a drink at every pub and every dance, they found me, and who should I meet but the captain again, catching the liberty boat back. We pretended I was just leaving the ship, and he swallowed it all. I spent the rest of the night trying to get the stuff we were called to get. Just like the Comedy of Errors, but it took ten years off my life." I relished that experience as the one time I had got the better of the skipper.

Our pleasures ended abruptly. Plymouth sustained a full-scale air raid on the night of May 29. We had our first clear sight of enemy planes outlined by searchlights against the sky, and we could hear antiaircraft gunfire close by. Two days later small boats called LCVPs (Landing Craft Vehicle Personnel) came alongside and put aboard our ship a company of U.S. Army troops. They were 186 enlisted men and sixteen officers of the 115th Infantry, 29th Division, under the command of Major Victor P. Gillespie. Members of the Maryland National-al Guard, these men had been in the war almost from the beginning of American involvement. They were seasoned by fighting in North Africa and Sicily before moving to England to prepare for the invasion of France. Each man brought either a machine gun or a carbine and a heavy pack. They were to be the reserve assault troops for the invasion, we learned. Our once roomy ship was now suddenly crowded with soldiers. "Since the troops have been using the troop officers' stateroom," I wrote Diana, "I have been forced out and have to room with the captain, who is personally the most disagreeable human being I have ever been forced into association with. The other officers are fine, and that keeps my existence from being too trying."

All liberty was canceled and tight security went into force, meaning no outgoing mail. Our ship and other LCIs moved to a new anchorage farther downriver at Jenny Cliff Bay, and then we traveled in convoy out into the Channel to another anchorage in Weymouth Bay. Blustery weather gave the troops a taste of what a Channel crossing would mean, and many were violently seasick. At Weymouth we waited a week for a signal to move, but the weather continued to be rough. Our galley being too small to cook for the soldiers, they lived on their 10–in-1 rations, which soon had to be replenished. Either this invasion was poorly planned, we concluded, or else it was being held up by bad weather. Trying to keep in fighting trim, the troops did calisthenics on our well deck. We ourselves were woefully ignorant of the strategy in which we would play a part, but the skipper left for a hush-hush meeting with higher-ups ashore and came back to brief us hurriedly on the plans for the invasion.

The skipper finally, with great reluctance, showed us junior officers the charts he had been given of the English Channel, maps of the Normandy coast, and even profile views of the coastline where we would land, based on reconnaissance photographs. They showed every church steeple, hill, and ravine, and, along the shore, the ominous serried rows of beach obstructions the Germans had planted there in the zone between high and low tides. There were tetrahedrons, hedgehogs, and sharpened stakes driven into the sand to obstruct a landing, facing outward to puncture the bows and bottoms of landing craft. Long before our prospective landing around 11 in the morning, we were reassured, Army Rangers and Navy frogmen would have gone ashore, before dawn or even the night before, to defuse or explode the mines, destroy the hedgehogs and other beach obstructions, and wipe out or capture any artillery strongholds guarding the beaches.

We already had some apprehension about the approaching invasion because of the disastrous Dieppe Raid in 1942 by British and Canadian troops to test the German coastal defenses. We knew that the Allied forces had been repelled, but wartime security had prevented our realizing what a total failure it had been. We had no idea that only about a month before our arrival in England there had been a similar disaster at Slapton Sands, a little beach just three or four miles from Dartmouth. During a mock landing there at night by American landing craft and troops, a dense fog rolled in and under its cover German submarines and surface craft stole in and opened fire on the landing craft, sank ships, killed many soldiers, and wreaked havoc. By a miracle of wartime security the disaster was covered up and the local civilians even evacuated and interned in order to prevent a leak that might damage Allied morale on the eve of invasion.

FIVE

The Real Thing

Sitting in our tub for five days in Weymouth harbor, we got acquaint-ed with the 115th Infantry troops we were to carry into the beach. Their work would begin where ours ended, at the water's edge, and they seemed remarkably fit for it. After their initial tests of battle in North Africa and Sicily, they had spent two years in England honing their fighting skills. As Clark said in his diary, "The whole outfit was truly a trim bunch of soldiers, from the officers down and after seeing this fine group of fighting men that beachhead we were slated to capture became all the more tangible." A top sergeant gave us GI haircuts, which our crew promptly labeled "the invasion special."

We had expected to cross the channel on June 3, but on that day we learned that D Day—a new term in our vocabulary—was postponed until June 5. Later yet, word came that D Day would be delayed one additional day on account of bad weather in the Channel. We began to wonder if it would ever occur. For us, D minus 1 was "the longest day." The soldiers grew restless in their cramped quarters below decks, and not only because of the delay. Their equipment was so bulky that movement in the troop holds was difficult and poker games almost impossible. The air down there grew stale, and more and more soldiers sought fresh air and elbow room on the outer decks. We Navy people were also keyed up. We had rehearsed enough. We were ready for "the real thing." But we also felt some apprehension about how well we would meet the chal-lenge. From the captain down to our seasick cook, our entire ship's com-pany had played the fool in one way or another ever since the ship was commissioned. Thoughts and fears of fouling up again ran rampant during this period of inaction. The coming battle would put us to the test.

Our first question on the morning of June 5 was whether this would be D-1, the day of departure? The water was still choppy behind the breakwater of our little harbor, and we could imagine how much rougher it would be in the open water of the English Channel. A cloud blanket and haze limited visibility to perhaps a mile. By noon, however, no word of further delay had reached us. The troops got their gear in order, camouflaged their helmets, and were all set. At 1630—late afternoon—the signal came from the flotilla flagship to get underway and fall into line with other LCIs. We weighed anchor and took our station behind the 541 and in front of the 557. We soon found ourselves in the port column of a tremendous convoy gradually taking shape, extending eastward from Weymouth to the Isle of Wight.

The invasion fleet was too large for us to visualize, but it was certainly reassuring as to the safety in numbers. We could see battleships, cruisers, destroyers, and others of every kind and size, stretching around us and on out of sight. Hundreds of minesweepers crisscrossed in front of the convoy searching for underwater mines to destroy. Meanwhile in the sky overhead we heard the reassuring drone of Allied planes, each marked with a white and a black stripe to make for easy identification. It was reported that 6,000 bombers and 4,500 fighter planes were to take part, surely enough to sweep the skies of the diminished Luftwaffe, to destroy German ground troops defending the Normandy coast, and to provide complete air cover for the invasion.

Proceeding eastward along the English coast for several hours while day turned to night, the convoy then wheeled southward toward the Bay of the Seine on the Normandy coast. The sea stayed rough, but the clouds began to break, revealing a full moon that gave us a brighter light to steer by and a brighter outlook. Though we did not know it at the time, the full moon had been factored into the invasion plan. Greater visibility heightened the reassurance we gained from the magnitude of the armada around us, probably the largest gathering of warships in the history of humankind. We had the feeling that, whatever danger might await us individually, our enterprise was going to succeed. If our enemies were ten feet tall, so were we.

Around midnight we heard the first sounds of explosions ahead, either bombs or naval guns, and far ahead on the horizon we could see bright yellow flashes. Flares lit up the sky. The drone of planes overhead was now almost continuous. In the moonlight we saw wave after wave pass overhead, then the sky became overcast again. Nobody aboard slept that night. We didn't even think of sleep. We junior officers took our four-hour turns at watch, but the skipper was continually in the conn and in charge throughout the voyage. Most of the soldiers became seasick, and undoubtedly some of them even longed for dry land more than they feared the enemy lurking there.

The convoy slowed from twelve to eight knots in the small hours of the night, as we approached the transport area about ten miles off the Normandy coast. There the convoy column broke up, and the LCIs began a series of circling courses opposite our sector of beach, awaiting the first landings scheduled for the break of day. A brisk wind blew, and a rough sea bounced our flat-bottomed tub as we wheeled around waiting for the curtain to go up on the colossal drama of invasion. Would it be a smash hit or a flop? So far all seemed to have gone well. We assumed that our bombers had hit their targets onshore. But many a soldier was rushing up from the troop holds below to lean over the rail and vomit. And not all of them made it to the rail. We wondered if they would have any strength or fight left in them when they hit the beach.

Reveille sounded on our ship at 0600, though few if any needed to be aroused, and morning chow at 0630 gave us Navy guys, at least, stomach for the fight. It was about then that the first wave of assault troops was hitting the beach, while those aboard the LCIs were held in reserve for a second wave. Our officers and crew made ready for beaching whenever the call came, and the troops went through their own routine of preparation. Meanwhile, we continued our monotonous circling offshore, riding smoother or bumpier depending on where in our course we were, whether wind and wave were hitting us forward, amidships, or aft. This circling continued all morning, giving us in effect a front-row seat for the early stages of D Day. We were close enough to see and hear the thunderous fire of 16-inch guns from a battleship and a cruiser offshore, and explosive bursts on the cliffs and hillsides near the beach indicating that their shells had found targets. We were too far away to discern enemy movements or the landing of small LCVPs on the shore. Maybe there wouldn't be any resistance, we hoped in one breath, but common sense reasserted itself in the next breath and we accepted the probability of bloodshed.

As is often the case in warfare, we participants in the D Day landings understood little of the "big picture" or even our part in it, but the Allied generals and admirals did indeed have a grand strategy, and military historians over the years have carefully researched how it all turned out. There were an infinite number of venues for the second front the Russians had pleaded for all through 1942 and 1943, including Winston Churchill's pet project of opening up the "soft underbelly" of Europe through southern France or Greece. The Allied military planners had come by 1944 to agree, however, on landings along a hundred-mile stretch of the Normandy coast between the ports of Cherbourg and Le Havre. This was consistent with the American preference for a direct assault on the heart of Germany's strength, and every year after Pearl Harbor the American component in the Allied war effort grew until it was dominant. The Soviet Union threw its weight behind the American position through its repeated demands for a major second front, needed to divert German divisions from the eastern front.

Though the Allies had agreed on a target area, they took steps to confuse the Germans about the time and place of the landings. More reconnaissance planes flew over the Calais area, for example, than over the Bay of the Seine or the Cotentin Peninsula, but those planes that flew over the prospective landing area had the best aerial photographers available, who observed and photographed every square inch of the coast. The charts we received for the invasion noted the many fortifications and beach obstacles blocking our path, and Navy frogmen went stealthily ashore the night before D Day to blow them up. When our convoy sailed eastward along the English coast before turning sharply southward, that was a feint intended to create the impression that it was headed toward the Pas de Calais. There were five landing areas for the Normandy invasion. The westernmost, designated Utah Beach, was on the east side of the Cotentin Peninsula south of Cherbourg.

Next, to the east of the Cotentin Peninsula, was Omaha Beach, where our ship was headed. Both of these beaches were assigned to the American forces. Farther along the coast to the east were the British beaches, Gold, Juno, and Sword. Because of the element of surprise, resistance to the initial landings on four of the beaches was relatively light, but Omaha Beach was strongly defended and the outcome of battle there was uncertain for at least the first day.

Omaha Beach was divided into sectors—code-named Fox Red, Fox Green, Easy Red, Easy Green, Dog Red, Dog Green, in that order, reading from east to west. Charlie was the code name for the sheer cliffs of Pointe de la Percée and Pointe du Hoc to the west of Omaha Beach, honeycombed with concrete pillboxes for artillery guns. These cliffs were scheduled to be scaled and seized during the night by a specially trained unit of the U.S. Rangers. Our section of beach was Dog Red, an ominous name, we thought.

Unknown to us, many of the Allied calculations, particularly for Omaha Beach, had gone awry. The German defenders suffered little from the heavy Allied bombing. Forced by the cloud cover to bomb blind, and fearful that unloading too soon would hit the oncoming invasion fleet, most of the bombers unloaded on territory several miles inland from the beach rather than on the forward defenses along the shore. Also, the German defenders had the advantage of holding the high ground, the cliffs and hills that rose some 200 feet above the beach. And, instead of a single German division defending the beach, as the Allies had anticipated, there were actually two divisions. One of them at the time of the assault was engaged in an invasion drill, and it was relatively easy for them to segue from dress rehearsal to the show itself.

The skipper sounded general quarters at 0925, and officers and men scrambled to their battle stations, each with his life jacket and helmet. We were ready, but the circling continued for two more hours. Finally, at 1145, we received the beachmaster's call and started toward Dog Red. Just then we saw our first casualty. As Cotton Clark described it in his diary, "My first sight of death in this war in its reality came as a body of a soldier was seen floating atop the water close by our ship. The feeling which came over me is hard to describe but for the first time I guess the thought of hitting the beach gave a certain uneasy feeling and one thing was clear—this time was the real thing." The worst aspect of this casualty was that it was probably preventable. All the Navy personnel wore the classic kapok "Mae West," but the Army issued its troops a less cumbersome rubber life belt around the waist that they were supposed to loosen, slide up under the armpits, and then inflate with a compressed-air cartridge, forming the equivalent of the inflated inner tube often seen around swimming pools. These life belts turned out to be a technological disaster. Many of the soldiers at Normandy, either because of shock from an explosion or panic from loss of footing, inflated their belts without loosening them, causing their midsection to float high in the water and forced their head and feet down. The soldier we saw in the water apparently drowned in this manner, as he floated face down with his butt in the air.

We manned our beaching stations, and the soldiers lined up on the well deck ready to disembark in an orderly manner. At 1155, having already dropped our stern anchor and paid out cable, we struck the beach alongside our sister ship, the 541. Almost dead ahead was the little town of Vierville, its buildings now out of sight in the steep hills just behind the shallow beach. To our right were the sheer cliffs of Pointe de la Percée. Busy with our tasks, we hardly had time to take in the scene, but we noticed a major problem right away. Instead of our bow hitting the sand close to shore, we were thirty or forty yards out. The beach was too shallow for us to get any closer. We would have to make the best of an awkward situation. I had a clear view of what followed, from my beaching station on the starboard side of the gun deck. As soon as the starboard ramp was lowered, Seaman first class Lawrence D. Olin, who had volunteered for the task, stepped off into water up to his armpits, carried a small anchor ashore, and drove it into the sand at the water's edge. Attached to the anchor was a sturdy line the troopers could cling to, to keep their footing as they made their way ashore. The water between the ramps and the shore had periodic swells high enough to sweep men off their feet. Olin made it back to the ship, half-walking and half-swimming through the surf, his head barely above water.

Meanwhile the troops put four army life rafts over the side to help them carry heavy gear ashore. As soon as Olin had climbed with some difficulty back on the ramp, the troops began their disembarkation. It was now high noon. The first soldier into the water was Major Gillespie, the company commander. Soon he and a line of other soldiers, heavily loaded with weapons and other gear weighing between 80 and 110 pounds, were struggling toward shore, grasping the lifeline desperately as swells lifted them off their feet, moving forward with agonizing slowness. It took fifteen or twenty minutes for the first men to reach shore, and it seemed like hours. Cotton wrote in his diary, "As the men started on that trip down the ramp the face of each told a story in itself. Some looked as though they were going to a church wedding, others serious looking, most, however, joking and wondering 'what the hell was taking so long.' The spirit of these soldiers was wonderful indeed and you couldn't help feeling as though a spirit [such] as this would never be defeated." Clark forgot to mention that the reason some of the soldiers smiled was because they were so glad to get back on land after all the seasickness.

Finally the last four men, the medics, perhaps the most heavily loaded of all, were on the starboard ramp ready to disembark. The alongshore current and the swells had been battering the ramps against the ship's hull ever since we had beached, and suddenly the force of a huge wave bent the starboard ramp at its highest point and twisted it off its housing. The ramp fell into the water, still attached to its cables, and banged repeatedly against the hull. As the ramp fell, the four medics hesitated for a moment in confusion, then jumped clear of the ramp into water up to their necks and occasionally over their heads. They struggled there, too far away to grab the lifeline, close to drowning in the churning water. Seaman first class Bob Starkey, a redheaded, overweight Irishman whose duty had been to assist the soldiers off the ramp, lowered himself into the water, held the lifeline taut, and stretched out his hand far enough to help the bobbing medics reach the lifeline and struggle to shore. It is doubtful that they would have made it without his help. He was a brave man but not much of a swimmer, and he had quite a struggle getting back aboard the ship through the breakers, arriving utterly exhausted. I wanted to help him but my duty was to remain at my station on the gun deck.

Cotton Clark, whose beaching station was on the forecastle, the forwardmost part of the ship next to the ramps, supervised the cutting of the cables holding the ramp to the ship before it could ram a hole in our bow or hamper our retracting from the beach. We regretted losing a part of ourselves and adding to the beach obstructions, but we would have been unable to cruise in open water with the ramp dangling and banging. Then we started to retract from the beach preparatory to returning to the staging area offshore.

We had been so busy with our own beaching and aiding the disembarkation of our troops that we had little time to feel fear or even notice what went on around us. We could hardly fail, however, to hear the artillery fire constantly whistling overhead and exploding. Hearing the heavy gunfire of our battleships and cruisers lying offshore, then seeing geysers of water from exploding shells all along the waterline ahead of us and alongside of us, we assumed that by some ghastly miscalculation our own warships were firing at us. We figured out eventually that these shells exploding around us were fired from the dreaded German .88 guns that were supposed to have been knocked out by our bombardment and naval gunfire. Unbeknownst to us or to the Allied high command, shortly before the invasion the Germans had ingeniously mounted .88s on a short railroad track just behind the hills and thus were able to move the guns frequently to evade Allied counterfire.

It was not until much later that we learned that the American troops at Omaha Beach faced the strongest German resistance and had ten times the Utah Beach casualties, and that our sector of Omaha, Dog Red, was the most fiercely contested. The military commanders at Omaha Beach had deliberately chosen to attack head on rather than by flanking or subterfuge, in a situation where the defenders held the high ground, and the dogfaces had to pay with their blood the price of this foolhardy arrogance. American troops of the first wave who had reached Dog Red in early morning found most of the beach obstacles still in place, and most of their artillery and tanks were dumped unceremoniously into the water by the unexpectedly heavy offshore wind and current. Many small landing craft also capsized and packed against the German obstructions to form a barrier to further landing. Unable to secure the beachhead, most of the first wave were either killed or pinned down and exposed on the flat beach near the waterline, while the Germans from the protected high ground raked them with artillery and small-arms fire. Our LCI wave, therefore, was equivalent to a first wave at Dog Red; it was our troops of the 115th Infantry who, after heavy casualties, secured that stretch of the beach.

We could see, as we went in, the debris of the earlier struggle. At the waterline was almost a solid line of small craft put out of action, and the shallow water was crowded with half-submerged tanks, capsized small boats, and remaining beach obstacles. Among the obstacles were a few of the many-pointed hedgehogs, but the most persistent obstructions were sharpened wooden stakes driven into the sand between the high water and low water lines and protruding outward and upward. We had to pick our way carefully between the obstacles and wreckage. Our ship's company was unscathed, however, unless one counted a piece of spent shrapnel that hit a signalman in the butt. Some of our companion ships were not so lucky. The ship immediately to port of us, LCI(L) 492, took an indirect hit from an .88 shore battery about midships on her well deck. We saw troopers there who had been standing ready to debark, falling to the deck from the impact of the explosion, but we could not judge the extent of damage. Down the beach we saw an LCT afire, and in the distance what appeared to be an LCI ablaze. Dead American soldiers lay on the shallow beach, most of them neatly stacked like cordwood, possibly for use as cover for living men pinned down on the beach.

The tide of battle was shifting, however, while we were beached. We could see through binoculars a file of American soldiers moving slowly forward along a ravine leading to the top of the plateau above the beach. Houses along the shore were partly demolished, and gaping shellholes pockmarked the hillsides that loomed over the beach. A lone American tank had survived the trauma of landing and moved along the beach firing what sounded like a popgun compared with the heavier fire overhead. It soon took a hit, blazed and smoked. A single bulldozer moved near our beaching point, and some twenty German prisoners marched under guard along the shore. What glimpses we got gave no clear sign as to the outcome of the battle.

As we retracted from the beach at 1228, our skipper had an opportunity to show his mettle and to gain a better standing in our eyes than his petty arrogance had achieved. One of our sister ships, LCI(L) 553, which had beached several ships over to our port, sent us a blinker message that it was in distress and needed our help to get off the beach. It was unable to retract from the beach and would soon be high and dry, as the tide was going out, and asked us to give it a tow to deeper water. Without hesitation, the skipper signaled his willingness to help, even though the shells were flying and landing near us, and we might be hit at any moment. Moving out a few hundred yards, we dropped our stern anchor again and headed in toward the 553. The strong along-shore current, however, the same one that had torn off our ramp, swept us off course and out of reach of the 553. We fired a Lyle gun, a little popgun that fired a ball with a light line attached, to which a heavier line or cable could be attached if we hit our target. We fired a second time without success, but the 553's Lyle gun reached our deck, and we passed our bow anchor cable over as a tow line. This cable, attached to the winch on the 553's fantail, was intended to tow it off the beach as we winched our own stern cable and retracted. We revved our engines for additional towing power, but the 553 did not budge.

Artillery fire from shore continued to rain around us, and there were surely some silent prayers that we would soon move out of range and that the skipper would give up trying to dislodge the 553. The skipper, however, remained calmly determined to rescue the other ship. As Clark later wrote in his diary, "By this time the gunfire was really getting hot. Two LCI(L) together made a good target. The enemy had our range alright. The bullets were dropping close to our side and usually about amidship. Shrapnel was flying about furiously, and we found it together with shells & rocks blown from mines on our decks. Our men worked fast and wonderfully well under the first gunfire they had experienced and had it not been for unusual circumstances we could have towed the 553 off the beach." After several more tries, it became clear that the ebbing tide and some underwater obstruction, possibly a half-track tank that had never made it ashore, were blocking the retraction of the 553. Finally, at 1255, we abandoned the effort, severed our cable connection, and hightailed it away from the beach to join the other LCIs of our flotilla in the transport area offshore. We had been at the hotly contested beach for more than an hour. "I thanked my lucky stars that I came out of that ordeal alive," Clark confided to his diary, "because I fully realize that only one person could have brought us through safely. I thanked Him plenty."

The 553 never did get off the beach. After the tide went out and left it high and dry, the crew abandoned ship and huddled on the shore with the troops, and sometime in the afternoon it took a direct hit from the German artillery. After several days, when further efforts failed to rescue it, its personnel were evacuated to England and reassigned to other LCIs. Meanwhile, in midafternoon of D Day we joined nine other LCIs in a reciprocal course back across the Channel, the sounds of gunfire fading away behind us. We were not running away from battle but going back for another load of troops. This time we sailed without escort, and anchored in Weymouth Harbor at 0308 on the morning of June 7. After nearly two days and nights without sleep, we dozed heavily for about three hours until reveille started it all again at dawn.

Emory V-12 at Dobbs Hall, 1943. H. L. (Mitch) Mitchell, last row, first on left. Author immediately in front of Mitchell, and "Sonny" Williams, midshipmen's school roommate, is to right in front of author.

Author and four roommates at Emory V-12, at author's home in Decatur, Georgia, summer 1943. From left: author, Parr, ?, Mitchell, David.

Emory V-12 roommates at a party at the author's house. From left: the author, his sister Harriet, David, the author's sister Stella, Parr.

Midshipmen on training cruise, Long Island Sound, January 1944. Author at lower right.

The newly minted ensign, in Navy greatcoat, February 1944.

I hope you have a license. Do you?

That picture you sent was of an LS[T] ... of the landing craft, which one of us ... sizes depending on their use. They all ... like screws, than anything else. The LCI ... pretty ship ... with ... bow and graceful lines. It carries ... troops. Then the LCV carries jeeps, peeps, vehicles, etc. the LCP is a small personnel ... the LCVP's carry both, etc. etc. But ... for LCI duty. I may get sent to ... Florida, Solomons, Nd, or San Diego, Ca ... of Little Creek, so don't count on me ... up to HC very often. Damn it! I ... to be in the Mediterranean or Pacific ... zone by May. Then again I mig[ht] ... DE school with 4 months training.

Romantic sketch of an LCI. From a letter to Diana, Feb. 1, 1944, before seeing one.

An LCI underway at sea. Courtesy of the National Archives.

Diana and her dormitory, 1944.

Ensign Harold W. "Cotton" Clark writing home, 1944. His future wife Gloria Gambill in photo.

Some of the ship's company at Plymouth, England, May 24, 1944. Front row, from left: the author, Olin, Petergal, Jones, Pisaneschi. Back row, from left: Mohr, Dwyer, Ensign Davis, Ensign Clark, Rost, Polick. (See pp. 80–81.)

Crew members in the mess hall. Front row, from left: Rost, Smigielski, Hoylo, Brown, Foster, and the new mascot (Salty the cat jumped ship in Plymouth). Second row: Dwyer, Anderson (seaman 1/c), Patton, Burk. Third row: King, Carlson, Anderson (motor mac), Candeto.

LCI(L) 555 underway in a fog with troops aboard.

LCI(L) 553 landing troops at Omaha Beach on D Day. It later received two direct hits and was left a wreck on the beach. (See p. 73.) Courtesy of the National Archives.

SIX

Do Not Fire
unless Directly
Attacked

"I am 'OK,'" I wrote Diana in a hasty V-mail the morning after D Day. "P. S. We were in the assault force." I sent a similarly brief letter to my parents. A few days later I volunteered a few more details, but none that would give aid or comfort to the enemy. "I was eating one of your candy drops when we went into our beach," I wrote Diana, "and it really gave me a shot in the arm—not the kind it sounds like, however." On our first day back we tied up to the Weymouth dock for some hasty repairs. A working party from ashore replaced the ramp we had lost on the beach and the bow anchor we had cut loose when we passed its cable over to the 553 as a towline.

While we were docked, fifty cases of K rations arrived, and close behind them a fresh shipload of troops. We moved out to the Portland anchorage awaiting our sailing orders, but because of a mixup in our orders it was after midnight when we set off again for Normandy. The LCI(L) 557 simply blinked us saying it was getting underway, and our skipper agreed to go too, apparently without sailing orders or escort. Two British LCTs joined us. It was probably foolish and risky to sail off without orders, but luck was with us and we muddled through. If there were any German subs in the Channel, they were probably looking for bigger game. An hour out of port one of the LCTs collided with a tug, but neither was seriously damaged. We soon joined up with ten other LCIs and LCTs and proceeded to an anchorage off Omaha Beach, where we caught a few more hours of sleep.

General quarters lasted for about an hour after midnight. Gunfire was plentiful, and we could hear planes directly overhead. The protecting ships sent up a brilliant barrage of antiaircraft fire, and we saw three planes go down in flames not far away. Evidently Allied forces had secured the beach by then, for we heard no more from shore, and we rested peacefully during what remained of the night. Conditions along the beach were a sharp contrast with our experience only two days earlier. There was also a contrast in the quality of troops we carried. Clark remarked caustically in his diary: "This group of troops are a supply outfit, carrying 30 officers in this unit. The number of meat heads I've never seen before. There were Lt. Colonels, & Colonels at every corner. This outfit is about as sorry [as] the first was good. Heaven help them once they get on the beach!" In the afternoon of the next day, small beachcraft carried our troops ashore and we moved to a better anchorage. General quarters that night lasted only seven minutes, an indication that at least the shoreline part of the invasion was going well. After a good night's sleep, marred only by an early morning air raid in which four planes were shot down, we returned with six other LCIs to Weymouth around midnight of June 10 and tied up again at the Weymouth pier. The following night, for the first time in two weeks, liberty parties went ashore for four and a half hours of freedom and solid ground.

During the six weeks after D Day, LCI(L) 555 and many other ships settled into a routine of shuttling troops and supplies across the Channel to the Normandy beachhead. We did this until harbor facilities were cleared for larger vessels on the Normandy coast. Weymouth was our home port for the first few weeks, then we moved to Poole and its nearby resort town of Bournemouth. We noticed on our liberty nights that the success of the invasion had greatly improved English attitudes toward the Americans. We were no longer the occupying army but liberators from a long war that had nearly exhausted them.

Changes on the far shore gradually made our method of transporting troops obsolete. As the Germans evacuated the Cotentin Peninsula in Normandy they blew up Cherbourg, the only port in the area, leaving it a mass of twisted steel and sunken ships that would take months to clean out before large ships could use it. The Allies had anticipated this at least a year before the invasion, however, and carried out secretly a plan to construct their own artificial harbor at Arromanches a few miles east of Omaha Beach. In the interim, the Americans sank obsolete British cargo ships in a large semicircle in the shallow water off Omaha Beach. The sunken ships served as a breakwater, and a pontoon bridge connected them with the shore. This temporary harbor allowed large troopships and freighters to unload, but it was only the first step. A heavy storm on June 19–23 soon breached this makeshift haven. Meanwhile, British engineers brought to Arromanches what they called a Mulberry Harbour, huge hollow concrete sections that barely floated as tugs towed them slowly down the British west coast toward the Normandy beachhead. Starting out well before D Day, they arrived at Arromanches in the days following D Day and were sunk in place to form a more permanent temporary harbor. In our various trips across the Channel we watched the American and British artificial harbors unfold and gradually spell the end of our usefulness. They were both vulnerable to storms, however, and served only until the natural harbors of France could be cleared.

Meanwhile, in company with other LCIs and LCTs, we carried American troops to Utah Beach on June 13 and brought another shipload on June 17. On June 25–26 we took three British naval officers aboard as liaison while we led a slow convoy of seven loaded British LCTs, a trawler, and two tugs across to France. We returned to England as escort and leader of sixteen empty British LCTs, at a speed of only four and a half knots. On these leisurely voyages we plied our visitors with questions about their earlier experiences of amphibious operations at Dunkerque after the fall of France in 1940. The sea-lanes we followed were now mineswept, but occasionally an alert watch officer would spot a floating mine that had been dislodged by rough weather from its underwater moorings and floated on the surface. Once while on watch I encountered a floating mine dead ahead and swerved to avoid it. Wind and current, however, bore it down upon us, and we avoided it so narrowly that I could see clearly its perfectly round shape and the little triggered tentacles that would have exploded if we touched them. We missed the mine by about a foot and left it bobbing in our wake.

In my correspondence with people back home, I put on a brave and hopeful face. I recall writing a rather maudlin letter to my father on the eve of D Day but fortunately cannot remember the details. In other letters, though, I struck a bluff and hearty note, hinting at danger but avoiding specifics. This was not from fear of censorship, for we officers had a code of honor on that score. Our letters went in the mail stamped "Passed by Naval Censor" with our initials, but by a double standard we never actually read fellow officers' letters, only those of enlisted men. As communications officer I was the ship's official censor and read all of the enlisted men's mail, but my own letters were stamped and initialed by Harold W. Clark.

"I've seen enough of the 'master race' lately to dispel any feeling of their superiority that anyone might have," I wrote Diana, though the only Germans I had seen were some prisoners of war we carried briefly from the beach to a waiting transport. "There are a number of 'True Stories' I can tell you," I hinted broadly, "that will beat even the paratrooper hero" of her hometown. My suggestion of derring-do stopped just short of the absurd, and a few days later I wrote more truthfully, "Don't worry about my safety because the chances are mighty good for us right now, nothing like the dangers the front-line soldiers have to face for days at a time. Our worst dangers are over in a day or so and after that work is only routine with a minimum of danger."

"I've taken up smoking a pipe in my spare time," I wrote. "I find that not only does it make a man ten years older, but it keeps me awake at times when . . . lighting is the only thing that will save me from complete oblivion. I was so sleepy one night last week that I slept through general quarters in an air raid that came off very badly for Jerry." That was a somewhat mythic version of the actual event. During the hurry-up period following D Day, while we lay at anchor off Utah Beach on June 13 after disgorging our troops, we awakened to the sound of general quarters and chattering gunfire. I didn't sleep through it all, but like other sleepers I was slow to reach my battle station. By then the sky was bright with searchlights and tracer bullets, and a few planes circled overhead. We joined in with a few fitful rounds of our 20-millimeter guns, probably far short of the range of the planes, but the excitement was soon over. The planes we and other landing craft fired on turned out to be not the Luftwaffe but our own reconnaissance

planes. Next morning all landing craft in the area received the embarrassing message, "Do not fire unless directly attacked." We never
learned whether we had actually bagged any targets that night, but a
year earlier during the invasion of Sicily a disastrous exchange of
friendly fire occurred between American landing craft and planes.
American planes from North Africa flying low over the island had
suddenly appeared above the beach area, and the LCIs and LSTs there
shot them down. In a combat situation, we ninety-day wonders often
flunked the plane recognition course we had taken in a dark room at
midshipmen's school, mistaking Allied planes for enemy planes.

Weymouth was used as a hospital center in the days following D
Day, and we saw many boatloads of wounded men arrive at our pier.
Some walked ashore with a white bandage on head or arm or moved
along on crutches. Others arrived on stretchers or as dead bodies. The
faces of the wounded bore a haunting look of personal defeat. They
brought back to mind those half-forgotten pacifist views of war that
we had heard in the thirties and disregarded in the early forties. "I
wondered if it was worth it all to give the supreme sacrifice," Clark
pondered. "It made me think and ask myself just what we're fighting
for. The passing of each of those 'shoes' told a story in itself and I
wondered how each face looked, if I knew them, and how much sor-
row and suffering would result from each stretcher. It made me want
to do something real big for these men but yet I knew that only one
person could do just that. I still feel that He takes care of each man but
that faith is certainly challenged with so many incidents as this. I'm
trying not to become bitter over the whole rotten setup. God, give me
strength."

In the enforced leisure just before D Day I took some photographs
of our pirate crew, but it was some time before I could get them ashore
to be developed. Sending my rogues' gallery snapshots to Diana, I asked
in return for pictures "of you digging in your father's victory garden,
or giving blood plasma to the Red Cross, or selling War Bonds," cli-
chés about the things those on the home front were doing to further
the war effort and boost servicemen's morale. I also teasingly upbraided
her for lacking sufficient concern for my safety. "You were supposed
to groan and moan and pray that I was safe and carry on in a highly

hysterical manner on D Day, crying 'Fireman, save my Whiskey.' Instead, to my chagrin, I find out you aren't worrying at all, not even crying in bed." "Whiskey" was a reference to my embarrassing college nickname, Whiskey Lou, acquired after a drunken caper at a fraternity dance.

"Do you picture me in dress blues and visor cap?" I asked. "If so you'll probably be sadly disappointed at my appearance in the new photographs soon to be released. A fur-lined jacket, dungarees or grays with no tie, a pair of brown Army shoes, and usually several days' growth of whiskers complete my ensemble for underway." I enclosed a group photograph and comment that, despite its straining for satire, gives a clearer description of our crew and officers than memory can now dredge up. "I'm the wop-looking guy in the skivvy-shirt in the bottom row right," I wrote. "The one next to me is Olin, the worst birddog and sack-hound on the ship. I have just finished pushing a 'deck court' for him for AWOL. Next on left is 'Pete' Petergal, the seaman who painted a picture of Dopey of the Seven Dwarfs on our conn. Needless to say, he is called Dopey. But the jerk next to him, Jones, the pharmacist's mate, is the poorest excuse for a man that God ever gave life to in an absent-minded moment. Dominic Pisaneschi, the ape-face last on bottom row to left, is probably the best seaman and most conscientious worker on the ship. King Kong above me is Mohr, who can hardly spell his own name but tries hard when you dog him 24 hours a day to do every simple task. Joe Dwyer, in blues with the Duty Belt on is another of our best seamen. Curly Davis, the next one, is our Engineer Officer. Born and bred in the barbarian environment of Ohio, he hates Roosevelt and is convinced that he is ruining the country and is the worst crook in a crooked Democrat party. . . . He is more fun than a barrel of monkeys." I continued: "The next one, Exec. Cotton Clark, says to tell you he isn't fat—he's just chubby. He's the Vanderbilt boy I've mentioned before, third baseman on the baseball team. He's really a nice guy. Next is Rost, Bosun's mate in charge of the crew. He's the guy that wakes the bugler up. Polick, last on left, dressed up for liberty, is on my watch underway. He kept us laughing all the way across the Atlantic. On his haunches above is Sarge, U S Army, aboard to guard Army supplies for the troops who were to come aboard, but

he slept most of the time. We are a pretty rowdy looking Pirate crew."
I have no idea why I described "Doc" Jones so unfairly, unless it was
to impress Diana.

We found it hard to describe our combat experiences or seafaring
life without violating the censorship rules, but I made an oblique stab
at it. "The tale of our latest excursion into the sea is reserved for my
grandchildren around the fire on a winter night," I wrote, "but I can
hint at a few things, such as floating life jackets, air raids, stunned
floating fish, a duck with oil on its wings which couldn't fly, life-jack-
ets and K-ration boxes in the water, ships looming out of the fog, and
robot planes." For lack of reportable news, I sometimes indulged in
fantasies of the home front. Hearing that Diana had caught the bridal
bouquet at a wedding, I groaned at the possibility of her marrying
someone close and available. I described for her my nightmare of her
marriage to a mutually disliked acquaintance. I imagined the corpulent fellow waddling down the aisle, singing in his pretentious manner "Here comes the bride, here comes the groom," Diana all in white
like a pure lamb led unwilling to the slaughter, his friend Ape-Face an
usher, his corpulent mother bustling around Diana like a hippopota-
mus in a mud-wallow. "When the groom was to say 'I do' he could only
grunt like a pig because of the tight stays," I wrote. "But the repulsive
show went on until the minister asked if . . . [anyone objected to the
marriage], the whole picture faded away, because in a loud, clear voice
you said, 'Your honor, I object. That is a leading question.'"

Almost simultaneously with the D Day landings, when their planes
had been virtually cleared from the skies, the Germans launched the
first of their secret weapons, the unmanned V-1 rockets aimed at London. The Germans also had in production a larger, more accurate V-2
rocket that would have wreaked havoc in England if the Normandy
invasion had not captured the French coast and destroyed the launch-
ing pads for both types of buzz bombs. Even so, for some time the V-
1s terrorized London, which had already taken much punishment. Both
at sea and in the English ports we saw a number of these "robot planes,"
as we called them, passing overhead, but they were after bigger game
in London. Once, on our way across the Channel, we saw British and
American fighter planes trying to tip the wings of V-1s and throw them

off course, but enough of them got through to create turmoil. Clark, who was on watch at the time, was so busy watching the action overhead that he ran the ship into a buoy, causing a loud disturbance in the crew's quarters. The crew immediately dubbed him "Buoys" Clark, a name that lingered only a short time. Clark was too well liked to keep a derisive nickname for long.

By late June, our invasion service largely over, we moved into a shallow harbor at Poole, formerly a fishing port, adjacent to the sizable resort town of Bournemouth, until the Navy could decide what to do with us next. Overnight liberty became the rule. Two officers and half the crew had to be aboard at all times as usual, but we all had liberty on alternate nights for more than a fortnight.

I tried during this period to do what had been impossible before, to cultivate a closer acquaintance with English people. How I hoped to do this is lost to memory now, perhaps by natural charm and youthful enthusiasm. Somehow I wangled dinner invitations from middle-aged couples, met English girls, went to dances. On one social occasion I engaged in a lively clash of stereotypes with some Labourites I had met. I had assumed they were loyal, nonpolitical adherents of Churchill's wartime coalition, whereas actually they could hardly wait until the war was over to overthrow his government. Similarly, when they learned that I was a Roosevelt supporter they assumed that I was a radical reformer of their persuasion. They had an exalted image of the New Deal as more radical than it was, and were unaware of the breadth of Roosevelt's coalition that included southern Democrats. If I were for Roosevelt, they reasoned, I must love Marx and hate capitalism. I must be ready for the revolution that would follow the war in both countries. I managed politely to conceal my discomfort at this misunderstanding, and couldn't bring myself to explain why most southerners voted Democratic. I was both attracted and repelled by what I heard from my Labourite hosts. I managed to get safely away from capture by them, but their heretical talk had a delayed influence on my political reorientation. I felt more at home and less challenged by the tenor of dinner conversation with a middle-class couple I met while buying souvenirs. To supplement their meager rations at dinner I brought canned goods, sugar, and chocolate from the ship's store. We discussed the war, not politics.

"This little village by the sea has a charm that can't be described," I wrote Diana rather tritely. "The people here are much friendlier than anywhere else in this self-contained little island where I've sought shelter. They are talkative, hospitable, happier, and more attractive. In short, this is sho nuff a hot liberty town." Reading between the lines, she might have guessed the real reason for my enthusiasm, that I had met a good-looking girl at a dance. Unlike my earlier female acquaintance in Falmouth, Kay was well educated, at least as mature as I was, and too respectably middle-class to be seducible. Kay was her nickname, but she was actually named for an African town where her father had been a colonial administrator. She had found it easier at school to adopt a more conventional English name. She was a nurse in a local hospital, but was usually off duty in the evenings, and we spent many hours of cultural interchange and light banter. On our first date she lured me to a concert by the local philharmonic. I groaned at the prospect of "amateur night," but the orchestra turned out to be surprisingly professional and played before a packed house. My view of the English people changed in many subtle ways under Kay's tutelage, and our wartime friendship blossomed fast. We dated as often as I could get liberty, and she introduced me to all sorts of nuances and class differences in British attitudes. She was half-apologetic about fish and chips, a lower-class snack but too good to be passed up on account of snobbery. She also invited me to a more formal meal at the nurses' dining hall. It was delicious. Particularly memorable was the salad—my first leafy food after months of living from can to mouth. I took Kay to the movies, kissed her in the moonlight, necked a little, and soon sailed away. To our surprise, we became pen pals, and corresponded off and on throughout the war and for a short while afterward. I suppose that made me a two-timer, writing to two girls at once to keep loneliness at bay. It wouldn't be the last time I did that.

While in Bournemouth on liberty I shopped feverishly for a "distinctively Britannic" present for Diana. I found a sweet shop that also sold a little china and crystal on the side, and pleaded with the proprietor not to close until he had sold me something very British. The shopkeeper and his wife tried for an hour or more to sell me some Dresden cups and saucers, their idea of elegance. I insisted that Dresden was not English enough for me, however it might suit them. Tea-time arrived and they were too polite to get rid of me, so they invited me to partake. We sat around drinking cup after cup from their Dresden china until I wanted never to see either tea or Dresden again. But I had a wonderful time with the old couple, and had a real Anglophile glow on. They invited me to dinner the next time I had liberty. Just then my eye fell upon an object they hadn't tried to sell me. I was told it was an antique Waterford honey jar, dating from about the eighteenth century, and they were obviously reluctant to sell this heirloom to an American. An old lady had been walking by the shop every few days for the past month, they told me, stopping to gaze at the honey jar and wishing she had the money to buy it. With the air of a villain who holds the mortgage, however, I refused to be turned away by this pathetic story and demanded the honey jar anyhow. While I was paying, they told me the price they had quoted was in guineas. I had never heard of this particular coin of the realm, and learned the hard way that a guinea was more than a pound. We shared a laugh at their little trick, and I paid up. To seal the bargain we each had a piece of their Devonshire butterscotch.

Meanwhile, my troubles with the skipper continued. Now that we had risen above our former selves during the D Day landings, I had assumed that the skipper was in a mellower mood and would raise his estimate of his junior officers. I was shocked, therefore, when Flinn informed both Davis and me that he had given us unfavorable quarterly fitness reports. He was required by *Navy Regulations* to inform us of an unfavorable evaluation and allow us the opportunity to file written responses. I suspected that Flinn himself had received an unfavorable fitness report from the flotilla commander and was simply passing the blame down to us. Only Cotton Clark was spared a blot upon his record. Curly Davis didn't bother to file a statement. His morale was so low that he didn't care. He hoped to be transferred to shore duty anyhow, and be home by Christmas to see his wife and infant son. I, on the other hand, refused to accept the captain's judgment of my performance. In my statement I pointed out that we had proven ourselves competent on D Day, that when we had strayed from the convoy on our Atlantic voyage it had occurred on Davis's watch, not mine, and that it was the skipper who had issued the written order that separated us entirely from the convoy. The skipper tried to argue me out of my statement, but I insisted on his acceptance and transmission of it along with his evaluation. I am not sure that he did not privately change his own report in order to avoid having to submit mine, because in the next quarterly report he gave me a satisfactory evaluation, and I was later promoted on schedule to Lieutenant (j.g.).

On the eve of my twenty-second birthday, we learned that instead of returning to the States on the way to the Pacific theater, we were to proceed to the Mediterranean. This delighted me, for my appetite had been whetted for further travel. To Curly Davis, however, this was a devastating blow to his plans for family reunion. He and I had only recently talked, while serving as the duty officers, about our two chief topics of conversation, the state of the war and the state of the weather. He had bet that we would be home by Christmas, that Hitler himself could not keep us away. Now he had to accept the rotten hand the war had dealt him, and his morale collapsed. Our ship moved to Dartmouth and took on a ninety-day supply of dry provisions and fresh food. There was about to be a lengthy detour on our journey home. We didn't know why the Navy was sending us to the Mediterranean, but we could guess.

We moved in convoy toward Plymouth, our last English port of call, and ran into a fog so dense that it reduced our visibility to nil. We could no longer see the other ships in the convoy. Hoping that the other ships were also brought to a halt by the fog, we anchored off the Plymouth breakwater and rang the ship's bell every minute to warn any other ships that might sail into us. The fog lifted several hours later, and we proceeded up the Tamar River past Plymouth to our old pre-invasion anchorage at Saltash. Next day we got underway for a new theater of war. In the large and diverse convoy, our ship was the guide ship for the other LCIs.

SEVEN

Go to the Head of the Bay

Our convoy sailed south southwest out of Plymouth, skirting the French and Spanish coasts but well out of sight of land. On our fourth night out the sky lit up with a shower of shooting stars, some of them as bright as fireworks and looking closer than they were. The farther south we traveled, the calmer the sea and the balmier the weather. We gradually disrobed until the uniform of the day was shorts, a skivvy shirt if necessary, and sandals cut down from workshoes. Discipline relaxed along with the dress code, and soon Skipper Flinn had to hold a Captain's Mast to try Donnie Nance, an electrician's mate from Myrtle Beach, South Carolina, who had profanely refused to carry out an order from the skipper. Found guilty, of course, he lost his petty officer's stripes and part of his pay. The skipper reduced him to his lowest possible rank of fireman 1/c.

We had hoped to stop at the Rock of Gibraltar, just out of curiosity, but our convoy sailed right past it. The water changed color from Atlantic green to Mediterranean blue. As we moved east along the North African coast in the night, we briefly lost our convoy again. I refused to relieve Davis until we could ascertain our position. I got a fix on a lighthouse and another on a star, and where their lines crossed, if my navigation work was accurate, would be our ship's location. My result showed us directly on top of a rock! Fortunately my calculations were slightly in error. We soon found the other ships, but after Clark relieved me he had another narrow escape from other rocks. Thinking the rocks were another ship, he sent a blinker message in their direction, a slight misunderstanding that became a shipboard joke. The skipper once again gave me as well as Davis a reprimand for poor navigation, even though the incident had happened on Davis's watch. For once, the inscrutable Flinn said nothing to Clark about signaling to a rock.

We sailed on to Bizerte, Tunisia. Two years earlier it had been the scene of bitter tank battles after the Allied invasion of North Africa, but now was a humdrum little supply depot and amphibious base. We took on fresh produce and other supplies, and a Navy paymaster came aboard for a long overdue payday. We were disappointed that no mail was waiting for us, but touching shore at least gave us a chance to send outgoing letters. Liberty parties went ashore for two evenings. There was little to do in Bizerte, but Tunis was nearby.

My own liberty included a ride to Tunis on a Navy bus. We went through the Kasserine Pass, a major battle site of the North African campaign, where the bleaching hulks of German and American tanks gave silent testimony to the destructiveness of war. Nearby were the ruins of an ancient battle site, Carthage, but they were not on our itinerary. I had dinner in a bare little French restaurant in Tunis. The food was good but the red wine gave me a blinding headache for a day and a half. A large part of my evening was used up waiting for a bus back to Bizerte. A huge, fierce, and very drunk Army sergeant waited with me. Pacing and lurching like a caged lion, he glowered at me and screamed over and over, "They taught me to kill, and I want to kill! They taught me to kill and I want to kill." He was more crazy than drunk. The alcohol just permitted him to express some inner rage. Though he was not a typical soldier, the sergeant illustrated a difference in the psychological impact of war in the different services. The schooling in violence of combat soldiers and marines was direct, whereas the Navy and Air Force killed enemies by long distance, abstractly, out of sight of the blood and guts. During the sergeant's tirade I made myself as inconspicuous as possible, for fear of becoming an object of his irrational rage. As he said, he had been taught to kill. Soon after we boarded the bus, however, his drunken rage faded into a drunken stupor.

I would later be in Bizerte on several other occasions, but always too busy for liberty. I made the most of this brief visit, however, in a sort of travelogue to impress Diana. "I've seen the desert camels," I wrote, "also the primitive huts, irrigation system, Casbah, veiled virgins, and a sort of harem. I'll tell you about them when I get back." I never actually saw a harem, and fraternization with Muslim women was virtually impossible. I do vaguely remember seeing a few veiled women rustling through the narrow streets. An Armed Forces pamphlet warned ominously that molesting Arab women was a capital offense, so I played a safer game with the stereotypes created by the movies. Cotton Clark in his diary rattled off a similar but less colorful list of sights: "Wonderful sightseeing trip. City itself, marketplace, park scene, gun implacements, 'vino [vin?] rouge', irrigation, vineyard, farms, shops, food, bombed."

We got underway again for Italy on a few hours' notice, sailing with other LCIs past the western edge of Sicily and then along its north coast. At night we could see the active volcano of Stromboli glowing on the northern horizon. At dawn the second day we entered the port of Salerno on the Italian mainland, a little town set like a jewel at the foot of steep hills, many of them crowned by churches or monasteries. A liberty party went ashore, but it was my night as duty officer. Clark got to nearby Naples and saw *Madama Butterfly* at the San Carlo opera house. He also recorded in his diary: "First Coca-Cola since 1 Apr. 1944."

While at Salerno we learned that Jack Flinn had been promoted to full lieutenant, news that gladdened every heart. It meant that his days aboard our ship were numbered, his new rank being too high for an LCI skipper. In time he would have to be transferred to a larger ship. The skipper smiled broadly at the news before he remembered himself and readjusted to his usual sour puss. The tinkle of merry laughter was heard from stem to stern that night as we contemplated a future without Flinn.

Speculation about the skipper's future soon gave way to more urgent business. That another invasion was in the wind was signified by our having to strip the ship again, putting our personal gear and surplus supplies ashore as we had done before the Normandy invasion. Twenty-five cases of K rations arrived, and we knew they were not for us. While we were in the Salerno anchorage I donned my bathing suit and dove off the fantail into the milk-blue water, swam about a mile to the beach, dried off there for a while, and swam back. It was fortunate that I returned when I did, because the ship was dragging anchor, and just after I returned we weighed anchor and moved farther out. Next day we came in to the dock and took on forty smoke pots to supplement the little fog generator we had carried on our fantail but had never used. The purpose of these floating smoke pots was unmistakable. At some invasion in the near future, part of our duty would be to carry them through possibly mine-infested waters and drop them at intervals to create or deepen a smoke screen. We wondered what this new duty would do to our chances of survival.

On August 5, after three days in Salerno Bay, we got underway, passed Capri, the newly activated volcano of Vesuvius, the busy harbor of Naples, on to the fishing port of Pozzuoli in the northeast corner of the Bay of Naples. We had never heard of Pozzuoli, and Cotton Clark even misspelled it in the ship's log. We soon learned, however, that in Roman times it had been a heavily used port, then known as Puteoli. It became our home base for the next few months, and was well suited for landing craft, with their shallow draft. Pozzuoli was all of southern Italy rolled into one. It had a lively fish market, and was also the market town for surrounding farmers and a working-class suburb of Naples, some six miles away. The war and American occupation had interrupted its fishing economy, but it quickly adapted to the catering needs of American landing craft. The name of our bosun's mate, Rusty Rost, became a byword in the streets of Pozzuoli because of the bargains he struck in trading American goods for fresh tomatoes, watermelons, beans, and squash in the local market. Many poor, olive-skinned people crowded Pozzuoli's narrow, smelly streets, but their vitality and cheerfulness saved it from seeming a slum. Unknown to us, Sophia Loren was then an illegitimate teenager growing up in Pozzuoli. On our arrival there we thought of Italians as the enemy, but they soon totally disarmed us by their friendliness and their obvious relief at being out of the war. By the time we left Pozzuoli, we considered them our friends, but how they viewed us we had no way of knowing. Occasionally when we walked through the narrow streets in town on work details, we could hear female voices from the upper windows of houses calling invitingly or plaintively for "Rusty." On the eve of our final departure, Rost's many Italian friends gave him and his buddies a farewell party with plenty of vino. Officers were not invited. We were probably still "the enemy" to both Italians and the crew.

As we moored along the breakwater at Pozzuoli with our sister ships the 554 on one side and the 557 on the other, an Army second lieutenant came aboard with a working party carrying twelve days' supply of C rations—nearly the worst kind the Army had to offer, totally unlike the 10-in-1 rations used in the Normandy invasion. The K rations we had already stored would serve as backup for the C rations. The work detail also brought Army blankets, supplementary rations, and the same lifebelts that had been such a disaster in Normandy. Close behind them came the troops, a company of the 179th Infantry, First Division. They were at least as seasoned as the company we had carried into Omaha Beach, having fought through the North African, Sicilian, and Italian campaigns. We got underway almost immediately to practice beaching near Salerno. We beached and retracted, unloaded and reloaded our troops all day, and tested our smoke pots. Anchoring nearby, we went through our landing drill all over again the next day, and then returned to anchorage in Pozzuoli. Unlike the tight security before the Normandy invasion, this time we had liberty every night. Maybe this was because thus far we knew nothing to reveal to an enemy about our destination. There was much speculation as to whether we would invade southern France or establish a beachhead beyond the battle line in northern Italy.

Soon after we got underway, it became obvious where we were going. We headed to Corsica and anchored overnight in Ajaccio Bay, nesting with two other LCIs. From there the only logical landing spot was southern France. The weather being extremely hot, I seized the opportunity to swim ashore for a short stroll on the beach. That evening an Army chaplain and a Navy chaplain came aboard to hold religious services. It was evident from the many ships crowded there that Ajaccio was the rendezvous point for the invasion, and it was while there that we learned officially of our role in the invasion of southern France. We would land our troops in the Bay of St. Tropez near the town of St. Maxime.

Our troops were fresh from combat in northern Italy, and somewhat war-weary compared to our Normandy troops. Some had malaria, and three of them were so ill that they were put ashore in Ajaccio. "They are a fine bunch of fighting men, know their objective, and intend to achieve same no matter what the cost," Cotton Clark wrote in his diary. Cotton had a romantic view of dogfaces. We all admired them, but after a week of sharing their C rations we were anxious to get them on the beach and return to our regular eating habits. Our skipper was, if possible, even more cantankerous since his promotion had seemingly legitimized his style of command. His latest outburst was against Curly Davis for some minor infraction. "To me this seems poor psychology on the eve of an invasion," Clark noted in his diary.

We got underway about sunset on August 14, saw flashes of heavy gunfire around 0300, and by dawn next morning were in sight of the French coast. Our charts for this invasion were not as detailed as those for the Normandy landings, perhaps a reflection of the haste with which this strategic maneuver was improvised. The American forces in northern France, having broken through the German defenses, were racing toward Paris, and the southern France invasion was intended to create a diversion that would prevent German occupation troops there from moving north to help stem the Allied drive.

Lying offshore, we sounded general quarters in the early morning and took our beaching stations. We waited all morning, however, for our call into the beach. The weather was warm and the sea smooth, in sharp contrast to our Normandy experience. All around us were ships of many kinds, sizes, and nationalities. We saw the battleship *Nevada* on our right, firing broadsides from its sixteen-inch guns into the beach, and on our left the battleship *Texas* was doing the same. Rocket ships hurled a tremendous amount of flak against the shore defenders, who offered little apparent resistance. The whole shoreline seemed to be going up in smoke.

At noon our ship received its call into the beach as part of a second wave of landing craft, and we touched bottom at the beach at 1243, a little distance to the east of the small resort town of St. Maxime. It was then that I came as close as I would ever get to qualifying for a Purple Heart, for my teeth! As we approached the beach, which seemed to be uncontested except for occasional shell-bursts and the rattle and pop of small arms, I stood at my beaching station on the starboard side of the gun deck. Several enlisted men, the gun crew assigned to the 20-millimeter gun nearby, crouched behind the semicircle of quarter-inch steel plate sheltering the gun, while I stood foolhardily erect, protected only by my Mae West. A member of the gun crew grabbed me by the back of my belt and pulled me down with them, saying apologetically something like, "Excuse me, sir, but you don't want to be a dead hero, do you?" My front teeth were full of porcelain fillings, and when the gun crew pulled me down, my upper lip and teeth struck the edge of the gun turret. A numbness set in, hardly noticeable at that moment of high adrenalin. A few hours later, however, when during a moment of respite I popped some dried-out caramel Walnettos from our ship's store into my mouth, the fillings began to come loose in the candy. I wondered whether this combat wound would qualify me for a Purple Heart. The thought brought a crooked grin to my sore lips, but I was too busy to pursue it. For the next year I was too busy and too isolated even to see a Navy dentist about my decaying teeth. Otherwise, our beaching was uneventful. "A piece of cake," the British would say. "A piece of candy," I could have replied.

The water was calm, without real surf. We touched bottom in waist-deep water only fifteen yards from dry land, and our troops filed ashore in good order, unmolested by gunfire. We spotted a few German dead on the beach and about thirty German prisoners, but only four American casualties. Retracting from the beach, we returned to the staging area, tied up alongside a transport, the SS *Marine Robin*, and took aboard a second load of troops, some 300 men from a headquarters company.

We made a dry beaching at a new spot. Since this group had much gear to unload and kept us on the beach for quite a while, we took turns wandering along the beach. To our right was a machine-gun nest, possibly the most heavily fortified spot on the beach. Dead Germans lay in pathetic attitudes all around the gun like rag dolls carelessly thrown by a child. They had probably been hit by naval gunfire before any Americans had set foot on the beach. We were stunned by this and other signs of violent death, but that did not stop members of our crew from looting rings and other souvenirs from the bodies of the dead. A few days later I wrote Diana: "When we went ashore to collect souvenirs I'll have to confess the only souvenir I took back to the ship was a white pebble from the beach. This business of looting the dead enemy who died fighting, who died a hero's death no matter what cause they may have fought for—that's a little too much for me. Nevertheless, scavengers on the ship did a pretty good job of it and brought back some mighty interesting things." A few days later, however, I stooped to taking a souvenir, a cloth patch. At least it was from a live German, a prisoner. "You can still see the outlines of the imperial eagle, but the swastika got torn off," I wrote. "The prisoner who gave it to me tore it off in a hurry as he was going over the side. It's for combat infantrymen only, and is worn above the left breast pocket. You probably don't want it, which reaction I can fully appreciate. If you don't, save it for me, though."

An air alert sounded that first afternoon, and we laid a smoke screen over our area of beach. We dropped a floating smoke pot for good measure. We worked all night and all the next day, unloading transports and carrying their human cargo to the beach. On one occasion we were sent to the beach to take wounded to a hospital ship, but when we got there we could find none to transport. They had probably been picked up by another ship. We went ashore and gawked at the forlorn German prisoners herded in large numbers into a barbed-wire enclosure on the beach. The majority were said to be Poles and Czechs forced into German army service, mostly middle-aged men and young boys, a sign that the Germans were scraping the bottom of the manpower barrel. They had probably sent these questionable troops to the south to free more combat-ready troops for the struggle in northern France. At any rate, the prisoners we saw didn't show much fight, and were probably not sorry to be captured.

That night, we tied up alongside a French transport to take a load of Free French troops into shore, and had great difficulty getting its crew to understand the phrase "take our lines." Just at that moment an air raid siren sounded, and we could see ten German bombers, flying low, dropping their bombs on the newly arrived transport ships. Ships all around us opened up with antiaircraft fire, and bombs exploded around us in great numbers. A ship about a hundred yards away received a direct hit, and bombs landed in the water about fifty yards from us, sending up a column of water. After two bombers went down in flames the others flew away. We and other ships with fog generators somewhat tardily laid such a thick smokescreen that we could see nothing whatever, neither the enemy planes nor our own ships nor the beaches. The smoke screen was probably unnecessary, for the Germans were running out of planes.

During and after the air raid we took about 300 troops aboard, mostly Moroccans or West Africans, "the roughest, toughest looking group of humans I've ever seen," as Cotton Clark described them. "They were almost wild looking creatures, each armed with a bayoneted Springfield rifle. From head to foot their clothes & equipment were U. S. Most all were dark skinned, tall and big boned." Included in our troopload and more or less in charge was an irascible American brigadier general named Swain, and also a detachment of fifty French WACs—petite, feminine, and stylish in their perfectly fitted uniforms. We summoned up what little French we knew to give the WACs our solicitous attention. One of the French WACs was out of her head, screaming insanely every time she heard a gun or a bomb. We wondered whether she could safely be taken into a war zone, but her comrades told us they would take good care of her. They said she had gone crazy when her entire family was killed in the war, but was determined to return to French soil.

We settled General Swain comfortably in the officers' wardroom, while we undertook in the thick smoke screen we had laid to find our landing spot. At this point we committed one of the errors by which our ship earned its nickname of USS *Dopey*. While we were alongside the French transport, Commander Warburton, our flotilla commander, ordered us by blinker to "Go to the head of the bay," where a beachmaster would guide us into shore with signal lights. The skipper called me to the conn. After all my humiliation at his hands, I was flattered to learn that the skipper wanted my advice. "Harlan, you are supposed to be so smart," he said with a sarcastic twist, "what does he mean by 'the head of the bay'?" A pun sprang to my lips, bypassing my brain. "Well, skipper," I answered, "where the head is, there will the mouth be also. I'm not sure what he means, but it logically follows that he must mean the mouth of the bay, the outer end, like a river mouth." "I guess you're right," the skipper said with his best imitation of a chuckle. He set our course toward the outer edge of the bay.

We wandered off through darkness and smokescreen to one side of the mouth of the bay and, seeing no light signal waving us in, then crossed to the other side. We muddled thus for an hour or two. Meanwhile, it was my duty to keep the general happy. Every few minutes he would put his cigar down on his coffee saucer and ask when we were going to land. "Any time now, General," I would say, pointing out the difficulty of piloting through a dense smoke screen, trying to pacify him as one would a restless child. Finally, exasperated at my evasive answers, he demanded to break radio silence. I took him to the radio shack across from the wardroom, and we reached the flotilla commander on the voice radio. The general impatiently grabbed the mike from my hands and shouted, "This is General Swain! I want to speak to the Commander personally. . . . Commander, we've been wandering around in the dark for hours and none of these god-damn incompetents know their ass from their elbow. Can you get us ashore and out of the hands of these morons?"

The commander called me to the mike, explained testily that the head of the bay was at the opposite end from the mouth, and demanded to know who my commanding officer was. I told him, "Lieutenant Flinn, sir." I could hear an explosion at the other end. He demanded to speak to the commanding officer. I told him the skipper couldn't come right then, that he was in the conn trying to find his way through the smoke screen. The commander said, "Tell your commanding officer to report to me in person as soon as you have unloaded your troops." I had to relay this message to the skipper, but fortunately he was too crestfallen to shoot the messenger. Now that we knew where the head of the bay was, we quickly found our beach.

Clark's attention meanwhile was focused on the French babes. "One thing which made me stop and think," he told his diary later, "was the sight of those 50 French gals, carrying a pack of some 60 pounds, walking down those ramps in the darkest of nights, and knowing exactly nothing of what was waiting for them. I guess I'll never forget the funny feeling I had when a little gal took me by the arm and she and I made a hand chain for the other gals coming down the ramps. She clung to my arm as though she didn't intend to turn it loose. The Wacs were afraid of a wet beaching which would have been very difficult for them considering their packs. When I told her that we had hit dry land and there was 'no water' she smiled and said 'Oh bonne,' snapped her shoulders back and left the ramps like a real beachjumper, ready indeed to take her place among the French soldiers. We all had much admiration for these gals, certainly a wonderful example of fighting spirit. I couldn't help wondering how American gals would react to these conditions and I dismissed the thought from my mind with the hopes that they would never have to face such circumstances as these. This beach was in good order, the shouting of French officers offering the only confusing elements."

As soon as we had unloaded our restless passengers, we tied up to the commander's flagship and informed the officer on watch that our skipper was now ready to report to the commander. The commander had apparently hit the sack by then, because we got no reply. After waiting for a humiliating hour, we tried again. The commander finally sent us a curt order, "Get on back to work," as though in carrying out his earlier order we were simply malingering. "Me and my big mouth," I thought, blaming myself for my bad advice to the skipper. Hanging our heads at the head of the bay, we did get back to work. We worked all that night and all the next day. This made three days since we had been to bed, and the entire ship's company were half-dozing at their beaching stations. In all, we carried seven troop loads into the beach in a twenty-four-hour period. Red alerts sounded nearly all day, and planes were frequently overhead. To make matters worse, the wind whipped up and a driving rain pelted us. The lightning of a severe electrical storm made everybody uncomfortable by setting about thirty barrage balloons afire. War was turning out to be purgatory, if not quite hell.

Most of the troops we carried were American infantrymen, but on several occasions we carried French troops, including one shipload of Vietnamese troops under French officers. We still called them by their colonial name, Indo-Chinese. They had not seen home since 1940. On the way toward the beach one of the French officers boasted about the absolute loyalty of these colonial troops, not to France but to him personally. "If I ordered any of them to jump overboard he would do it at once," he said. To prove his point, he barked out an order in Vietnamese to one of the troopers, who immediately began climbing over the rail until called back. We took that demonstration with several grains of salt. For one thing, we knew he knew we couldn't understand his language, so he might have told the man to *pretend* to go overboard. We also doubted the loyalty of the Indo-Chinese to their colonial overlords.

Working as we did for days without sleep, through general quarters and smoke screens, we were certain to run into further trouble, and we did. Just after we had dropped our stern anchor prior to a beaching, an LCT suddenly loomed out of the smoke and crossed our bow so closely that we had to back full speed. This caused our anchor cable to foul in our screws, and we had to let out 150 fathoms of cable and cut it before we could get it clear of the screws. Hardly had we recovered from this mishap than another LCI retracted from the beach into our starboard side, putting a V-shaped hole through our hull four feet above the waterline. From Troop Compartment 3 it was now possible to see daylight, and in rough seas we would ship water through the hole. Stuffing some rag waste into the gaping hole, we continued our work.

Finally, just past midnight on the third day of invasion, the fourth night since our last sleep, we ran out of transports to unload and went to our rest at anchor in the Gulf of St. Tropez. We remained at anchor all the next day, but that night general quarters sounded again. We got underway, made more fog all over the west side of the gulf, and despite our embarrassment at Normandy in a similar situation, we opened fire with our 20-millimeter guns at enemy aircraft, or what we believed to be enemy aircraft. A mitigating circumstance was that they were probably out of our range.

After the first few days of the invasion, we carried more personnel from the beach to the transports than from transports to beach. On one occasion we carried out German prisoners to a transport for shipment to a POW camp. Clark noted in his diary, "These men were pathetic looking, clad in rags almost, each had a two weeks beard. Most every one was suffering from a cold and an eye disease. There were very young looking boys and rather old like men in the group. Of the ones talked to, they were convinced of Hitler's doctrines. Considered the American soldier unfair, since in one incidence a Jerry had been stripped of watch & wallet by Americans. Great many Poles, Russians." Rost, the bosun's mate, tried to force a German officer with a dirty bandage on his head into the same quarters as the enlisted men, over his vociferous protest. I had to explain the Geneva Convention, which Rost had never heard of. I learned later, from the boasting about souvenirs, that members of our crew had looted from the prisoners.

We also carried casualties to a hospital ship offshore. About 120 were able to walk aboard, and seventy-one others had to be moved by stretcher, some of them with very serious wounds. Included were five wounded German prisoners, but from their demeanor it was impossible to tell the Germans from the others. All had the personally defeated, hangdog, pathetic look about them that I had seen earlier among our own Normandy wounded. War wounds were a grim leveler. The hospital ship was only three weeks out of the States. We pumped its personnel for the latest "hot dope," and ogled the nurses.

Lack of sleep took toll of our tempers, and cross words if not actual disobedience became common. The junior officers tolerated a degree of informality, but the skipper made no concessions even to the special circumstances. W. L. "Bill" Moyle, the veteran enlisted man who had recognized land in the Azores on our Atlantic passage, lost his temper under the strain of our hard work and mumbled "You son of a bitch" under his breath in response to an order from the captain, and Flinn heard him. Not one to pass up a chance to punish, Flinn called a Captain's Mast, found Moyle guilty of insubordination, and sentenced him to loss of the next four liberties. Actually, that was extremely light punishment.

Our ship itself began to break down under the strains of a week in the beaching area. Two of our eight Cadillac diesel engines became inoperative because of a faulty saltwater pump. We lost so much power that our attempts in heavy weather to moor alongside a transport were unsuccessful, and we also had trouble beaching because of diminished power and heavy surf. Part of our difficulty was that, as a result of all

98

our beaching activity, we had buckled the plates in the forward fuel tank and broken the weld, and seawater flooded in and mixed with the fuel. We beached in an attempt to assess the underwater damage, but we were ordered off that beach. We moved to another beach, found and sealed the water leak in the fuel tank, got our engines in full working order, and tried to return to work. Instead, we were ordered to anchor nearby in Bourgnon Bay. That evening came another general quarters and another smoke screen. We went east to Cavalaire Bay in a vain search for fuel and fresh water. Finally we borrowed some fuel from our sister ship, the 552, and made plans to return to Italy. At the last minute, however, our destination was changed to Oran. On August 24, after nine crowded days at the beachhead, we took off across the Mediterranean.

EIGHT

A Blue Pennant
She Did Win

Limping away from the southern France beachhead, moving slowly in convoy toward Oran, we coped with our fuel shortage by cutting off four of our sixteen engines, two on each side. Midway across the Mediterranean our gyro compass became inoperative. That was not a crippling handicap, however, since we were in convoy. We just had to keep the other ships in sight. At Mers-el-Kebir, on the outskirts of Oran, we went into dry dock to repair the many kinds of damage our ship had suffered during the invasion. Workers welded a steel plate on our bottom where the old welds had buckled, repaired the hole in our bow above the waterline, and applied a coat of paint to our bottom. We moved out of dry dock then, but our ship continued to receive the equivalent of an annual physical. Workers repaired the compass, straightened the mast, and gave us 150 fathoms of new stern anchor cable to replace the tangled one we had left at the beach in southern France.

While in Oran we passed our remaining smoke pots over to U.S. Army custody, a sign that the western Mediterranean had ceased to be a war zone. Liberty every night for the ten days we spent in Oran was another sign of changing times, but so many places were off-limits to servicemen that there was little of interest to see or do. Our crew, however, with less dignity to maintain than the officers, managed to find trouble ashore. One morning Lawrence Olin, the erstwhile hero of our Normandy landing, was honored by his second Captain's Mast for being AWOL. Olin had returned from liberty one morning after a night as guest of the shore patrol. His punishment was mild, the canceling of all further liberty in that port.

I did not entirely avoid the dives and fleshpots of Oran, but I remembered the aftermath more clearly than the experience. After consuming a quart of champagne one night, I awoke at 0600 next morning to find myself officer of the day. To the tune of a hundred drums somewhere between my ears, I dashed for water. By the time I had downed two or three glassfuls of the fatal liquid, I was as drunk as the night before. But duty called, and I reeled dizzily out on deck. I was in charge of morning colors—a muster of the crew on the gun deck, calling of the roll, and saluting the ensign as it climbed the mast at exactly 0800. Fortunately, it was the bosun's mate who called the roll, for I could only croak. I leaned at about a sixty degree angle as I saluted the ensign and dismissed the ship's company.

Having become, in my own words, "a maker of history," I took this as a license for prophecy. In a rather pompous letter, I told Diana to expect a postwar depression. "So I hope you are going to be ready to cope with larger problems than you have ever had to face before. All war can do is avert disaster. It is not progressive in any sense, and the barbarism war gives birth to is hard to stamp out in the years of peace. Piracy and vandalism are the inevitable after-effects of war, and the whole world is likely to be grabbing everything in sight." A few days later, I uttered another profound cliché: "War is a pretty ugly affair, and I wish I could believe this were the last one. The inventiveness of modern times, though, is moving too fast for economic and political developments to cope." I could have said that in spades if I had known about the A-bomb in my future.

While we were in dry dock, all the mail that had been chasing us since we had left England arrived in several mailbags, and we had a feast of homesickness. By the time I had finished reading my back mail, I felt as if I had left my real life back home, and the war I had been living through was just an endless dream. Diana wrote that she had received the honey jar I had sent from England, and liked it. "The couple who [sold] it to me," I wrote her, "told me all about their little cottage out on the Knightsbridge road about three miles from Bournemouth. They were awfully nice to me, and asked me to tea or dinner any time I could go, with a little Scotch that had been aging for years."

Diana's birthday present was Antoine de Saint-Exupéry's *The Little Prince*. At first glance I saw it not only was a children's book but, worse yet, looked the part. I hastily hid it in my quarters for fear my shipmates would catch me reading it. "Speaking of that damn book you sent me," I wrote, "I don't know which of us sent the most inappropriate present. I think it was myself but that baby book ran me a close race. It has ruined my reputation with the crew of the good ship 'Dopey.' I haven't looked inside it yet, but have put it in the very bottom of the drawer. Forgive me, please, for telling you the truth." It was two months before I could bring myself to read it, and to my surprise I enjoyed it, though it was a bit fey. "What you might call 'out of this world,'" I then wrote. "Thank you sincerely this time." Even so, I returned it to the bottom of the drawer.

On September 6 we took aboard eighty-six Army enlisted men and eleven officers and headed back to southern France with four other LCIs. The troops included a military police unit and members of the Quartermaster Corps. The sea was rough, and many of these landlubbers were seasick throughout the three-day voyage. During our absence of some two weeks, the appearance of the beaching area had changed dramatically. Everything in sight was now under American control, and we saw many German prisoners under guard. French civilian refugees also crowded the beach awaiting the next developments in their disrupted lives. We unloaded what Army rations we still carried, presumably for feeding the refugees. We set out again for Pozzuoli, where we took on fresh provisions, including a cornucopia of fresh vegetables and melons, and jogged down to Salerno to collect the personal gear we had put ashore before the southern France invasion.

On September 13 at Pozzuoli the skipper, Jack Flinn, finally left our ship to take command of an LST. Clark, as executive officer, took over command of our ship, and I became the executive officer. Flinn's departure created mixed feelings on all sides. Shortly before his departure he finally gave me a favorable quarterly fitness report, though he still didn't relent in his unfavorable assessment of Davis. This redeemed him partially in my eyes, but I felt no regret to see him leave. I could not bring myself to feel any loyalty or affection for this arrogant man who had blamed others for his own shortcomings. All three junior officers were glad to see him leave, but to our surprise he hated to leave us. "Captain cried when leaving," Clark wrote in his diary. Was it possible that he was human, that he had a heart? Or was it simply that the occasion cried out for a sentimental tear or two? Maybe Flinn regretted leaving a situation he had mastered and feared the prospect of a new command. The tears of that son of a bitch are still a mystery to me after fifty years.

Flinn's departure laid new responsibilities on his junior officers, whose self-confidence had been lamed by his carping. "Really didn't want to assume command but orders came," Clark told his diary. "To date I had docked the ship one time and was skeptical about my ability. . . . His leaving left me with a deep feeling of responsibility but I was determined to get [give] it all I had. Spent rest of day getting gear squared away. Harlan made exec." Officers and crew alike sensed that Clark would have his own style of command. He had always been popular among crew and officers and would have been elected skipper if the Navy had allowed democracy. We made every effort to help him succeed. I discovered that becoming executive officer simply added to my duties as fourth officer, since we received no replacement for me in that post. As I wrote Diana, "I have not been able to get rid of my numerous and tedious jobs as communications, supply, commissary, and ship's service officer. But so far I've survived the ordeal."

The day after Clark assumed command of the ship, word passed among the LCIs at Pozzuoli of the presence of Captain John N. Opie III in the area. He was the chief of staff of all the amphibious forces in the European theater. It could be anticipated that he would arrive at any time without warning to inspect our ship, and he was reportedly a crusty old sea dog. A story circulated that on one ship Captain Opie inspected there was a man without a haircut. After finishing his inspection, the captain sent a note that the haircut was unsatisfactory and that he would be back in half an hour. When he returned and the man's hair still wasn't cut, he called for clippers and shaved the man's head himself. Clark made hasty preparations for inspection and gave a pep talk to the crew. They rose to the challenge of their new and more popular skipper and made the ship spotless, but it all ended in anticlimax, for Captain Opie never turned up. This incident illustrates, however, the sea change in morale brought about by the change of command, in that everyone aboard tried to help Cotton Clark succeed.

Clark faced a more concrete challenge when we got word that we would be transporting additional troops to France. He decided to move the ship to a new dock where ramps would make it easier for the troops to get aboard. Shallow water in the little Pozzuoli harbor made maneuvering difficult, and in his maiden attempt Clark made what he described in his diary as "a sorry docking." In each of several efforts to get to the dock, the wind carried the ship away, and Clark was finally forced to return to his original dock. "Remained here for the night," he recorded in his diary, "discussed [disgusted] at myself for a job so poorly handled."

Meanwhile I put my aching back into my own expanded duties. As communications officer I was required to keep our codes and ciphers up to date, changing them every month, so one morning in September I had to go by a little Toonerville trolley from Pozzuoli to the Navy RPIO office in Naples. The trolley left every hour on the hour, the half hour, or almost anytime the motorman chose to lean over the throttle. I climbed aboard a car teeming with local civilians and clung like Dagwood to the pole by a single, scrawny left arm. Every five minutes the funicula screeched to a semi-halt and an army of unwashed local peasants from every village for miles around swarmed over my newly polished shoes. Finally we were disgorged into the squalor of the Naples streets, and I waded through garbage for an interminable morning and on into the afternoon, searching for the elusive Navy publications office. Finally at one o'clock, hot, tired, and famished, I found the place, opened my mail sack, and begged for my secret and confidential publications. I was told I had to wait until the issuing officer came back from chow. Finally I got my documents and found my way back through the sweltering city for the return trip.

I soon made my peace, however, with that part of Naples built on higher ground. On a liberty night I discovered the Orange Grove, a nightclub taken over by the American military. It was located on a hill overlooking the city, with a breathtaking view of Vesuvius and the bay islands from Capri to Ischia. I got a ride back to Pozzuoli that night with a drunken soldier who almost killed me on the mountain curves. One afternoon I also visited "Little Vesuvius," a small volcano near Pozzuoli, and the San Carlo opera house in Naples. I never had time to visit Pompeii or the Isle of Capri.

One day an LCI came into port loaded with Russians rescued from a prison camp in France. "These men were desolate looking, being half-starved by the Germans," Clark wrote in his diary. "However they were in good spirits and treated us very friendly. We gave them food and cigs and they were very appreciative. Their hate for the Germans is as intense as previously believed."

Too soon, just as we were beginning to enjoy ourselves, we returned to the war. Fresh troops for France arrived, and our destination was not the beach this time but Marseilles, newly liberated and its harbor cleared for use. Most of these troopers had been wounded in battle in northern Italy and had just been released from hospitals and rest camps. They were on their way to join their old outfits or to be used as replacements in other units. They seemed tougher than any of the GIs we had seen, and indifferent to their fate. They might have been more concerned had they realized they were on our skipper's maiden voyage, and that his self-confidence had been shaken by his losing battle with the Pozzuoli dock. "To say I was a bit dubious at the thought of getting 202 men safely to Marseille would be putting it mildly," he confessed to his diary. "Of course no one aboard had ever been there before and we knew absolutely nothing as to what to expect. I had my orders, a determination to get there and back safely, and already a couple gray hairs just for 'security' measures."

Just before getting underway, Clark and I went over to LCI(L) 667, which was to make the trip with us, to confirm a rumor that Arab prostitutes were aboard, being transported to the front lines by the French government to "service" the African troops and thus keep them from seeking sexual opportunities with French women. "The story proved to be true," Clark wrote in his diary, "and never in all my days have I seen such filthy, discussing [disgusting] sights as these women. There was goats aboard, ragged hags, and really more junk than you could name. Many girls were very young, looking to be around 15 and were

largely from Casablanca." I saw the same women he saw, and my rec-
ollection is that many of them were attractive. We speculated about the
high time the crew of the 667 would have en route with those prostitutes, weather permitting.

Clark's maiden voyage was not without difficulties. We got underway about dusk, and by the same time the following day we successfully navigated through the strait between Sardinia and Corsica. Then
came a dark night and difficult station-keeping. Clark stood watch along
with the other officers, since there were now only three of us. Not a
star was in sight, and the sea was rougher than at any time since we
had approached the Azores six months earlier. In meeting the high
waves, the ship swung at 40 and 45 degree angles, nearly capsizing.
Almost everyone aboard was seasick, and the decks were awash with
seawater, vomit, and loose gear. The arrival of dawn relieved the station-keeping problem, but then came torrential rain. Our foul weather gear was no match for wind-driven rain, and we whose duties required standing watch outside were totally soaked. At dusk on the
second day we could barely make out land to starboard, the islands
outside of Marseilles harbor. We hove to in Marseilles Bay until dark,
awaiting orders to proceed. The rain was still heavy and driving, and
the visibility poor.

The bay was crowded with Liberty ships, and we had to zigzag
around them following our convoy leader. Around 2000 we received
with relief a message to anchor, though this presented a new dilemma. Our skipper had never anchored a ship before, and this was a dark
night in a crowded harbor. He finally found a suitable spot and dropped
the hook, "hoping and praying," he wrote, "that daylight wouldn't find
us rammed against a big ship." He had passed his most important test,
however, in that the crew made every effort to help him. As he came
below without a dry thread on, he found that one soldier was in the
throes of appendicitis and another was sweating heavily in a relapse
of an old case of malaria. A signal to a nearby Liberty ship brought a
doctor almost immediately, and the sick men were taken ashore.

Early next morning we got word to enter the harbor and *beach*. We
hadn't figured on beaching in a major harbor, but Clark now girded his
loins for his first try at beaching. He had seen Flinn do it a hundred

times, but it was a different matter to do it himself. The harbor was crowded, there were sunken ships in abundance, the channel was narrow, and the wind was still blowing, but Clark handled the ship as if he had practiced, and in short order we beached, unloaded, and retracted. Anchoring in the bay, Clark gave a long sigh of relief and claimed the skipper's privilege of taking the first and only liberty in Marseilles. This meant I had to stay aboard until we departed next day, but Clark had earned it. We were soon back in Pozzuoli and off to the Orange Grove.

For a week beginning on October 1, I was transferred for temporary duty on another LCI which, because of promotions and transfers, was short of officers. During my week aboard, it journeyed to St. Tropez carrying a new load of prostitutes for the French Senegalese troops. These women, of skin color from ebony black to chocolate brown to yellow and white, seemed to have prepared for a picnic. They brought with them baskets of fruit and vegetables and many pet animals—parrots, cats, rabbits, even a sheep. Not only in skin but in apparel and baskets they had livelier colors to challenge the usual drab blues and grays of our naval vessel. I did not fully appreciate the experience at the time—I tried to force it into the stereotypes of racism. "We carried a load of Senegalese savages," I wrote Diana, "who brought along pet rabbits to eat raw when they got hungry. Only they met the antithesis of hunger during most of the trip . . . and as we glided finally into port and the world stopped heaving and rolling, I wish you could have seen those two hundred woolly heads peering cautiously out the escape hatches."

After I returned to duty on the 555, we went on another interesting voyage carrying a company of 200 Brazilian troops and nine officers from Pozzuoli up the Italian coast to Livorno (Leghorn). They were part of the token forces the Latin American countries were hastily contributing to the war effort in order to secure United Nations membership in the approaching peace conference. The Brazilian soldiers, however, didn't think of themselves as token, for they were going to face the German troops on the battle line then just north of Livorno. The major in charge spoke excellent English, as did the chaplain, a jovial priest who seemed like a Hollywood stereotype. They were all from Rio, and had just reached Naples after a sixteen-day voyage on a transport.

Toward night of the first day, the sea got rough, and nearly all the Brazilians were seasick. Davis was also seasick, as usual, and almost out of his head. He got lost from the convoy when the flagship ordered an emergency turn and Davis did not execute it correctly. He had also cut speed, so we were soon not only far off to port of the convoy but far behind. It took several hours at full speed to reach our place again. Clark and I took all the watches from then on, past Elba and Monte Cristo. The return of calm weather cured the Brazilians almost instantly of seasickness, and they began to play stringed instruments and sing their lively songs. They showed particular gratitude to Cotton Clark. As he wrote in his diary, "the officers gave me some Brazilian candy and many coins. They autographed a Rio postal card and seemed not to be able to express their appreciation enough. They called me 'Their Captain' and such stuff. Welcomed me to Rio and their homes."

Livorno had been bombed into rubble by Allied planes. We were now only a few miles from the front, and we manned our guns for the first time since the invasion of southern France. We had no chance for liberty and had to console ourselves with a smooth voyage back to Pozzuoli. On the way back we sailed close to a half-dozen waterspouts, the marine equivalent of cyclones. We didn't know enough about them to be afraid. On reaching Pozzuoli, we were posted almost immediately to Bizerte.

It was obvious by then that peace was returning to the western Mediterranean. Ships could now sail with their running lights on. And, as always in peacetime, the Navy "brass" was ready to return to spit and polish. We got the scuttlebutt as soon as we reached Bizerte that the regular Navy was back in charge. Going around in shorts and sandals or without a hat was out, and snappy salutes and Navy regulations were de rigueur. I was put on report for walking around the base without my hat, and I was by no means the only one. Maybe we had gone too far in placing proper dress and decorum a distant second to winning the war. An army officer we had carried into the Normandy beach wrote us from France that he was facing similar problems as peace broke out. The French Resistance was taking care of the Germans before his troops could reach them, he wrote, and his chief concern was keeping his men rounded up and focused on the war, because whenever French civilians saw them they fraternized, embracing them and showering them with fruit and wine.

The war was now passing us by, but the Navy remembered us. Word went out that all the LCIs at the Bizerte amphibious base were to be inspected. Clark and I led the crew in an orgy of cleaning, chipping, scraping, and painting. The Navy had a word for what we became— "shipshape." We made our decks so spotless that we wouldn't walk on them for fear of dirtying them; instead, we swung from girder to girder through the deckhouse. In addition to my cleaning duties, I stood watch eight hours a day, drew provisions, supplies, and small stores, and brought our codes, ciphers, and other records up to date. All this furious activity seemed trivial compared to our former work putting combat troops on the beach, but the prospect of inspection made cleaning our ship a contest with the other LCIs.

After two days of furious cleaning, a Navy captain named Gregor came aboard with nine aides for a white-gloves inspection. The crew mustered on the gun deck, and Captain Gregor inspected them for haircut, uniform, and shoeshine. He toured our galley, storage holds, troop compartments, and the quarters of officers and crew, and gave the same close scrutiny to the other landing craft. "Captain very nice but 'henchmen' raised plenty of trouble," Clark noted in his diary.

Late that evening word came that our ship, USS *Dopey*, had won the contest and had been awarded a special pennant for "battle efficiency and trim." The award ceremony followed the next day. Vice Admiral H. K. Hewitt, commander of U.S. Naval Forces, Northwest African Waters, formally presented the pennant to our ship as the outstanding LCI in the Eighth Amphibious Force. Our crew mustered on the gun deck and Rost piped the admiral over the side with his bosun's whistle and all hands came to a hand salute. The admiral saluted our colors and shook hands with our proud skipper as the pennant was unfurled. Then Clark led the admiral and his inspection party over the entire ship. "Admiral a very gracious man and had nothing but praise for the ship," Clark noted in his diary, but he was relieved to see the admiral piped ashore. Even I abandoned my usual ironic detachment. I wrote Diana, while sending her a photograph of the pennant, "I'm really right proud of the whole bunch of us, and of that flag flying from the main truck of our yardarm—blue with white letters and that thing on the left is an eagle."

Not all our ship's company shared in our self-congratulation. Five days later, Clark made a cryptic entry in his diary that probably was connected with the inspection: "Heard through no false [fault?] of anyone, of Davis' 'stab in the back.' Considered it a foul blow and figured I could never feel the same toward the guy." The offense Clark so vaguely referred to was probably some embarrassing remark by Davis to the captain or the admiral during inspection. And Clark did later forgive Davis whatever offense he had committed. When interviewed decades later, he did not even recall the incident.

We came in for much good-natured ribbing from the officers of our sister LCIs. An unknown bard on the 557 wrote a mocking doggerel poem in rhymed couplets, "Ode to USS LCI(L) 555," the chorus of which was:

> A blue pennant she did win,
> For battle efficiency and trim!

It recounted our shaky shakedown cruise in the Chesapeake, our getting lost at sea, "Smilin' Jack" Flinn's troubles with Commander Warburton, and the rest of our checkered career. It lampooned each of the officers. Of Clark it sang:

> Now new Captain Clark was a shy young shark,
> But eager for liberty like every young lark!
> When duty called he was not there,
> Some tomato in Oran was smoothing his hair!

Curly Davis was

> Quite a lad, but not for the Navy,
> When underway he tossed up all of his gravy!

And I came in for my share:

> The fourth officer, hair unruly and black,
> Spends one out of two days in the sack!

Young and brilliant as Harlan may be,
The Navy wants men who at night can see!

Just as we were learning to wear our hats while ashore, we forgot all that again as soon as we received a new assignment, to go to the newly opened port of Toulon in southern France and carry troops from larger naval vessels into shore. We were the lone LCI to make the trip in company with a minesweeper, the USS *Steady*. We carried diesel parts and officers' gear and a lone passenger, a French civilian official.

Soon after leaving port, we headed into a gale of force 8. Anywhere else in the world it would be a hurricane, but in France it was called the mistral, a cold, northwest wind out of the Alps that swept across the Mediterranean and signaled the arrival of fall. Whenever the mistral hit, French fishermen secured their boats, threw their fishing gear in the corner, and headed for Marseilles or Toulon. Shopgirls took the week off to celebrate the change of season. Ours was among the few misguided vessels that actually went to sea during the mistral. Because the wind and waves struck our starboard side and thus gave a sort of twist to our pitching and tossing, we were constantly in danger of capsizing in the troughs of mountainous waves.

As soon as the storm blew up, Davis announced that he was too seasick to stand his watch. Clark and I, as the only two other officers, would have to stand his watch as well as our own, each standing watch four hours on and four hours off, all through the storm. Ordinarily a storm excited me as a challenge of man against nature, of willpower against windpower, but this was no ordinary storm. Its onslaught was so furious that I came to doubt whether our flat-bottomed tub could handle it. We might capsize or break in two as our bottom slapped the water with such great force and splash.

Throughout my watch, my signalman and I were out in the weather, constantly cleaning our binoculars of the salt spray so as to keep the more seaworthy minesweeper in view, in waves so high that our ship was periodically swallowed up in the troughs of successive waves. The howling wind caught the whitecaps, streaked them along the top of the water, and dashed them as spray in our faces. We were constantly soaked, not with rain but with the salt water that the wind tore away from the waves. At the peak of every monster wave our bow would heave halfway out of the water and dive into the trough below, while our stern lifted out of the water and the engines shuddered as the screw spun momentarily in the air before settling into a repetition of the pattern on the ensuing wave. After the wind had screamed and torn at our clothing throughout a four-hour watch, we were ready to howl back. Clark and I vied in cursing Davis at every change of watch, and then went below to try to get some rest and new resolve in the few hours before our next watch. The gyrocompass went out of commission again, rendering navigation impossible and making it absolutely necessary that we keep the USS *Steady* in sight. Fortunately, it lived up to its name.

As rough weather took its toll on officers and men, I faced a discipline problem during a night watch. When the ship spun around under the impact of a particularly large wave, I shouted down the tube into the pilot house, "Hard left rudder," in an effort to bring us back on course. "Hell, no, I won't do it! Are you trying to capsize us?" shouted Moyle, the gunner's mate, who was on watch in the pilot house. This was direct, willful disobedience, according to *Navy Regulations,* the Bible of correct procedure. Everything in my training called for me to insist on obedience, even though my order had been wrong. Common sense, however, dictated otherwise. I changed the order to thirty degrees left rudder, and the ship slowly swung around again to follow our lead ship.

As soon as the ship had righted, I told Moyle to get another enlisted man to relieve him and report to the conn. Meanwhile I sent the signalman off for a cup of coffee so that Moyle and I could talk alone. I reminded him that he had already been punished once for insubordination and that a second offense would bring a stiffer penalty. I had no intention of prosecuting him for disobeying my order, I said, because he was actually correct as to the facts, but other officers might not be so reasonable. And I could not allow my orders to be routinely challenged, because discipline was essential to the proper conduct of a ship at sea. I would forget this incident, I said, if he would promise in future to show more diplomacy. If he thought he was in the right, he should point out what was wrong with the officer's order rather than refuse outright to obey it. A reasonable officer would then change the order, but if he didn't the order must be obeyed. Moyle agreed that what I said was reasonable, and I never again had any more cases of refusal to obey my orders, though other officers were probably put through a similar test.

The storm shook our port ramp from its housing, and it hung by its cables and bounced against the hull until Rost and a work detail cut the cables and let the ramp sink to the bottom of the sea. "The ship continued to take its beating," Clark noted in his diary, "—sometimes I was dubious of its staying in one piece." As the storm wore us down, Clark and I found it harder and harder to stay awake on watch. Before we fell asleep, however, on the third day we reached Toulon. "We made it, by the grace of Neptune," I wrote Diana. Our ensign was a good index of the severity of the storm. It had been brand new at the beginning of the voyage, and in three days the mistral had whipped it so hard that its stripes were worn off all the way back to the stars. The wind tore off sixteen of its twenty-two inches. I kept it as a souvenir of the voyage, and by the time we reached port, I felt in about as bad shape as the ensign.

Since Clark and I had stood all of Davis's watches in the storm, we required him to stand watch all three days we were in Toulon. Unfortunately, we were too busy for extended liberty in the only city I had the opportunity to visit in France. It had been heavily bombed, and the harbor was crowded with sunken ships. There was plenty of wine and French bread, however, the trolleys were running, and the American officers' club was in full swing. I got into town long enough to walk the streets and glance in the shops for a few hours. The people had suffered privations during the war, and their clothes were often ragged, but I was struck by the stylish flair the French women gave to their limited wardrobes.

Going alongside a Navy repair ship, we received some quick repairs of stanchions and plates where the loose ramp had damaged our hull. Repair of underwater damage, however, would have to wait for a while, as we almost immediately received a shipload of transferred Navy personnel and set off to Oran. The weather had calmed as though there had never been a storm. After only a few hours in Oran we picked up a load of troops for transport to Bizerte. In the aftermath of the fighting, it seemed, we were becoming the seagoing equivalent of a bus. At Bizerte we put our passengers ashore and also our steward's mate, C. B. Richardson, for a few days in a naval hospital for a flare-up of syphilis. We were not convinced that he was cured, and resolved to replace him when we got back to the States.

While we were in Bizerte our fourth officer reported for duty, Ensign Russell Tye, a tall, baby-faced young man from Batavia, Ohio. A recent graduate of Berea College, he was and looked as fresh out of midshipmen's school as I had been six months earlier. "A simple sort of jerk," I wrote Diana, "but determined to 'make good.' I guess he'll fit in pretty well, and will be good for standing watches going back across." Tye turned out to be far from simple and was several years older than I. Though he had a ready laugh and a friendly manner, unlike the other officers I had served with he had intellectual and political interests and like to talk. He and I shared the junior officers' quarters for the next year and a half, and whiled away the hours on the long voyages of the next year talking politics, economics, and literature. I kept my upper bunk with its porthole view, while he took over the lower bunk. Tye had the distinction of attending midshipmen's school twice. He first went to the one at Columbia that I had attended, but caught the mumps and had to be transferred to a naval hospital on Long Island. When he recovered, the Navy sent him to the first midshipman class at Northwestern University, where he graduated and got his commission. He crossed the Atlantic on an aircraft carrier to Casablanca and then took a train across North Africa to reach us at Bizerte.

While in Bizerte we learned the results of the 1944 presidential election. Like other servicemen all over the world, we had sent home absentee ballots weeks earlier. Political debate, at least among the officers, had been lively. As southerners, Clark and I might be described as "circumstantially Democratic," though I had begun to consider myself more as a liberal New Dealer, and I think Clark was moving in the same general direction. I had no use for the southern conservative carping about New Deal welfare programs and wartime labor demands that were said to be ruining good field hands. Davis, from a small town in the hills of southern Ohio, had been a Republican all his life. As far as I recall, he was the only Republican aboard. Our straw poll among the crew had already anticipated Roosevelt's election for a fourth term. "'Old Smiley' Roosevelt seems to have come through like a champion in the election," I wrote Diana. "The first thing I heard this morning was Davis shaking me and hollering, 'Dewey wins by a landslide! Hooray!' I guess he decided that was the only way to get me up. But if so, it failed to accomplish its purpose. I just groaned and muttered, 'You must have heard the German propaganda broadcast,' turned over and went back to sleep. We heard that the election was conceded by the gang-buster a little later in the morning."

When we moved to a dry dock in the Bay of Tunis, a few hours away, Tye had his first and only bout of seasickness, an experience shared, of course, by Davis. We had discovered a quarter-inch hole leading to the fuel tank. The ship's bottom below the first troop compartment in the forward part of the ship was badly buckled in several spots by the battering storm. Not only were there leaks from buckling and cracked welding of the hull plates but even the structural I-beams bracing the hull in two forward fuel compartments had buckled from the impact of the waves. The repairs we needed were too tall an order for the dry dock. So we returned to Bizerte and soon got orders to the more extensive naval repair facilities in Palermo, Sicily.

As we sailed into the harbor at Palermo, I was surprised to hear my name boomed from a loudspeaker at the harbormaster's office, "Welcome to Palermo, Ensign Louis Harlan of LCI(L) 555." I hadn't known I was such a celebrity! The voice turned out to be that of a longtime family friend from Atlanta, Johnny B. Roberts, now an Army captain in charge of a Palermo hotel converted into an officer's club. As we moved toward the dry dock to moor, a gusty wind presented Clark with his most serious challenge yet. He made three passes at the dock, and each time the wind threatened to wreck the ship. Finally he called for a tug, and it arrived to save him from further red-faced embarrassment. We all reassured Clark that it was just part of learning the ropes.

Palermo had suffered some of the damage of war, but its people seemed to adjust easily to the American conquest. It was a complex modern city. Although it had a Mafia criminal element and one of the worst slums in Europe, it also had a thriving cultural life. American cigarettes brought some $10 a carton on its thriving black market. "Only people dealing in black market can survive or prosper," Clark noted. "Communistic trends very apparent. Shortage of food appal[l]ing. Mothers nursing on street, kids & men picking up cig stubs."

Though Johnny B. was supposed to be *my* friend, he struck up instantly a closer rapport with Cotton Clark. He introduced us to the social life centered around the officers' club. We met his beautiful girl-friend Vera, whom he later married and brought home to the States. She spoke excellent English and worked at the American consulate. She had been a university student until her father was killed in the Allied bombing. I went to two dances arranged by Johnny B. and attended by attractive and respectable local girls, who, fortunately for me, knew English. I also attended a performance of Verdi's *La Forza del Destino* at the Palermo opera house. We had an enjoyable week away from the war. "America is too youthful and alive for this," I wrote Diana about Palermo, "because the beauty of this place must be the crumble and decay of one civilization after another. I give up—I can't describe it." Palermo meant to me "liberty 2 out of every 3 nights—wine, women, and song." We spent Thanksgiving there, without work except for the minimal watch-keeping. Turkey and homemade ice cream were on the menu, and that evening I saw a Sicilian basketball game.

We returned, after the lively social life in Palermo, to the aridity of Bizerte, sat there doing nothing for a week, took some Navy person-nel and sacks of mail to Oran, returned to Bizerte for another monot-onous week, then moved on to Oran for a week. On these voyages, Clark took Davis's watches without complaint and required Davis only to deal with emergencies in the engine room. This was not a satisfac-tory solution, though, because the smell of diesel oil usually set off a fresh attack of Davis's seasickness. It grew worse over time, in direct proportion to his homesickness. Mail call occasionally relieved our boredom, but the brass sensed a need to conduct navigational maneu-vers offshore to keep our minds occupied. We spent days practicing what we already knew.

Rumors began as early as December 12 that we would soon be re-turning home en route to the Pacific theater. Buoyed by that prospect, the crew worked hard to prepare the ship for the voyage, in Bizerte and then in Oran. Christmas came, however, and still no sailing orders. We swallowed our disappointment and made the most of the holiday, decorating the ship with Christmas crepe, bringing a tree into the deck house and decorating it. Stine the cook stayed up all Christmas Eve baking, and we had a wonderful Christmas feast from the ship's larder, supplemented by ice cream made with roasted Algerian almonds. The thriller movie *Laura,* with Dana Andrews and Gene Tierney, showed on the base. Even so, it was a lonesome Christmas far from home.

NINE

A Visit to the Home Front

Two days after Christmas 1944, word passed among the LCIs at Oran that a convoy conference for the voyage home would be held at 1300. Skipper Clark, on his return from the conference, assembled the ship's company and told us we would sail the very next day for Charleston, South Carolina. Jubilation broke out among the crew, and we all went about our tasks of preparation with a light heart. When I asked an enlisted man what he looked forward to most, he gave the usual answer, "Fresh milk and good old American white bread." We learned that many of the LCIs would remain behind. "Hated to leave Flot. Eleven," Clark wrote in his diary. The rest of us didn't give a damn. Next morning, the convoy commander inspected our ship and declared it ready to sail. We securely lashed everything above decks and much in the holds below, in anticipation of rough weather on the long voyage home, and left Oran that afternoon in a large convoy. The weather was as rainy and rough as it had been the previous April when we set out on our first transatlantic voyage. It took us three hours to get into station.

That night the rain ended and the moon came out, but the weather was rough enough—any weather was rough enough—to make Davis seasick. Clark stood watch for Davis during much of the voyage, though Davis's spirits were better now that he was going home. Now that Tye completed our officer complement, however, it was easier for the skipper to take his turn at watch. Flinn would never have done so, however, and that was a measure of the difference between him and Clark.

Around midnight of the second day out, we passed Gibraltar and entered the open Atlantic. The weather improved for a day, but then the wind and the rain returned with the arrival of the new year. We wondered how much the world might change in 1945. Because the Battle of the Bulge had begun just before we left port, we were not optimistic about an early end of the war in Europe, much less the war against Japan. We assumed there would be several more years of war.

On January 6, after almost a week of rougher and rougher seas and dark nights, Tye the tyro strayed from the convoy when enemy submarine reports caused the convoy to engage in evasive maneuvers. The entire convoy was soon in disarray. Tye called for the skipper to rescue him. Clark increased speed, finally reached a minesweeper serving as rear escort, and received the blinker message, "Follow me, pour on the coal." Two or three hours later we regained our station. But the rough weather was taking its toll on everyone, as it was difficult to eat and impossible to sleep. Overdoses of coffee became an absolute necessity. The decks were slick with spilled food and worse, but there were many laughs as food and people constantly slid about. Davis crawled briefly out of the sack to stand watch but almost immediately lost station, and Clark had to take the last three hours of his watch. Clark wrote in his diary that he was "beginning to wonder if losing station was a nightly occurance [sic]." The bad weather had by this time put us one day behind our dead reckoning position. "Loss of sleep and untidiness of ship trying my patience," Clark noted. "Gradually losing faith in human nature."

Improvement in the weather restored the faith. Gear that had been strewn on the deck was picked up, bedding aired, and decks swabbed down. The days passed more easily, but too slowly to suit us. We had seen enough of the ocean and were eager for shore leave. As we sailed north of the Sargasso Sea, an abundance of seaweed floating in the water suggested proximity to land, but that was a misinterpretation born of optimism. On January 13, however, still east of Bermuda, the convoy split in two. The larger group headed toward Norfolk and we, under the leadership of the USS *Achelous,* followed a more southerly course toward Charleston.

The weather remained pleasant except for occasional squalls. We once had to reduce speed to six knots because LCI(L) 528 had the 946 in tow while the latter worked on engine repair. It was discouraging to creep along at such slow speed now that we were so close to home and the sea so smooth, and we hurled a few curses at the stravager. Then the same thing happened to us. Our engines shut down and we had to accept a tow from another LCI. I stood on the bow directing seamen in running our bow anchor cable out to attach it to the stern of the towing ship. As soon as it was attached, the forward speed of the other ship caused the cable suddenly to snap taut and threaten to break and whip back at us. The seamen ran for shelter inside the forecastle, but I was too far away to get there, so I dove into the water instead. If the cable had snapped, I would have been regarded as the quick-witted hero of the occasion. Unfortunately, however, it did not snap, and I was criticized for leaving my duty station without good reason. As I floated back to the fantail, the lowest deck on the ship, and clambered back aboard, I began to regret my quick recourse to water. I consoled myself by recalling an earlier occasion when that had been the right move. One night as Cotton and I were returning from liberty, we saw a drunken sailor fall off the dock into the water between two ships moored close together. As the water was rough, the sailor might be crushed between the two ships. Pausing only to hand over my wallet and kick off my shoes, I dove into the water and used my lifeguard technique to grab him by the chin and pull him out of danger. That was how it was in the Navy, a hero one hour, a goat the next.

On January 16 we sighted seagulls, a surer harbinger than seaweed of nearness to land, and some of our convoy continued on to Miami as we turned westward toward Charleston harbor. We said our good-byes by blinker to those on our sister ship, the 557. They had hardly passed out of sight when our rudder went on the blink and we had to stop all engines until it was repaired. Fortunately, the sea was calm, with only leisurely swells. Once repaired, we hurried to catch up to our small convoy. At 0700 we passed the first buoys marking the channel into Charleston harbor.

All was well at first. Exuberant at finally reaching home, we passed under the Cooper River bridge, picked up a Coast Guard pilot, and docked at the Naval Ammunition Depot to unload our ammunition. After the storybook port towns of Europe, I was shocked by the industrial ugliness of the American scene before us. "It's ugly, but it's ours," I muttered under my breath. It was not until some time later that I saw the more attractive Battery area of Charleston. Next day we moved further upriver toward the Charleston Navy Yard, towing LCI(L) 529 alongside us until it could get its engines started. After ten minutes the other ship was able to cast off all lines and proceed on its own. Perhaps it was this distraction, or possibly our feeling after two ocean voyages that we were old salts who could handle any navigational problem, or maybe it was just the careless optimism of youth that led us into the waiting jaws of disaster. Skipper Clark was in charge in the conn, and I was also there following the harbor charts as we navigated upstream. Half the ship's company lined the rail in their dress blues, ready for two weeks' leave. The mood was festive.

As I followed the chart and checked the channel buoys ahead, I remembered, of course, the seaman's three Rs—Red Right Returning. In other words, the red buoys should be on the right when returning to harbor. As we passed a red buoy on our starboard side I could see another red buoy ahead and called it to Clark's attention. What I failed to notice, in reality and also on the chart, was another red buoy far off to port where the channel zigzagged. We were taking a shortcut through shallow water when we suddenly hit an underwater sandbar head on and came to a shuddering halt. Clark frantically reversed the engines, but too late. Having sailed safely through hell and high water, here we were undone by paradise and low water.

The tide was going out, and we were soon high and dry, and later even higher and drier. After about an hour a small tug arrived but did not have enough power to tow us off. A larger tug also failed. Late afternoon turned to dusk. The sandbar emerged from the water at the bow, and then amidships. Terns gathered and skipped around our bow in search of sand crabs. I appreciated the irony of our situation but could not raise a laugh from anybody else. The crew, dressed in their best, muttered mutinously. If we bothered to eat chow that night, I don't remember it. Some may have chewed a few nails. Finally, at 2346, nearly midnight, the tide came in sufficiently to float us free of the sandbar. Taking no further chances with us, a Navy Yard tug tied up alongside us and towed us to the pier. By then it was too late for the leave party, which included Clark and me, to get our back pay and our leave orders. We had to wait until morning. The manner of our arrival home was certainly ignominious, but not out of character!

My two weeks' leave in the winter of 1945 is largely a blur in my memory nearly fifty years later, with only a few letters remaining to help my recall. Clark ended his diary with our arrival in Charleston, and it would have been of no help anyhow on *my* leave. I do have my handwritten itinerary: "to Atlanta to Chapel Hill to Wilmington to Atlanta to Chapel Hill to Atlanta to Charleston." It is hard to believe now that I made seven train trips in fourteen days, but that was probably an accurate record.

I can remember only a few set scenes through the blur. First I went home to see my proud and anxious parents in Decatur, a suburb of Atlanta. I played as well as I could the role of emissary from the battlefront, though in fact our engrossment in our own little corner of the global war, and our very limited engagement with the enemy, had left me woefully ignorant of the strategy and geopolitics of the war. The folks back home actually had a clearer view than we on the scene. I had seen some of the ugliness of war up close, and I *knew* war in a way no civilian could, but I had no synoptic view of it such as I might have gained from reading the daily papers. While on leave I learned more than I taught about the war, and what I learned contradicted the stereotypes of 4Fs, goldbricks, and "feather merchants" who were the stock characters of servicemen's thoughts about the Home Front.

The imperatives of the war era, following swiftly upon the Great Depression, brought major changes in the lives of most Americans, whether military or civilian. Some changes became permanent, but others disappeared as soon as the war was over. My father's ambition and initiative, which had been submerged all during the depression years under the necessity of providing for a wife and five children, was revived in the flux of the war. He was no longer burdened by five children, who had left for the service or for college. Because the military and war agencies overcrowded Washington, the federal government about 1943 decentralized some of its old-line departments to make room for the war agencies. The Atlanta regional office of the Department of Agriculture, where my father worked, became a hub of feverish activity during the war. My father rose in rank and power, from being head of the lowly hay, feed, and seed division to being the agricultural marketing director and second in charge of the Atlanta regional office. He dealt with major cotton producers and the biscuit companies that made the Army rations. His wartime work became the moral equivalent of soldiering. Besides, he and others in regional offices really believed in decentralization, and the war gave them an opportunity to pursue their regional dream of, perhaps, permanently decentralizing the federal government, a dream that would later cost him much grief as soon as postwar bureaucratic realities reasserted themselves and the centralizers returned to control of the department.

My mother, who had been a teacher before she married, founded a nursery school early in the war years that also doubled as a day care center. Her day involved not only instruction but a noon meal featuring homemade soup, a nap, and transportation from and to home to help parents absent all day doing war work. My two sisters—one in college, the other a high school senior—became service volunteers and social butterflies during the war. They both worked with the local USO to entertain servicemen at dances on nearby bases several times a week, and visited local hospitals to comfort wounded soldiers. The girls also published a monthly family newsletter, *The Harlan Times,* to keep their scattered brothers in touch with home and each other. Never before or since did my family members feel so *needed* as during the war.

My visit home was an intrusion on these busy people, but they were delighted to see me still in one piece. My mother now had a gray streak in her formerly coal-black hair. She was now fifty—"half a century" she laughingly told her nursery school children when they asked her age. The stress of war work and anxiety about her sons—my brother Buddy was in the Battle of the Bulge—gave my mother at least some of her gray hair. Once a pacifist, she now proudly displayed the little flag of a "three-star mother" in the front window. At her insistence I went to an Atlanta studio to sit for a formal portrait photograph in my white uniform. Looking at it now, I believe I never looked handsomer, in fact, never so handsome.

From home I headed as soon as possible to the University of North Carolina in Chapel Hill, where Diana had transferred after two years in the women's college in Virginia. She was majoring in English, had joined a sorority, and worked as a writer and artist on the campus literary magazine. I still have several issues of the magazine with her marginal notes. In Chapel Hill I stayed at the Carolina Inn, then managed by a family friend who had developed tuberculosis and moved there for the climate. Her classes and other obligations prevented my monopolizing Diana's attention, and I had much time to myself, waiting for her to be free. My most vivid memory of that trip was our horseback ride. Diana was taking riding lessons to meet a physical education requirement, and took me to the stables where we arranged for two horses to ride around campus. When she asked what sort of horse I wanted, I pretended I'd never met a horse I couldn't ride, concealing the fact that I had met very few horses in Decatur and had only ridden horseback a few times when visiting my father's farm. We chose two spirited horses and climbed aboard, but they began to gallop even before we were firmly in the saddle. I managed to stay topside and guide my horse's general direction, but no matter how hard I tugged the reins I couldn't slow him down until he tired himself out some half-hour later on the far end of the campus. Fortunately, Diana was having nearly as much trouble with her horse, but she must have suspected that I was no horseman.

During my visits with Diana at Chapel Hill, I sensed a subtle change of feeling toward me that I had already suspected from her recent letters. She was now more coy than responsive. It was as though she still liked me but did not love me, was not in love with me. Though she denied there was another man in her life, that was probably only to spare my feelings. She talked more now about a career after college, and that was probably her true intention. But my bones told me she was in love with somebody else. Maybe, I thought, I was just someone for her to play with while waiting for Mr. Right. Maybe, maybe. When love goes out the window it leaves a lot of maybes behind. Maybe she was doing her bit for the war effort by keeping up my morale. That would be the wartime thing to do. My head was full of doubts, but I dreaded certainties even more and did not pursue the truth. As if to prove to myself that her kisses were as generous as ever, I caught her cold. We were physically that close, but there was a psychic distance between us. She was keeping her options open for whatever the postwar era would bring. I silently resolved to respond in kind, but did not tell her for fear of losing what remained of my claim upon her.

From Chapel Hill I took a night train to Wilmington, Delaware, where my older brother Allen was a captain in the Army Quartermaster Corps. I wrote Diana a long letter about this trip, in hope of exciting her interest and perhaps jealousy: "I was lucky enough to get a reservation on the 'Southerner' to Wilmington, and had my seat tilted back for a nice sleep when this female sleeping in the next seat started flopping all over me in her sleep. Every time I'd get almost to sleep her head would be on my shoulder and her knee in my side. Not bad-looking either but not exactly my type and besides I was interested in sleep at the moment, so I devised a clever plan. I raised my seat about an inch or so above the level of her seat so it would be slightly uncomfortable for her. Where there's a will there's a way, though, and the battle went on. Just about the time I was about to give up through sheer exhaustion she 'woke up' and started sitting on her side. Then the first call to breakfast came like a death-knell to my sleep. I was asleep when she woke me up and insisted that I have breakfast with her. 'You look hungry,' she said to me. 'Madam, that is the secret of my charm,' I replied, but to no avail. I paid the check. When I arrived in Wilmington I would have felt like hell if I had been able to feel anything."

Allen met me at the station and took me to his apartment, where I met his beautiful wife Betty for the first time. They had married in Miami while I was in midshipmen's school. She nursed my cold during the next two days, while also working an eight-hour day and cooking all the meals. From a younger brother's perspective, Allen seemed rather pompous and self-important, and his raw-boned frame had filled out to fit his new role. "Allen is quite the big shot," I wrote Diana, "with five offices on the base and three WAC stenographers and phones ringing every two minutes and him dashing around from one phone to another. He gets quite a bang out of it, though, and is remarkably efficient. The Army has really made a changed man of him. He's fat now, but not really fat, because he is as powerful as the boa constrictor that has swallowed an elephant—or do you remember him?"

Though snow and slush were six inches deep in Wilmington, I recovered enough from my cold to attend Allen's office party at the base. He arranged for me to date a sexy stenographer who worked for him, and I soon found out how sexy. She showed me little attention at the party, climbing all over Allen on the dance floor, embarrassing him in front of his wife. I drove her home in his car, however, and she apparently decided that, having struck out with the boss, she might as well take on his little brother. We did some heavy necking in the front seat and then crawled into the backseat. She pulled off her panties and was ready to have sex, but I had drunk so much and had such a cold that I was totally incapable of erection. This was a new and embarrassing experience for me. The harder I tried, the more I panicked. She tried all her tricks, but we finally had to give up. I got back to Allen's just in time to eat breakfast and catch my day-coach back to Atlanta, sleeping most of the way.

I visited the Emory campus in my uniform, showing off my ribbons and battle stars. I stopped by the library where I had worked for two summers, the old frat house, the pool where I had swum for countless hours. On the steps of the library I met Professor Leroy Loemker, Emory's distinguished philosopher who had once had a powerful influence on my intellectual development. He had recently become dean of Emory's expanding graduate school. "The whole country is going to listen to you servicemen after the war," he said to me in a somewhat lecturing tone. "I hope when that time comes you will have something to say." At that moment I could not think of a thing I would have to say. I fell back into my old classroom shyness, groveling at the feet of the master. I mumbled something like, "I hope so, too," covering up my seizure of self-doubt. I wondered whether there was some hidden skepticism in his remark. Thus far I had thought of the war as my personal adventure, but maybe it was time I grew in wisdom. Perhaps all along I should have been studying the political and social significance of the war instead of just living through it.

I matured unevenly during the war, and most of me lingered in adolescence. As I hung about Atlanta waiting for Diana to finish her classes and be ready for another weekend, I returned to old haunts near her aunt's house in northwest Atlanta. One of our rendezvous was a

Toddle House on Peachtree Road. "It's still preserved in all its tacky glamour," I wrote Diana. "Do you remember when you and Margaret and Joe and I parked across the street and I tried to kiss you and you were very much embarrassed at the thought of such a thing? So we went across the street and got hamburgers with onions and sat on the steps outside watching a couple just wrestling away in a necking party?" I urged Diana to "study your head off" during the week so that I could monopolize her weekend, and particularly the evenings. Though the government had carefully studied the value of daylight saving, it seemed to me that "the field of moonlight saving hasn't even been investigated."

I made a final, frenzied trip to Chapel Hill to attend a dance and basketball game with Diana. Just before I left Atlanta I got a phone call from Cotton Clark, our conscientious skipper, who said he was already leaving home a day early to be sure he reached the ship on time. "Sounds like its Anchors Aweigh very soon after we get back to Charleston," I wrote Diana, "because Cotton said I might have to chase the ship all the way to the Pacific if I were a bit late." It almost came to that. After a busy weekend in Chapel Hill and a troubled good-bye, I took a bus, a train, and then another train due to reach Charleston in the small hours of the morning. The trains were so crowded that I had to stand up almost the entire trip. Finally about midnight I got a seat, depended on the strangers around me to wake me up at Charleston, and fell instantly asleep. The train passed Charleston while I slept, and I woke up just as the conductor called out "All Aboard" for departure from Savannah—the next stop beyond Charleston! I grabbed my seabag and barely got off the train, forgetting in the rack above me my heavy Navy overcoat, which I never saw again. Fortunately, where I was headed I would never need it. After a few hours of hitchhiking back to Charleston, I arrived at the ship and saluted the ensign a few minutes before the 0800 deadline.

Many personnel changes had occurred in my absence. Curly Davis had been reassigned to shore duty on Clark's recommendation filed months earlier in Oran. He had disappeared from our ken as completely as Jack Flinn, never to be heard from again. Years later, while living in Cincinnati, I went to his hometown but could find no trace of him, probably because he was somewhere out in the country milking his cows. About a dozen crew members were also reassigned, including Lewis W. (Bill) Moyle, the man who had recognized land. I was sorry for the ship to lose him because, in spite of the disciplinary problems he presented, he was one of our most competent sailors. Also transferred were Bob Starkey, the signalman who had carried the lifeline ashore at the Normandy beach, and Donnie Nance, who had gotten in trouble with the skipper because of his bad habit of drinking the battery fluid. Decades later I found his name in the phone book at Myrtle Beach, South Carolina, but when I called the number I reached his son. He had died in middle age. All the so-called troublemakers were transferred, but this was probably a mistake, for the troublemakers were often the most resourceful men. Nobody, however, regretted the departure of Bill Stine, our chronically seasick cook.

Our new arrivals also made major contributions to our ship's efficient operation. Our new engineering officer was Orie Todd, a middle-aged ensign who made in almost every way an improvement on Davis's performance. "Our new engineer officer has eleven Pacific battle stars," I wrote Diana. "He is an old Navy man of twelve years [service], worked up through chief machinist's mate. Seems like a nice guy, was on the Hornet for Doolittle's raid, and was one of the survivors of its later sinking." Todd had joined the Navy in the early days of the Great Depression. It was the only job he could find. He was at Pearl Harbor on the "day of infamy." When his ship sank from under him, he was commended for heroism in saving several men trapped in the engine room. He hated being an officer, after so many years of regarding officers as the enemy, but the only way he could get back home after years overseas was to accept a commission and undergo retraining. And he had needed to get back home, because the stress of war had taken its toll of his health and nerves. He seemed ancient to us younger officers, though he was probably in his early thirties. He was unhealthily thin, and may already have contracted the tuberculosis that caused his death a few years after the war. We tend to forget today how widespread and debilitating tuberculosis was in the 1940s.

Returning from leave with new determination to be a better executive officer, respected and feared by the crew, I started my first day back with an early morning inspection of the crew's quarters. I found five men still in the sack and restricted their liberty. Each had some kind of excuse, but the crux of the matter was that they were testing my resolve. If I let them off, we would have trouble from then on. A further complication was that one man did not return at all from liberty. "It's a shame too," I wrote Diana, "because he's a mighty good boy and a hard worker, and knows his job. But when he gets ashore he's doomed. As he arrived back in Charleston from leave the SP's grabbed him for wearing a leather jacket and hat not squared. I had to bail him out, but I tore up the report slip and sent him on his merry way. Then his next liberty he disappears and we will have to turn him in as a straggler. Probably he's back in Birmingham by now."

The steward's mate who had been with us in the European theater, Clifford B. Richardson, also began to complain anew of poor health—rheumatism this time—and limped whenever he saw an officer. He said his wife had to rub him with liniment all during his leave, and that he was too sick to go to sea again. I suspected that he still suffered from venereal disease, which had earlier put him in the hospital in Oran. We sent him to the Charleston naval hospital for observation and managed to get out of town before they could send him back to us. The next catastrophe that first day was the illness of our new ship's cook, Meligonis, instantly yclept "the Greasy Greek." He had been donated to us by the 554 after Stine had been transferred. He complained of "the shakes," and dropped all our china dishes. "He's as crazy as a bat, if you ask me," I wrote Diana. "He told me all about the bump he still has on the back of his head from a baseball bat. He has a wild, haunted look in his eye and gets seasick besides. The first dealings I had with him were this afternoon when he tried to tell me he wouldn't fix chow without an assistant. 'If you are asking for trouble, you've come to the right place,' I said, and he got this wild look in his eye. Has delusions of persecution, I think, but I'm not a psychiatrist and therefore not equipped to humor him. He told me, 'You officers are treating me like a convict. I don't want to go out to sea. When I got in the navy the psychiatrist that interviewed me started not to take me in the navy, but then he said I was qualified for shore duty only, and then he forgot to put it down on my record.' Finally I got him quieted down enough to serve chow, without an assistant. I'll try to get rid of him but it's a hard job."

The climax of that first day back at the ship was when a truck arrived and deposited on the dock a thousand-pound anchor to replace our lost stern anchor. It was at least five times heavier than we needed. I wondered whether I was expected to hoist it overhead, whirl three times, and heave it on deck. At nightfall the anchor still lay on the dock, along with a twenty-foot dinghy. Next day I managed to get a crane to hoist it into its housing, and we sported the largest anchor in the amphibious fleet.

As soon as Clark and I returned, Russell Tye was free to take a three-day pass for home. He was engaged to a girl he hadn't heard from for the entire three months he had been overseas. We had begun to think he had made her up. It turned out, however, that she had been addressing her letters to LCT 555, and we were on our way home before the error could be straightened out. During our absence on leave, he had arranged through the Navy to buy an engagement ring from a New York jeweler. He took off for Kentucky, and returned to the ship a happy man, officially engaged.

At Charleston we had a surprise visit from Lewis Mohr, a seaman we had transferred to another ship months before. We had nicknamed him Lewis Less, and Zero, on account of our low estimate of his mental acuity. We knew he could not read a comic book and steer a straight course at the same time. Staring dully at the dark blue of our new camouflage paint job, he grunted, "Guess y'all are going to the Pacific, huh? Huh, huh!" He thought that was funnier than we did.

Thoughts of the Pacific and the naval warfare there filled our minds as we prepared to get underway for Key West. On February 24, at the last minute before shoving off from Charleston, I expressed to Diana the conventional sentiments that wartime propaganda had placed in my head: "There are other men in the Pacific fighting the war in my place, and I can't help feeling I want to be there to help them. I wouldn't feel right unless I were going there. So all ahead Tokyo, and maybe now that the 555 is headed that way the war will be over shorter than anyone believes." After fifty years of hindsight, I'll take credit for the brilliant prediction in that last sentence, though I wish I had said "sooner" rather than "shorter."

TEN

Sylvia

Leaving Charleston, we skirted the sea islands and the Florida coast, close enough to see the surf breaking on the shore. The palm trees swayed, the sea gently undulated. We could ignore the roaring of our engines when Miami Beach lay before us, just out of reach, bathed in soft moonlight. The winter weather this far south was warm enough for us to stand watch in shirtsleeves. I conjured up images of tropical paradise on the nearby shore—"fresh sea breezes that sway the palm trees on the shore, cocktails two feet high, tennis in the afternoon and dancing in the evening, a swim every morning before breakfast." When off watch, however, I had to face reality aboard ship. We had two cooks, both too seasick to prepare meals.

Key West was our first port of call. There I saw that paradise at close range was slightly tawdry—"milky-blue water and coconut palms swaying in the breeze, tacky clip joints at every corner and one in the middle of every block. Beautiful suntanned girls everywhere I turn with summer dresses that look more like bathing suits than any other article of feminine apparel. . . . It's hot, though. At eleven thirty at night 'Ah'm sweatin' like a hawg in a butcher shop.'"

Key West under wartime conditions was lacking in glamour. It had been almost deserted all through the depression years, when few Americans could afford to travel there. The WPA built a highway from the keys to the mainland, thus giving employment to hard-hit Floridians, but then wartime gasoline rationing put Key West out of reach again. Houses needed painting, bars and honky-tonks were nearly empty, though never wholly empty as long as sailors were around. Ceiling fans provided the only air-conditioning in those days. Because Key West during the war depended almost entirely on sailors' trade for its living, most of the places of business were bars. The once and future resort awaited the arrival of President Truman and his loud shirts in 1946 to put it back on the map.

We spent long enough in Key West to change some personnel. The officers had quickly tired of making their own beds and serving their own meals after we lost our steward's mate. As executive officer it was my duty to find a new steward's mate ashore. The only one available faced a summary court martial for disorderly conduct while on liberty. To judge from the blue vocabulary he used, which the arresting officers wrote into the charges against him, he was truly an underworld character. Some of the words he used I saw in writing for the first time. It took pretty strong language to shock the Shore Patrol, but he had it. His appearance, however, made his language seem laughable. He was the scrawniest, meekest, most mouselike little man imaginable, and a policeman's blackjack had put a lump on the side of his head as big as a plum. With considerable misgivings we took him rather than do our own bed-making and cleaning up.

While we were in Key West a seaman who had been aboard for only two weeks brought about another personnel change by shooting himself in the left hand with the .45 pistol he carried on gangway watch. He claimed it was an accident, but we suspected that it was self-inflicted in order to avoid sea duty. The bullet passed through his hand, ricocheted from the gangway deck to the conn and then on to another ship tied up alongside us, and lay there spent on the deck. We got a stretcher to carry the wounded man to an ambulance and the base hospital, even though he was perfectly capable of walking. We wanted him to seem as wounded as possible in hope that the hospital would keep him. In view of our doubts about the cause of the wound, we transferred the man to the hospital for observation and left port before they could send him back. We also transferred a chronically seasick member of the engine crew.

As we continued south in company with four other LCIs to Coco Solo, Panama Canal Zone, calm weather offered our ship's cook another try at his job. He remained too seasick to prepare meals, however, and at Coco Solo we transferred him also to a naval hospital for observation. Altogether, our return to the States had caused us to lose good seamen and replace them in many instances with duds. Some of the new recruits, however, began to make themselves useful and earned their passage. While awaiting our turn through the canal locks, we got one overnight liberty in the Canal Zone. I settled for a few drinks and shopping for souvenirs, but some of the crew had high times in the low dives for which the Canal Zone was famous. They entertained us for days at sea with their tales of strippers fornicating with sailors on the dance floor, and even with a dancing bear. Some of the graphic descriptions sounded disgusting, but the eyewitnesses said one had to have been there to fully appreciate it. During our brief stay in Panama the LCI alongside us had a refrigerator failure. The temperature inside rose to 47 degrees, and the ice cream they had hoarded, as squirrels save nuts, began to melt. The ice cream dripped and flowed gently over the deck as they rushed it to our refrigerator for safekeeping. About the same time, I had a personal mishap. I discovered that a bottle of Clorox I had stuffed into my seabag in Charleston had broken, ruining my only suit of dress whites and making a hole the size of a fist through my blue coat.

We sailed through the canal in a single day, entering the first locks at 0920 and passing through the wide Gatun Lake and narrow Culebra Cut to another series of locks on the Pacific side that lowered us back to sea level in Balboa by 1535. We had hoped to get another liberty in Balboa, but our sailing orders took precedence, and we got underway that same night with two other LCIs for San Diego. In the Bay of Panama we sailed through a large school of whales. Somehow, in the large ocean, they seemed smaller than I had expected. About midway through the voyage, off the coast of Mexico, we hove to one day and took a swim in the open Pacific, posting a watch armed with a carbine in case sharks should appear. It was a thrill to realize that the bottom was a mile and a half below. We sunbathed all through the voyage, but every time we tried to sit on the weather decks we immediately bounced up again to avoid blistering. My tan was very uneven, however. As we sailed due north, my left side turned dark but the tan on my right side was so light that a good bath would probably have washed it off. If this continued, I thought, Pacific islanders might think I was a "halfbreed."

Keeping the crew active and efficient was part of my job as executive officer, but I found it particularly hard to accomplish in the tropical heat. To spur on the crew, I created an award called the "plush-lined purple heart," to be given each month to the enlisted man whose work on cleaning details contributed most to the efficiency and smart appearance of the ship. Rost, the bosun's mate, was the first recipient. I do not recall that there was a second.

We had acquired a new cook at Coco Solo, but he quickly became famous for the congealed masses of dough he served every morning as pancakes, sunny side up. Criticisms were so severe that he came to me for sympathy. "I didn't mind," he said, "when they called them collision mats or even shock-absorbers, but it was the last straw when Rost said this morning that I should go back to the synthetic rubber factory now and not wait till the war's over." I tried to comfort the cook, but he swore he'd never make another pancake as long as he was on the ship. I accepted that as a promise.

I recall now with embarrassment the wanton destruction of marine life we and the other ships traveling with us wreaked on that voyage. It fortunately did not occur to us to take target practice on the whales we passed on the first day out, but all along the coast of southern Mexico we took pot shots with rifles at blue marlin and giant squid three feet long. We thought we scored hits on some of the marlin, but by then they were too far astern to haul aboard. Farther along, we shot at sharks, and then at great sea turtles with spreads of five and six feet. I almost bagged a flying fish on the fly, but it was too fast for me. The helmsman began weaving out of station in search of other living targets for our sport, until the skipper looked up from his sunbath and spotted our zigzag wake. Clark raised hell, but it was not our threat to marine life that exercised him, only our wandering path.

During the leisurely voyage along the coast of central America, as we sat in the wardroom drinking coffee, our new engineer Orie Todd regaled us with stories of his days aboard the cruiser *Chicago* in these waters. I included one of his sea yarns in a letter to Diana. The cruiser *Chicago*, he said, once put into San Salvador for fuel and water. The commander of the Salvadoran army sent word from his villa overlooking the bay that he would pay a visit to the commanding officer. The ship became a buzz of activity, such as only a beehive or a regular Navy vessel can be. Deckhands dashed hither and yon carrying paint buckets, swabs, water buckets, brooms, cleaning rags, and shoeshine kits. When all was shipshape, they mustered on deck in their dress whites and waited all afternoon for the arrival of the general's sixteen-cylinder Packard. Meanwhile, he was taking his usual afternoon siesta. After waiting until sundown, the skipper finally said to hell with the general and retired to his quarters. Just as dusk turned to dark, along came a scruffy small boat, and sitting in the stern sheets was the general himself, wearing a three-cornered hat and enough gold braid to pay off the national debt. He was alone in the boat except for a case of rum, but this rum would soothe the ruffled temper of many a captain, commander, ensign, and seaman that night. The whole ship snapped to attention and six side-boys piped the general aboard. He and the skipper grabbed a bottle each and went off to discuss the broader aspects of Pan-American relations. As soon as they departed the scene, all hands made a mad rush for the rest of the rum. This story got a particularly good reception because aboard our own ship there was not a drop to drink, though that would change later during our Pacific sojourn.

When we ran into a storm off Baja California, seawater soaked into every part of the ship. My upper berth in the junior officers' quarters was next to a leaky porthole, and any time the sea was rough enough, as on this occasion, whenever water splashed over the bow some of it found its way into my bunk. I rearranged my position on the bunk so as to keep my head dry, but water now wet my feet and also splashed on the deck and into my shoes and socks. When I finally dropped off to sleep, the weather got so rough that the books bounced off my bedside shelf and conked me in the head.

On March 18 we reached San Diego. Almost immediately inspectors from the U.S. Department of Agriculture seized all our fresh fruit and what remained of the delicious Argentine beefsteak we had acquired in the Canal Zone. The inspectors feared the spread of fruit diseases and hoof-and-mouth disease, or perhaps the foreign competition.

Believing that we must be badly needed in the Pacific war zone, we expected only a short stay in San Diego, but we were there for two and a half months. We gradually realized that the Navy high command had come by then to consider the LCI obsolete as a landing craft. Combat experience in both Europe and the Pacific had shown that the smaller LCVPs and LCTs were more efficient in delivering men and machinery to beaches, and also were smaller targets for enemy fire. While the Navy brass considered how best to use our ship in the Pacific war, we sat in San Diego—at first in complete idleness, and then in vigorous training exercises on the offshore islands—exercises that taught us mostly what we already knew.

Meanwhile, overnight liberty was plentiful. Our first major excursion was to Tijuana, the Mexican border town about twenty miles to the south. One night, leaving Orie Todd on watch, Cotton Clark, Russell Tye, and I took the excursion bus to this den of iniquity and spent the evening in a rundown little honky-tonk, the Café Aloha. We bought a Mexican meal and many drinks, and leaned back to enjoy the floor show. There was a fan dance every hour on the hour, and a striptease on the half-hour. Tequila, known as "the Gulp of Mexico," was the drink of choice. It was rumored to be made from cactus and flavored with bee venom. The tequila caught in our throats, but what caught our eyes were the lively, unbelievably revealing floor shows. The high point of amusement was when a fat, middle-aged woman tourist tried to jitterbug and imitate the fan-dancer. We all shed some of our inhibitions as the evening wore on and the tequila took effect, and we wildly applauded the fan dancer, Wanda Mae, clearly not a Mexican. She must have observed my study of the "character" in her face, because sometime after midnight a waiter brought her note to my table, pointing her out suggestively. The note read: "Could we have the pleasure of meeting you? The two girls are lovely & would like to have some one to talk. Sign. Wanda Mae." I was too embarrassed in the presence of my shipmates to reply. I did dance with one of the girls, who abandoned the tease part of her routine and just came out on the floor naked. Not believing that the nipples were not covered with pasties nor that it was really pubic hair I saw in the dim light, I had to dance with her to find out. Sure enough, she was as naked as a jaybird, and her

bare nipples jiggled coquettishly as we danced. With two fellow officers watching me, and my head awhirl with sensations, I summoned my
willpower and decided I had gone far enough. All I took away from
Tijuana was a tequila hangover.

Since we had no serious duties in the early days in San Diego, only
one officer had to remain on duty each night. The others were free to
roam overnight three weeknights out of four, and both day and night
on Saturdays and Sundays. I could extend my liberty horizon to Los
Angeles. I took the train at first but soon learned that hitchhiking was
faster and cheaper. I stuck out my thumb and usually immediately got
a ride, up the coastal road past the closed-down Del Mar race track,
through the oil fields and orange groves of Orange County, to Los
Angeles or, to be more precise, to the fabulous tinsel town of Hollywood. Hollywood in those years had a special place in the heart of every
young American. It was our Emerald City, and I walked around there
as if in a dream. During my first day and a half in Hollywood, spent
entirely without sleep, I wandered through Earl Carroll's, Ciro's, the
Florentine Gardens, Grauman's Chinese Theatre, the Brown Derby, and
the Palladium. The movie "celebrities" must have been hiding out,
because the only ones I saw in that first star-struck weekend were Billy Gilbert and Penny Singleton—hardly Hollywood stars of the first
magnitude. I can't even remember now who Billy Gilbert was. But I
continued my star trek in the firm faith that, when I least expected it,
I would actually see an authentic star of movieland. In the meanwhile,
I would just look for girls.

A postcard I picked up at Earl Carroll's described it as the "most
distinctive theater in the world," with two famous orchestras and "sixty
of the most beautiful girls in the world." A deluxe dinner there cost
$3.30, but the cost without dinner was only $1.65. As Archie Bunker
would later say, those were the days! I sent the card to Diana with a
note, "It's all a trick to lure the innocent rustic, namely yo's truly."

On my second excursion to Hollywood, I took Russell Tye along.
We had a wonderful dinner by Navy chow standards, at the Hofbrau
Gardens, a Viennese-style restaurant on Sunset Boulevard. Then we
hurried to that mecca of servicemen, the Hollywood Palladium, a huge
dance hall featuring the big bands. Its main attraction, however, was

that lonely servicemen who came there could meet girls. It not only provided fabulous swing music but served as an informal dating service. I danced for four hours that night with various women and girls, "the long, the short, and the tall."

One girl particularly interested me. She belonged to the new generation of working girls seizing the opportunities for employment created by the demands of the war economy, though she was by no means the first working girl I had met. Wartime America was one big orgy of work. Her first job had been clerking in a department store, but on the spur of the moment she had recently switched to work as soda jerk in a drugstore, a previously all-male occupation. It was easy during the war to change jobs, as had not been the case during the preceding Great Depression. I laughed at the debonair way she described her mundane work. Her brother had been killed, she told me, in the Normandy battle of St. Lo. She wasn't pretty, but her patter was lively, in contrast to the skin-deep beauties I met that night who didn't have sense enough either to make conversation or to run from sailors. I kept her phone number, but I soon forgot her again as I met other girls.

On a second visit to the Palladium I met Sylvia, a small, beautiful Jewish girl with a light step on the dance floor and strong opinions on every subject we discussed, from what the war was all about to labor and the bosses, and on to Jews and Gentiles and southern accents and racial attitudes. Our conversation went on and on, with endless fascination because we were so different in background. Though educated only through the first year of college, Sylvia was far more sophisticated than I and older, with more experience in every category of life. She worked as head bookkeeper in a large wholesale produce company. Everything about her conversation challenged my conventional wisdom and punctured my platitudes, and all the while she whirled around the dance floor with infinite grace.

Sylvia later told me that she had almost turned down my invitation to dance, having become tired of the crowded hall and the insistent beat of the music. She required that I give her overweight girlfriend, a fellow worker in her business office and also the daughter of her landlady, equal time on the dance floor. I was glad to do so, because that was a sign of her strong and generous character. I escorted them home, or to be more precise, they gave me a ride in the backseat of their car to their house in Beverly Hills. I went along with the fiction Sylvia insisted on, that I was dating both of them, but I managed to get Sylvia alone long enough to make a date with her alone for my next liberty night. I took the bus back to San Diego, arriving at dawn. I was already in love.

As soon as possible I got back to Sylvia, who met me as we had agreed at the Los Angeles railroad station. As we wandered through the streets, she protected me from panhandlers in the public parks, warned me against the Mormon evangelist I had met on the train, and showed me Hollywood more effectively than I had been able to sight-see it on my own. At the Trocadero, we saw Rita Hayworth, my first authentic star, and the Johnny who called for Philip Morris—not together, of course. At a movie that night, by a curious coincidence, the newsreel reported a talent contest for a Hollywood contract, won by a girl from my hometown, one I had been in love with during my freshman year in college. She had trained for years to be an opera singer, and I felt somehow betrayed that she would give up her operatic dream to become a dime-a-dozen Hollywood starlet.

Sylvia was on further acquaintance an even more stimulating companion than I had imagined. My love grew by what it fed on, her conversation, and I was amazed at how clearly she thought on every subject we discussed. My pursuit of her soon became an obsession, as war's exigencies quickened the pace of wartime romance. In all aspects of appearance and personality Sylvia was a contrast to Diana. She was a petite brunette, about five three, weighing about a hundred pounds, and had an angel's oval face. She was vivacious and direct. "Does it bother you that I am Jewish?" Sylvia asked me the first time I danced with her. "Not in the least. I admire Jews," I answered. "My father says they are the real master race." In college, I told her, I got on so well with Jews that a Jewish fraternity rushed me and tried to pledge me. They couldn't believe that with a nose like mine I was not Jewish. My response to Sylvia's question was a half-truth that swept under the rug the fact that my father shared the anti-Semitism that was endemic in the society I grew up in. My father had Jewish business associates but no Jewish friends, and he once threatened to resign from the country club unless it ejected a man who merely looked like a Jew.

Probing further, Sylvia skeptically asked how I felt about Negroes. I responded with what seemed like wisdom at the time, that I liked them all right but that they, unlike Jews, were inferior. To my surprise, she disagreed with me, arguing that blacks were intellectually equal to whites but were held in check not by heredity but by discrimination. I found her too attractive to risk alienating, so instead of arguing back I began to listen. I discovered that she also had advanced views on Mexican-Americans, on the war, and on the social order in general.

I found it necessary to suppress or suspend all of my inherited prejudices in order to impress Sylvia and continue a dialogue so well begun. I always got an earful from her, and came to agree with at least part of it. I could hardly wait to get back to my ship to address a letter to Diana. It had always irked me that she had kept her freedom to date other men, while I had felt more or less bound to her. Now I tried to pique Diana into jealousy by hinting at my new involvement, but I did not want to break entirely with her because of my love for Sylvia. Anticipating a long tour of duty in the Pacific, I wanted letters from both of them. "I'm crazy about you, honey," I wrote flippantly, "but there's a man shortage, you know, and your Uncle Louie is taking full advantage of it. So don't feel tied down to me. I want you to feel free to do anything you want to. Only I wish you'd tell me what the score is, because I'm not even at the game." Reading this letter years later, I can sense that, while I wanted to pursue Sylvia, I also hoped to draw Diana closer to me through jealousy. It was Sylvia, however, who was now at the center of my waking thoughts, crowding out everyone and everything else, including my ship and the war itself. Fortunately, my ship in port did not require any extraordinary attention.

I devoted my liberty days to courting Sylvia, and cajoled additional days from the other officers. Sylvia and I became inseparable. We ate, danced, and went to movies together, using every moment our other responsibilities could spare. We ended every evening necking in her landlady's car in her driveway. For a while I alienated her friend and her landlady by my exclusive interest in Sylvia. Though they gradually came to accept it, they didn't like it. Sylvia found it less and less comfortable to live there with the two jealous women, but she mitigated the jealousy by including them in some of our activities such as meals and movies. I learned more about Sylvia by persistent questioning. She had lived in California all her life. As a child she had a curvature of the spine and underwent an operation to correct it, spending a year or more in bed as a convalescent. That explained her petiteness, but the operation must have been a resounding success, for she had a graceful figure and was a marvelous dancer. After we became closer friends and confidants, she told me an uncle had sexually molested her while she was convalescing in bed. She had an unhappy marriage before she was twenty and was now divorced. In many ways we were mismatched—she had not only lived longer but had suffered more and matured more—but we were too much in love to give these differences much importance. They would later loom larger.

As our necking parties in the car became more intense, I didn't know how to take the next step. I had had little or no experience of adult sex. Our affair would have foundered on my shyness and indecision if it had been left up to me. Finally, Sylvia confessed that she couldn't any longer stand so much sexual arousal without fulfillment. It was time we made love, but we needed a more ideal setting for our first time, or at least some place more secluded and more attractive than the backseat of a car. She proposed that we take a weekend trip out of town. I accepted with alacrity, and once we had decided on the course of action, the time quickly became the very next weekend. By that point in our discussion I was panting with desire. It had to be as soon as possible, and on her terms. I agreed to get a car somehow, if she would plan the trip. When she later said it was she who seduced me rather than the other way around, I hotly denied it, but it was true. I was still a boy, but she was a grown woman.

I thought I had a valid Georgia driver's license back at the ship, but when I checked it I found it had expired. I knew the car rental place in San Diego would not accept it, so in desperation I persuaded my shipmate Orie Todd to let me borrow his license and identity. He refused at first, and to overcome his reluctance I swore that if caught I would say I had stolen the license. Producing his license at the car rental place, I signed his name to the papers, took the gasoline coupons, and drove out in a reasonably good sedan. If I stayed out of trouble I would succeed in carrying off this deception, and I had the optimism of youth.

Reaching Los Angeles late in the afternoon, as if in a waking dream, I found Sylvia waiting with her overnight case. We drove to Long Beach and took the coastal highway southward, had dinner in a roadside cafe, and began our search for a motel. Ignoring the tourist cabins built in the early thirties that were beginning to show their age, we demanded for a motel. The motelization of America was in its infancy, but as usual California led the trend. At first casually, then desperately, we stopped at eight or ten motels, all full in spite of the wartime gas rationing. Our plans had not taken into account the popularity of coastal resorts on a truly gorgeous spring weekend. After we had searched in vain along Capistrano Beach and San Clemente, Sylvia suggested that we turn off the coastal road toward San Juan Capistrano, the old Spanish mission town, just the spot for a pair of stray swallows. There, about midnight, we found our trysting place, an upstairs room in a small hotel. I managed to sign the register in a shaky hand and took the key.

As the door closed behind us and we were alone in our own little world, we looked at our Spartan surroundings. A bare bulb hung from the ceiling above a narrow single bed. Who cared about these unimportant externals? The mystery of life was about to be revealed. I undressed in the bathroom and returned to a darkened room. Condoms were in my pants pocket, but some instinct prompted me not to use them. I slid into bed beside Sylvia and discovered by touch her perfect small body. To my surprise she was more beautiful naked than clothed. I murmured something such as "unaccustomed as I am . . . ," anything to cover up my trembling eagerness and panic. "Relax," she said, "we have all night." That broke the tension, and I made love to her then with a surer hand. Kisses and caresses segued into intercourse by some sort of magic. Sex and love together turned out to be more than the sum of their parts. My desire and hers blended into a shuddering mutual climax.

We lay there catching our breath, giggling about the awkwardness of the single bed. The act of sex had seemed like a dream, but I was wide awake and felt more alive than I had ever been. So this was love! And sex! I sighed with relief that I had met the challenge, but the golden glow suggested that sex was an end in itself. Sylvia whispered that our simultaneous climax on the first try was a rare occurrence. It must mean that our souls were in rhythm. Should I do anything differently, I asked, or anything I hadn't done? "More of the same," she murmured. There were more caresses, even daring body kisses. This was unexplored country for me, but I felt adventurous, and purrs of pleasure guided my way. Soon we were on our way to a recurring miracle, making the beast with two backs. Snuggled together in our own new world, we told each other a few of our innermost secrets. We made love again and again, never sleeping but rising at dawn refreshed. Perhaps the experience was not as unique for her as it was for me, but somehow our bodies tend to forget the sex act, so that it always seems as if for the first time, a bit of evidence for evolution by design.

The dreaminess, the sleepwalking, continued through the ensuing day. We had a late breakfast and explored the Capistrano mission, caressing the ancient stones as though they were a part of our coupling, fixing in memory every feature of the trysting place. We lay together on a grassy hillside in the sun, basking in one another's warmth and asking all the intimate questions we had withheld earlier. "How did you know about my hysterectomy?" Sylvia asked. "Is that why you didn't use a condom last night?" This was my first knowledge of it, as well as the first time I had ever heard a woman utter the word condom. "Oh," I said teasingly, "the Navy told us condoms were just for the prevention of disease." Then I told her the real reason, that I had wanted nothing to come between us, and if that led to our having a baby I wouldn't mind. "The hysterectomy doesn't seem to have lowered your sexual appetite," I remarked with a new frankness. She told me that uterine cancer had made the operation necessary, and that she took hormones regularly to keep her libido in balance. This was the first time I had heard of this medical miracle. That she could never have children added a certain sad poignance to our lovemaking. And yet, who knows, maybe my knowledge of it sowed the first seeds of our eventual breakup, though in the euphoria of the moment I refused to acknowledge it. I certainly wanted someday to have offspring to continue my genetic line, but I also wanted Sylvia, then and there. I ignored the contradiction between these desires. There on the grass, with my head in her lap, I shook away sleep so as not to miss any part of this extended moment. "You're beautiful," she said, gazing down at me. I certainly felt beautiful, if a beautiful woman could describe me thus. But male ego required a protest—men might be handsome but not beautiful. "You're the beautiful one," I answered, "I am merely handsome." "No, you're not handsome, your features are not regular enough," she said, "but to me you are beautiful. Beauty is something inside of you." I had to accept that as a compliment, but with the gender anxieties of youth I couldn't in the long run let myself to be measured by feminine standards. Beauty was a fighting word in the battle of the sexes in 1945.

That afternoon we took advantage of having a car, going to places formerly out of reach. I saw the yawning emptiness of the Hollywood Bowl, and Aimee's temple. Aimee Semple McPherson, Hollywood's mystic, had died mysteriously earlier that year. I wondered for a moment whether Sylvia had gone religious, like so many other Californians, but she assured me she was simply showing me the sights. She expressed the same secular outlook I had recently acquired. Reaching her house and driveway after dark, we climbed into the backseat and had a last exquisite "spot of heavy breathing," as Walter Matthau would later describe it in *Pete 'n Tillie*.

I headed back toward San Diego, fighting sleep now and finally losing the fight. While driving through a stretch where the highway divided around a grove of large trees, I fell asleep going sixty miles an hour. It must have been only an instant before I snapped awake and found that my grip on the wheel was firm, but the consequences of a crash would be not only death or serious injury but the discovery of my driving with a fraudulent license. Fortunately, servicemen crowded the roadside hitching their way back to their bases. I pulled over, picked up a sailor with a driver's license, and turned the keys over to him. Crawling into the backseat, I slept like a log until he drove the car into the rental location. I returned to duty with a song in my heart and my thoughts far away.

From then on until my ship left port, I spent every spare moment with Sylvia, but did not tempt fate with another rental car. Now that we had been properly in bed together, Sylvia felt that it was perfectly all right to make love in the back of her landlady's car. Our love would dignify the act. In fact, making love in the car became quite the thing to do. No more movies. We were content with each other's undivided attention. I continued to hitchhike back and forth for a while, but one night a homosexual gave me a ride into downtown Hollywood and made a grab at me while stopped at a traffic light. I pushed him away and asked as coolly as I could to be let out at the next light. From then on I took the late-night bus back to San Diego. It was often so crowded I had to stand up for the entire trip, and one night I was so sleepy I climbed into the overhead baggage rack and slept soundly until the bus reached San Diego.

The war soon intruded on my idyllic life. The Navy rediscovered our LCI and required us to take part in training exercises we thought we really didn't need after our extensive beaching experience in Europe. We beached for a while off Point Loma, North Island, and Till Beach in the San Diego Bay area. Then we broadened the scope of our maneuvers to the offshore islands of San Clemente and San Nicolas, inhabited mainly by wild hogs and seals. Over a period of about two weeks we practiced beaching, fire drills, collision drills, and abandon-ship drills, and tested the fog generator that had been installed on our fantail. We fired our 20-millimeter guns at the shore and at moving targets. What began as an exciting exploration of new waters soon became boring repetition. We found temporary relief from the tedium in an incident off San Clemente Island. At dusk we were about to drop anchor when our skipper thought to check the water depth on the chart and found that the bottom was several hundred feet below, too far for our anchor to reach. As we prepared to search for a shallower anchorage, we caught our breath when we heard the distinctive whine of the ship accompanying us paying out anchor cable. They had forgotten to check the chart. The whine grew higher in pitch as the anchor gathered downward momentum. As they reached the last few rounds of cable on the drum, we heard them jam on the brakes with a great wrenching sound and flying sparks. We had a good laugh at the other ship's expense. We beached so often that some welded plates on our bottom buckled and leaked, and we had to go into dry dock for our last week in the States. This inaction gave us a final chance for liberty ashore.

While we were moored in San Diego on April 12, our commander-in-chief Franklin D. Roosevelt died. We were surprised, shocked, and fearful of the future. Roosevelt had been our president since most of us could remember. We wondered whether the unknown Truman would be up to the challenge of world leadership. Though the war in Europe was nearly over, we still faced the Japanese, whose stature had grown enormously in our eyes after they expanded their empire after Pearl Harbor. Following orders throughout the armed services, Cotton Clark called a solemn muster of our crew in the mess hall next day. At the hour scheduled for Roosevelt's interment, we stood for a moment in silent prayer. Clark then gave a short inspirational speech extolling our fallen leader and urging us to redouble our efforts to bring the war to a successful conclusion. The German surrender less than a month later led to the celebration of V-E Day, but we were too busy beaching on San Clemente Island to take part in the jubilation.

On the day Roosevelt died, the .45 pistol used by the gangway watch disappeared. A search of the crew's quarters turned it up in the bedclothes of George Wright, the steward's mate we had recruited from the brig in Panama. A likable but emotionally unstable youth, he immediately confessed. We never learned any reason why he stole it. We had to place him in shore patrol custody awaiting trial in a summary court martial. A few weeks later the court martial convened on our ship under a Marine major, and I served as the court recorder. The court found Wright guilty and sentenced him to a bad-conduct discharge, and a week later he was shipped back home to Texas for the execution of his sentence. Wright's replacement was Ivey, a tall, powerfully built Texan who had had some experience in civilian life as a ranch cook. Despite the white prejudice against his color, Ivey quickly asserted himself as a natural leader of the crew. He was slow to anger but big and strong enough to put fear into the heart of any potential antagonist. He was also more mature than most of us, and gave wise counsel to officer and crew alike. And he knew more than the ship's cook about how to bake bread and pie. He was competent in everything that had to do with food. If institutionalized racial prejudice had not interfered, Ivey would have been the ship's cook instead of a waiter upon the officers. He served the officers' mess with courtesy and dignity and without servility. Altogether, he quietly challenged the racial stereotypes I had grown up with, and this reinforced Sylvia's admonition to me, to measure people by their character instead of their skin color.

We got word in late May that we would soon be underway for the Pacific theater. The commander of our new flotilla was so impressed with our skipper that he assigned two of his staff officers to berths aboard our ship, the flotilla engineering officer, Lt. (j.g.) Lorne D. Porter, and the group medical officer, Marine Lt. Edgar N. Johnson. They bunked in the troop officers' quarters where I had spent my early months on the ship.

Sylvia and I meanwhile made plans for our final night together. She borrowed a friend's car, and we drove down to Long Beach, where a couple who were her close friends lent us their spare bedroom for the night. What they thought of me I could only imagine, but they must have understood how much in love we were and how desperately we were trying to crowd a lifetime into a few short hours. After a very brief period of socializing, we disappeared into the bedroom and made love all night with the desperate abandon of wartime. We tried to abolish time, but time moved inexorably onward. Toward dawn, when I had to leave, we clawed at each other one last time. She began to beat on me and muttered bitter curses not so much at me as at the tempora and mores. The last few grains of time ran through the hourglass and we parted, not to see each other again for nearly a year.

"Until I hear from you again assuring me that you forgive me I'll not be too happy about my mood on our last evening together," she wrote in a letter I did not receive until I was several time zones away. I don't remember any longer what I was being asked to forgive. "You weren't at fault at all for the things that you said," Sylvia wrote. "We were deliberate in our gouging. The only explanation I can offer, and on a very humble platter, is that I knew it was the last time I was to see you and I was fighting the whole world on your hide." Like lovers everywhere, she thought we could create our own special language for our letters that would avoid any verbal misunderstandings. Every Sunday would be "our Anniversary." "A whole bunch of mmmm's means I'm snuggling up to you real close. How about you adding to our dictionary? I can do more with little noises, giggles & purrs than

Webster ever had time to define. Perhaps I'll have a chance to have some snapshots made soon and then you can see what you've been putting up with for a whole month. There hasn't been a month that has ever been so wonderful. May— May 27th—red letters. This June will be four hundred years long and then in July I'll hear from you. More mmm's." But that letter would be long in reaching me. Next day at noon we sailed out across the wide Pacific.

The blue pennant on mast of LCI(L) 555, fall 1944.

German prisoners, taken on the beach in southern France, one hour after the Allied landing. (See p. 93.) Courtesy of the National Archives.

Some crew members on the fantail. From left: Earl Anderson (motor mac), Joe Dwyer (seaman 1/c), Henry Busse (chief motor mac), Meligonis (seaman 1/c, cook's assistant), Kuhrt (cook).

Russell Tye and author, en route from Panama Canal to San Diego, spring 1945.

Ivey, steward's mate during the Pacific tour. Despite his menial duties, a leader of the crew.

Ensign Orie Todd, engineering officer during our Pacific tour.

A "bumboat," Vietnam, November 1945.

Loading Chinese troops, Do Son, Vietnam, November 1945.

LCI in convoy in South China Sea, December 1945.

Sylvia, enclosed in a letter of Dec. 14, 1945. "This was snapped when it shouldn't have been—yep, that's beer—and can you imagine me listening!"

Up a stump, Sadie Morton and author at Peabody College, 1946.

ELEVEN

Tropic of
Skin Cancer

Our ship churned and wallowed its way in convoy toward Pearl Harbor. The weather was calm and warm throughout the nine-day voyage. The only trouble was with our engines. After only a year and a half of service, the LCI diesel engines were breaking down at more and more frequent intervals under the amateur care of our engine crews. Whenever one ship in a convoy broke down, all the others had to reduce speed until it could be repaired and allowed to catch up. Halfway across, for three days running one ship after another fell behind the convoy while the rest slowed to four or five knots. There was no danger of enemy attack in this zone of the Pacific at this stage of the war, but such frequent breakdowns were cause for concern about how we would fare in a future battle area. The Navy's employment of half-trained engineers and mechanics was taking its toll. Our own ship performed better than before under the expert care of Orie Todd and Lorne Porter, but that didn't help us when other vessels were crippled. We might as well have been crippled, too.

Still, the time passed pleasantly in such good weather. We heard the entire repertoire of Orie Todd's modestly told but inherently exciting yarns of sea battles he had experienced in the early years of the war. On June 11 we sighted Oahu, rounded Diamond Head, and sailed past the colorful Waikiki beach hotels and the city of Honolulu to Pearl Harbor. We moored at West Loch for three weeks, with duties virtually nonexistent and a liberal liberty policy in effect for both officers and crew. The ship underwent minor welding and repairs, and as always there was much chipping and repainting of the ship's hull. Much of the time, however, was ours to spend ashore—only in short blocks of time, of course.

I spent most of my liberty hours in the shops and bars of Honolulu. Along Waikiki, one of the great beaches of the world, not yet ruined by overdevelopment, I watched the surfers with envy but lacked the time to learn the sport. I took a couple of afternoon swims, but most of our liberty time was after dark, when the bar of the Royal Hawaiian Hotel on Waikiki became my principal watering hole. At Pearl Harbor the main attractions were the rusting hulks of American battleships and cruisers sunk in the Pearl Harbor raid four years earlier. A few of them had been salvaged or cleared from the channels, but most lay partially submerged, grisly monuments of Japanese fighting prowess.

I paid a visit to an old family friend living in a little cracker-box house near the base, with a row of papaya trees in the yard. I quickly acquired there a taste for papayas, and as the ship was being outfitted for the next leg of its voyage I persuaded Russ Tye, the commissary officer, to procure a case of papayas for the officers and crew. I soon discovered that almost nobody else aboard cared for this unaccustomed, un-American delicacy, and I had virtually the whole case to myself. Tye condescended to eat a few, but I was the principal consumer. I particularly enjoyed my papayas with a large scoop of vanilla ice cream in the center. Before we left port I arranged for another case, and continued to enjoy them for a couple of weeks at sea.

We left Pearl Harbor on July 1 without mishap, heading for Eniwetok in the Marshall Islands. Maybe, we thought, we were finally ridding ourselves of our foot-in-mouth image, but there were new goofs ahead for USS *Dopey*. An LST served as our convoy guide. Even though we were now up to our full complement of officers, Cotton Clark took a regular turn at watch, and Lorne Porter stood a four-hour watch once a day, though not obligated to do so as the group engineering officer. With this relief on watch, combined with a peaceful ocean, our duties underway were light indeed. We added a day to our calendar when we crossed the international date line on the seventh day out. But we had no ceremony, since Todd was the only one among us who had ever crossed it before. Todd gave us all the ignominious details of his numerous dateline-crossings back in peacetime, when such ceremonies were performed with gusto.

At 0448 on July 11, the middle of the night, general quarters sounded, and three minutes later all guns were manned and ready. It was only a drill. That afternoon, on orders from the flagship, we had a repetition of general quarters, and each time we responded quickly and efficiently. We could take pride in our continued "battle efficiency and trim," but there was little or no need of battle efficiency. Eniwetok, toward which we were heading, had been secured by American forces a year and a half earlier. By July 1945 the Americans had retaken the Philippines, the battle for Iwo Jima was over, and the battle for Okinawa ended victoriously on July 2, the day after we left Pearl Harbor. Our forces were knocking on the door of the Empire of Japan. Island-hopping had left a few stranded pockets of Japanese on some islands, but the American Navy had long before swept the central Pacific of Japanese surface vessels through tremendous sea battles. Though the Japanese had lost most of their navy, they still had strong defensive capacity in their home islands. LCIs had played a prominent part in the island assaults, but the last and hardest battle still remained ahead of us, invasion of the Japanese home islands. It was for that assault, presumably, that we had been summoned to the central Pacific. None of us questioned the unconditional surrender policy of our national leaders, or the necessity to invade Japan.

On my twenty-third birthday, July 13, we sighted land about fifteen miles ahead. It was so incredibly flat that it was barely distinguishable above the horizon. Eniwetok atoll, our new home, was an irregular circle of small sand islands resting on coral reefs that had formed on the rim of a submerged volcano. Inside the island ring was the lagoon, a vast expanse of relatively calm, moderately deep water. Islands on the far side of the atoll were invisible, being only two or three feet above sea level so that the curvature of the earth put them below the horizon. We could not see even the tops of the palm trees on the other side of the atoll. The lagoon was sometimes choppy but never as turbulent as the ocean outside. We sat there as though becalmed for the next three months. We saw little of the Polynesians who inhabited these islands. United States authorities had removed most of them to islands out of sight on the other side of the atoll, to protect them from corruption by us servicemen. In this instance, our government showed more compassion than it would later show when the Marshall Islands were used for nuclear tests.

Our becalming at Eniwetok was not a punishment for shooting an albatross, or any such hellish act. We simply lay in wait to do our duty in the climactic battle in the Japanese home islands that would end the war. Meanwhile, we learned more than we wanted to know about the Japanese suicide pilots and their kamikaze planes, which had first appeared during the battle for Okinawa. Their desperate attacks on naval vessels signified for us the way the Japanese could be expected to resist our invasion of their home islands. Our own government's propaganda heightened our fears by emphasizing the fanatical nationalism of the Japanese. Scuttlebutt, the Navy rumor mill, had it that American casualty rates for the invasion of Japan were expected to be 30 percent, or even 50 percent. None of this was official, of course, and was probably wildly inflated. We also heard that no prisoners were being taken, that both sides were shooting down those who tried to surrender.

Meanwhile, in a lull that might precede a storm, we lay at anchor offshore, usually with four or five other LCIs moored alongside. Our idleness was not total. On orders from the skipper and those above him, we kept the deck crew busy chipping old paint and rust from the deck and sides, coating the hull with a bright orange primer coat and then applying a final coat of gray-blue. The brighter, bluer water of the Pacific called for a lighter shade of paint than we had used in the Atlantic. In addition to the cleaner look a new coat of paint gave us, painting was considered therapeutic for the crew. It kept the men busy enough to dispel some of the discontent, quarreling, and homesickness. It also gave them healthy exercise. It was good for both mind and body. One trouble with this theory was that the tropical sun made our steel deck as hot as a frying pan. And nobody whistled while he worked. We abided religiously by the old Navy saying, "Nobody whistles aboard ship but a bosun's mate or a queer." And there would never be enough paint to cover all the heat, the inaction, and the anxiety about the combat that lay ahead.

Soon after our arrival at Eniwetok I learned of my promotion from ensign to lieutenant (junior grade). I don't recall the date, and the event passed without ceremony, since at that stage of the war more ensigns were being promoted than the Navy knew what to do with. As I recall, Cotton Clark gave me his extra pair of silver bars for my shirt collar, and much later I acquired the shoulder-boards and the additional half-stripe on my sleeve. Though my promotion was unceremonious, it was highly significant to me as a recognition that maybe I was a competent naval officer after all. This question had troubled my mind ever since our mishaps in the Atlantic and Jack Flinn's unfavorable fitness report. On July 27, I got my first letter from Sylvia addressed to me as Lieutenant (j.g.). Notice of the promotion must have been two or three weeks before that.

Sylvia and I exchanged many long letters, writing to each other almost daily since I had left San Diego. Our correspondence was arrhythmic, however. Time and distance between us made it impossible to engage in a dialogue. At least a month passed between question and answer, and we were forever casting our feelings for each other into the time-void between us. As she put it, this was the fault of "the gremlins" who were everywhere promoting discord and "messing with Mister In-Between." But it was more than that. I was also sending her mixed signals from a divided, two-timing heart. All I now have of our correspondence is her letters to me, but she occasionally quoted my words back to me. In one of my first letters to her, on May 13, I said: "I don't understand you, nor you me. Perhaps it's better that way." What in the world did I mean? What signal was I sending? Again, she quoted from my letter: "A friendship outlives most love affairs." These were only a few random negative signals in an ocean of affectionate outpouring of supportive phrases, and to a large degree they were simply efforts on my part to sound sophisticated, but it took a month to amend any thoughtless word. And she, who knew her own mind better than I knew mine, would accept none of these compromises from a young man in over his head. She wrote to me: "I should, if anyone can, recognize your moods. And I feel that I do. But at times I feel red-cheeked after reading your letters as tho you're slapping me for something I know nothing about. Why do you say I was a fool to fall in love with you? It is one of the few right things I've done in my life. And why say good bye—ever? Isn't it your idea—your words 'A friendship outlives most love affairs.' This is more than friendship—a knot has been tied, fat boy, and it isn't for you alone to untie. The entwined ends are duplicates—how will you know which one is yours? And you can't risk guessing—you might in error destroy the end that belongs to me. That is not your right." The reference to "fat boy" was a comic exaggeration, of course. I then weighed about 140 pounds. She was even thinner, but rounder, and had a bigger heart.

A classic instance of our problems of communication was Sylvia's birthday present to me, a handsome wooden music box that played a Strauss waltz. I still have it and treasure it. I thanked her "for the tunes I played on the music box before my conscience took hold." Then I said, for reasons I cannot now fathom, "But I can't accept gifts from you, darling." What could I have been thinking of? Compared with our strong bonds of affection, a gift was a mere token. I must have been in the tropical sun too long. She sent me a typed copy of my letter, adding a little note at the bottom of the page: "I have lost my place in my dream."

Somehow, we got past that crisis, and I never returned the music box. But it was symbolic of my indecision and her certainty. "There is nothing to forgive, darling," she wrote sometime later with typical generosity. "Neither of us meant any hurt. I know I didn't and as for your own little fox hole of hell if my permission for you to 'come on out' will help—you may have it."

After we had been at Eniwetok about three weeks and had about run out of decks to paint, on the night of August 6 an air alert sounded on the naval base. We blacked out our ship, but ten minutes later the alert ended. We assumed it was just a drill. The next day we passed through the entrance channel of the atoll into the open ocean for tactical maneuvers and drills, then returned to anchor. This little maneuver must have had some connection with the dropping of the atomic bomb, though what the connection was we never learned. Almost immediately afterward, we heard over the Armed Services radio American forces had dropped an atomic bomb of great force on Hiroshima on August 6. Four days later we heard that the Japanese had offered to surrender. When the news report of the surrender broke into the Armed Forces radio music program I thought at first that the announcer said "rejected" instead of "accepted." I was just summoning up my reserve of intestinal fortitude when Todd remarked: "Don't pinch me now. Let me dream a while longer." "What the hell are you talking about?" I asked, and he explained to me that the war was over.

Russell Tye was the only one aboard who had the least idea what an atomic bomb was, and he didn't know much. We cheered anyhow at the news that we wouldn't have to invade Japan after all. We learned more chilling details about the bomb a week or so later, when we got our copies of *Time*'s overseas edition, the skinny one without advertisements. I do not recall any ambivalence on my ship about the ethics of the A-bomb or the way it was deployed. We did feel awe of its power, and a vague uneasiness about the danger of such power in the hands of errant mankind. But the dominant emotion was relief. There was no celebration of V-J Day aboard our ship, because we lacked the required ingredients—women, liberty, and booze. Like most servicemen, we waited to see if the Japanese terms of surrender would meet the "unconditional surrender" standards set by the Allies two years earlier. They did so, with the acceptable modification that the Japanese would be allowed to keep their emperor. When the surrender was signed on September 2 aboard an American battleship, the *Missouri*, in Tokyo Bay, we followed the stirring occasion via Armed Forces radio.

Back in Los Angeles, when the announcement brought all work to a halt, Sylvia's boss took his "girls" out to dinner. All the bars and liquor stores were closed, but they somehow found a bottle of whiskey for a drink before dinner. In the time between the A-bombs and the surrender, Sylvia wrote me, "I have been accepting dates and with an injustice to the inviter if it was known he was entertaining 'two.' The last is something you will 'not like to hear but will want to know.' Many things would be made easier for me if I didn't love you so much." Though Sylvia broke the news gently, some part of the artificial edifice of our wartime lives was already crumbling. Pining for a faraway love, the main theme of wartime popular songs, went out of style abruptly.

Though the war was over, we servicemen were stuck at our posts until our ship could be brought back to the States. So we remained at anchor week after week, expecting any day to get orders to return home. Our impatience grew daily. Apparently the abrupt end of the war had caught Washington by surprise, and victory in the war gave encouragement to dreams of American empire, of a new Rome on the Potomac. The Navy brass seemingly had no blueprint for demobilization ready, or at least none hasty enough to keep pace with our impatience. Meanwhile, we occasionally got ashore for a few hours' recreation. Officers had access to the officer's club at the naval base built by the Seabees on Eniwetok Island.

Enlisted men had to content themselves with a few hours on the sunbaked sand at nearby Runit Island, where the beer ration was two warm cans per man. An officer had to accompany the enlisted men, and Tye and I usually volunteered. Two beers were better than none. While the men wandered around the island hunting half-ripe coconuts that had fallen from the palm trees, we spent our time in the remarkably clear water offshore. Russell Tye had our only snorkeling equipment, but I had goggles that allowed me to see the myriads of colorful tropical fish swimming in the shore waters or in the crevices of the coral reef a short distance from shore, where it dropped like a precipice toward the ocean floor below. The water was of a comfortable temperature, and I spent hours exploring the chasms of the coral reef. Another pastime was collecting the hundreds of varieties of seashells that the tide cast up on the beach. There were occasional disciplinary problems as some men got drunk by buying beer from others, but most of the problems were manageable.

As time passed, we managed to get ashore more often. When large fighting ships such as cruisers and carriers came into Eniwetok for rest and recreation, they frequently used LCIs in the demeaning role of liberty boats. We would carry three hundred or so sailors at a time from these big ships to shore for a few hours of recreation. On another occasion, I took our ship's dinghy to the beach. Actually, I swam from the ship to shore while Russell Tye rowed the boat. A storm came up while we were on the island, and the wind was against us as we tried to row back to the ship. While Tye manned the oars, I dove into the water and pushed the stern of the boat while swimming. As we made slow headway, we saw ahead that our nest of ships was dragging anchor and then getting underway to move to another anchorage. We managed to make our way to another LCI, which gave us a tow to our own ship. We crawled on board greatly relieved not to have been swept away by the wind and current.

There were few highlights in this period of tedium and tanning. Now that the war was clearly over, we began more and more to think and behave like civilians who happened to be in uniform. Outwardly, of course, we continued to be naval personnel, but our thoughts were in a different world. On August 19 we entered a floating dry dock for a check of our bottom and for minor repairs, but as we left the dry dock on our way to anchorage we hit a timber floating in the water, four feet long and two feet thick. It gave us a heavy jar and jammed the port screw, so a few days later we had to return to dry dock for replacement of the screw.

As we sat at anchor day after day, personnel changes began to occur. Our medical officer for LCI(L) Group 109, a Marine lieutenant, was detached in mid-August for reassignment, and six weeks later so were Orie Todd and Lorne D. Porter, engineering officers of our ship and Group 109 respectively. We received no replacement for Todd as our engineer, but Lt. (j.g.) Harry E. Tourtillotte soon reported aboard as Group 109 engineering officer, and he agreed to also serve informally as our ship's engineer. About a month later Lt. (j.g.) Philip Rubin reported aboard as group medical officer.

All through September and into October, we expected any day for our ship to be ordered back home. The war was over, after all. Peace had broken out. We did not endorse or even clearly foresee an imperial mission for the United States, least of all a full-scale cold war with our late allies the Russians. Meanwhile, Washington had promulgated a point system for the mustering out of servicemen. They would be separated from the service on a schedule based primarily on length of service, time overseas, and marital status. This worked to the advantage of some of our enlisted men but was of no help to the officers, whose duty required them to remain with the ship until it could be brought back to the States for decommissioning.

As time passed without any indication of plans to bring us home, our morale sagged. To bolster it, our LCI group quietly and informally modified the strict Navy rule against drinking aboard ship. Under regulation by the skipper, we requisitioned cases of beer from the naval base on Runit Island, and every day at sundown everyone aboard was authorized to drink one can of beer. To avoid any overindulgence, a rule forbade anyone to trade his beer privilege to anyone else. We assumed that this beer allowance would apply only when the ship was stationary, but we got the same daily ration while underway. I have no idea how far up the chain of command this bending of the rules was known, but I am sure that we reasoned that what the brass didn't know wouldn't hurt them.

Finally, in early October, word came that instead of heading home we were to proceed in the opposite direction—to Okinawa, along with about half of the other LCIs at Eniwetok. The prospect of new adventure only partly compensated for our disappointment at not returning home. But perhaps we could drown our sorrows. The night before our departure for Okinawa, the officers of our LCI group had a drinking party on one of the islands, while the enlisted men had a similar party on another island. I recall that, as we hit the sand that night, I ran into an officer from another ship who had been in my drill company in midshipmen's school. He held up a half-pint of Scotch he had been saving up for such an occasion ever since he had left the States. "Only half a pint?" I said scornfully. "I could chug-a-lug that much in a single swallow!" "You're just bragging," he replied, and we argued awhile until he finally dared me to do it. "Bourbon is my preference," I said, "but here goes." I drained the bottle, and that is the last thing I remembered clearly of that night. I do have a vague memory, later confirmed by others who were present, that I challenged a huge officer, a former "frogman" six feet four and as broad as a door, to a fistfight. Others tried to dissuade me, because the match was so obviously uneven. I was physically fit and drunk enough, but I was only a scrawny 140 pounds, mostly of skin and bones, whereas he must have weighed over 200, all muscle. But I absolutely insisted, as a point of honor. The whiskey did the talking. A crowd gathered around us as we stripped to the waist and squared off. As I rushed at him, I must have sobered up for long enough to realize what I was doing, because I fell flat on my face in the sand. I remember nothing after that, but Cotton Clark told me later he had brought me back to the ship at the end of the party using the fireman's carry. He said my head flopped limply back and forth on his back like the head of a chicken whose neck has been wrung.

I insisted next day on standing my watch when we got underway for Okinawa, though the sea became rougher by the hour and I had the worst hangover of my young life. The weather was even rougher the next day, but my condition improved. We took nine days to reach Okinawa, and it was stormy, rainy, and foggy the entire time. On arrival at Okinawa we learned the reason, that we had been on the periphery of a typhoon that had struck Okinawa with great force. We reached Buckner Bay and anchored. About a hundred ships were stranded on the beach, some of them as far as fifty feet inland. "We got in here yesterday afternoon," I wrote Diana, "and the place is a wreck. Hundreds of ships high and dry, the fleet post office blown away in the storm and letters scattered like bread upon the waters. . . . We're going to Shanghai, I think, maybe in a day or so." That was a bad guess about our destination, but I promised her that I would hunt in Shanghai "for your ebony god and a tomato can full of pearls." I expressed doubt about the scuttlebutt then in circulation that after we had left it "Eniwetok was washed away beneath the ocean by a tidal wave riled up by the typhoon," but I passed on the rumor nevertheless.

Next day I ran into Sonny Williams, one of the friends I had made during V-12 training at Emory and later in midshipmen's school. He had been on an LCT in Buckner Bay during the storm. He came over for a couple of hours' visit. "He's lost about fifteen or twenty pounds," I wrote Diana. "He and his crew were about the filthiest and most piratical-looking gang I've seen out here, with a pet parrot and a pet monkey. They hadn't had any fresh water since the typhoon. Sonny says they are always short of fresh water, and whenever it rains everybody rushes out on deck naked with a bar of soap. He really looked whipped down, and he says it's pretty hard on his nerves with nobody to talk to. All his crew talk or think about is tobacco, whiskey, and women." I added: "I guess you remember hearing about Sonny. He was my room-mate at midshipmen's school, and was over in Normandy with me. I haven't seen him, though, in twenty months. You remember when we bought some dubious demi-tasse cups in that little antique shop next to the Tri-Delt house? Well, that was a wedding present for Sonny and Martha. He told me about the typhoon and how when he slipped anchor and ran up on the beach three ships hit him with a bang and acted as a sort of buffer against the wind." Sonny's ship had to be towed back to the water. Before leaving our ship, he bummed forty-eight pounds of pork chops and a case of Coke, giving me in return a case of cigarettes he had lifted when his LCT was carrying ship's service supplies.

During the week we spent at Okinawa I passed up a chance to ride in a jeep through Naha, its capital, but I learned from Tye that it was 90 percent destroyed, a pile of rubble with hardly a building left standing. It occurred to me that the battle for Okinawa was the kind of combat I had escaped through the swift ending of the war. "The aborigines here are about the smallest creatures outside Ringling Bros. side show," I wrote Diana. "They are about the size and color of a half pint of Jamaica Rum, and they hate the Japanese even more than the marines do, and they were a big help in the occupation of the island." "I was ashore today," I wrote on October 22, "tromping around in the mud like a water buffalo, and I saw a native burial cave up on the hillside. So I clambered up there and furtively peeked into it. Some of them have Japs, rats, or bats in them. But this was as empty as a tomb. It had been burned out by a flame-thrower, I guess, because it was all black. There were some earthenware jars over in one corner. Somebody brought back a skull from one of them, but it's not the right size to play football with, so I made him get rid of it. There's a serious danger of disease germs from it starting an epidemic. Those burial vaults are about the most civilized structures the natives build. They are of stone blocks facing into a man made cave with a stone-tiled floor. The abode of the living is a tiny one-room hut made of mud bricks, and a thatch roof overhead. About ten to twenty people live in each one, and I think at night they must stack each other up like cordwood. It's amazing that any of them live. Every small child has a baby strapped on its back while it works. Mostly they grow rice in small fields, fifty or so workers to an acre." It is hard after the passage of fifty years to gauge the accuracy of my depiction of the Okinawans, but that casual reference to the skull makes me wonder about my own state of civilization.

Russell Tye and Philip Rubin spent a day hitchhiking with the Seabees over the entire island in jeeps and trucks, through the demolished capital of Naha, the crowded village of Ichikawa, and the farms of the countryside. Sweet potatoes seemed to be the principal crop. Though the war was over, there were still many Japanese soldiers hiding in the burial caves and woodlands to evade surrender. Tye wrote back to his girl Fran describing his trip. "One thing it is perhaps just as well that the States do not see," he said. "That is the condition of the Negro Seabees and soldiers. Their quarters are a disgrace to the Nation. It's conceivable that under some conditions, such unsatisfactory quarters must be used, but the comparison is the bad part. There is nearly as much difference in quarters for the Negroes and whites as there is in Negro and white homes in America. The Negroes have the muddy places and their tents are so poorly constructed that the only important difference between them and foxholes is that the tents keep most of the rain out. The camp areas look as if they were picked as the worst place possible."

On October 24, we began a five-day voyage to Manila, not Shanghai. We still had no idea what our mission was to be. Skirting the east coast of Luzon close enough to see its heavy tropical vegetation, we passed through the strait of Corregidor into Manila Bay and on to an anchorage near the city. We remained there for ten days. Along with the other LCIs, we practiced beaching one day, and picked up medical and other supplies, but most of the time we were idle, and free to enjoy liberty on alternate nights. While in Manila I ran into a boyhood friend since grade school, DeLoney Hull. He was an ensign, and the only officer aboard an LCT at Manila. He had graduated in the class following mine at midshipmen's school. I spent a night aboard his ship. He had just returned from a moonlight cruise on which his crew had invited girls from Manila. I took one large drink from the punch bowl and found it so heavily spiked with medical alcohol that I was barely able to stagger to a bunk before I fell asleep. Fortunately, I awakened in time to catch the early morning liberty boat back to my ship.

While we were in Manila, the first five of our crew members qualified under the point system for shipment home and separation from the service. From Manila we touched briefly at the naval base at Subic Bay, thirty miles away on land but about a hundred miles by water. There we learned that our destination was Vietnam, then vaguely known to us as French Indo-China.

TWELVE

Vietnam

Most of our struggles as a ship's company had been with the elements of wind and water, or with a conventionalized and largely unseen enemy, or amongst ourselves. What we did had little effect on others. During our brief three-week sojourn in north Vietnam, on the other hand, we took actions that affected the lives of many others. Even in Vietnam, of course, our actions were of little weight in the grand scale of history. Their chief significance was simply to illustrate how ill prepared Americans were in 1945 to lead the world and to wield the awesome power in their hands. I have a feeling, however, that such small actions as we took in small places were part of a causal chain that gradually set the Vietnam War in motion out of the ashes of World War II.

Our journey from Subic Bay with five other LCIs of Group 109 was uneventful except for the spotting of a floating mine. All five ships took turns charging the mine and firing their 20-millimeter guns at it. The mine never exploded, but it finally sank after two and a half hours of this diversion, and we continued on our course. After four days at sea we sighted land and located our destination, Do Son, French Indo-China, at the mouth of the Red River. Soon after we arrived, an American destroyer lying nearby asked our help in a medical emergency—appendicitis or a similar ailment—and we dispatched Philip Rubin, our group medical officer, in a small boat. He returned, mission completed, about two hours later.

We finally learned, in a somewhat garbled way, what our mission was, but did not understand its international implications. Chinese (Kuomintang) troops had received the Japanese surrender in Indo-China, including troops in Haiphong and Hanoi. Now that the war was over, these Chinese troops were to be evacuated to Liberty ships lying offshore, whose draft was too deep for them to reach shore, and our task was to ferry the Chinese from shore to the Liberty ships. We believed the Liberty ships would carry the Chinese troops to liberate Formosa, still held by the Japanese. We learned later, however, that these troops were actually shipped to northern China, where the Kuomintang was trying to wrest from the Communists the territory they had controlled since the late 1930s or had taken back from the Japanese. In short, the United States was taking sides in the Chinese civil war.

A day or so in advance of the expected arrival of the Chinese troops, our ship made a trial run from our anchorage off Hon Dau lighthouse through the shallow water to a long, rickety wooden pier at Petite Mirador, on Do Son Peninsula in the delta of the Red River. While we were docked there a British officer drove up in a jeep, a Lieutenant Commander Simpson-Jones of the Royal Navy, according to what he told us. He briefly spun a tale of having been an undercover agent of British intelligence for the past four years, working with the Indo-Chinese resistance behind the Japanese lines. He was so cocky and self-assured that we accepted his improbable story at face value. He offered Cotton Clark and our group commander, who had just arrived at the dock, a high time in Haiphong if they would transport him out to see some of his friends on a French hospital ship lying in sight offshore.

The skipper and commander accepted the invitation with alacrity. We got underway and moored alongside the French merchant freighter *Komtun.* There was no red cross painted on it, and it turned out not to be a hospital ship at all. It was probably loaded with munitions for the French side in the Vietnamese war of independence already beginning. Apparently Simpson-Jones just called it a hospital ship to make his request more plausible, and his involvement was simply a case of one European colonial power helping another. We were too naive to understand this or to question why Americans would want to abet their efforts.

Three minutes after boarding the French vessel, Commander Simpson-Jones returned with five high-ranking French officers. It was hard to tell how high-ranking, because they immediately began taking off their epaulets and other insignia of rank. Would we mind taking his friends ashore? Simpson-Jones asked. Of course not. They were our gallant allies, weren't they? They climbed aboard and we returned to our anchorage. The skipper, the LCI group commander, Simpson-Jones, and the five Frenchmen went ashore in our dinghy and crowded into a single jeep for the ride to Haiphong. As executive officer I was in charge of the ship until the skipper returned. It was my largest responsibility since I had joined the Navy. I promised to bring the ship into the dock next morning at 0900 to pick up the skipper and group commander. After a year and a half of service on this ship, I looked forward to my first opportunity to be in charge of docking it.

My responsibilities turned out to be heavier than I could have imagined. The jeep and its heavy cargo of brass was hardly out of sight when the signalman on watch received a blinker message from the flagship of our little task force, asking to speak to the skipper. I replied that the skipper was ashore and would respond as soon as he returned. Other messages came asking if the skipper were back yet, and there were also inquiries about the group commander. I sensed that they were in trouble. I replied as vaguely as possible that the commanding officer and the group commander were not aboard ship and that they would be in touch as soon as they returned. I answered all direct questions but volunteered nothing about where they were or the circumstances of their departure. Finally, exasperated beyond endurance, Commodore Edwin B. Hooper himself came alongside our ship in his gig about sundown and asked Tye, the officer on watch, whether or not we had gone alongside the French ship. Tye answered truthfully that we had. The commodore then said, with a certain edge to his voice, "Have the commanding officer and group commander report to me tomorrow at 0800." I came upon the scene at that point. "But, Commodore," I sputtered, "they aren't scheduled to return until 0900!" "My order stands," he replied grimly. The commodore also ordered Tye to go over in the morning to police a little island nearby that was being used as a liberty island by enlisted men, and to keep all Vietnamese off the island. Apparently he trusted Tye, the first person to give him straight answers.

Next morning at 0900 I climbed to the conn, upped anchor, and successfully guided the ship to the dock. The skipper and commander were waiting, and I told them they were already an hour late for a meeting with the commodore. I was so elated by my solo docking that I hardly noticed the pall my news cast over them, as I described the exchange of messages and surmised that in carrying those French officers ashore we might have created an "international incident." We tied up alongside the commodore's flagship, the two went aboard it, and in about a half hour they reappeared, looking considerably chastened. Cotton looked somber enough, not his usual jaunty self, but the commander was as white as a sheet. As the senior officer he had taken the main brunt of the commodore's tongue-lashing. Apparently that was as far as punishment went for the moment, but we later learned that the commodore threatened them with court-martial if an international incident developed. They were probably saved by the fact that the French and British, the only ones who knew what we had done, were pleased by this inadvertent American help in preserving colonialism, and by the fact that no specific orders had been issued by the commodore forbidding acts of friendship toward our wartime allies.

Once we were at a safe distance from the flagship, Cotton gave me an account of their adventure ashore. As their jeep headed toward Haiphong, they came to a roadblock and were surrounded by a half-dozen nervous Viet Minh rebels aiming guns at their heads. Followers of Ho Chi Minh, who controlled the countryside, they were clearly not playing games. But they were uncertain what to do. The Frenchmen all talked at once and Commander Simpson-Jones kept racing his motor impatiently, making trigger fingers even more nervous. At some point Cotton stood up and shouted in his limited French the only thing he thought might save his hide, "Je suis Americain!" The commander raced his engine again in an arrogant, pukka-sahib manner, and somehow they bluffed their way through the roadblock and on to Haiphong.

We never heard further of Simpson-Jones, but we did hear that the French officers we had brought ashore had negotiated with the Chinese general for the release of some 1500 French soldiers imprisoned by the Japanese and continuing in incarceration under the Chinese. They gave the Chinese general in exchange some rice carried aboard a freighter offshore, intended to be given away to relieve the famine in northern Vietnam. The Chinese general sold the rice instead on the black market, while the released French troops became a cadre for French reassertion of colonial claims in Indo-China, one of the turning points of a protracted civil war. Our ship and its misplaced friendship for the French played, of course, only a tiny part in this web of circumstance, but perhaps a crucial part.

In a letter a few weeks later to an old family friend, I gave a graphic description of our experience but revealed a limited understanding of its meaning. "Before the Japanese surrender they turned most of their arms and equipment over to the Annamites [Viet Minh]," I wrote, "who have political control over the northern part of Indo-China, under the Chinese military occupation. The few French civilians are huddled in Hanoi and Hai-Phong except the ones who are bull-headed enough to remain in their places around the countryside. The Chinese Army is rapidly being evacuated, and it is expected that open rebellion, murder, and lawlessness will break out very soon. In spite of the fact that we were neutral, several shots were fired at us, haphazardly, and an Army jeep was held up by one of the bandits that swarm the countryside. Some of the Japanese are still armed, and the Chinese are very careful not to offend the dignity of the Japanese. Starvation and disease conditions are appalling, and one Swiss civilian who had been stranded there during the war said the death rate was about one million a year. The country and the people were colorful, but I thank God I don't have to live there."

After we returned to anchor, Tye set out for the little island in a small boat and found it overrun by American sailors and by Vietnamese, including prostitutes. The commodore's gig was at the shore, and the man guarding it said the commodore had gone up the trail to the top of the steep hill, where there was a stone watchtower. Scared witless by this time because he had failed to carry out the commodore's orders to keep out the Vietnamese, Tye ran up the hill, some 500 feet, and to the watchtower. The commodore and another officer were seated on the roof at a folding table, watching the sunset and taking the evening breeze. Tye saluted and tried to explain himself. The commodore said, "Sit down, young man. You're kind of winded. Sit down and have a beer." So Tye had a beer with the commodore, vastly relieved that no court-martial seemed to be in the offing, and the commodore was apparently in a better mood than earlier. He never mentioned the Vietnamese presence on the island, and after finishing his beer Tye saluted and returned to the ship.

Two days later in the early morning we moored again at the small boat pier, now designated Beach Zero, to carry out our transporting of troops. Files of Chinese troops occupied all the space on the rickety pier, and other troops stood behind them up the road as far as the eye could see. They ate a meal from their rice bowls, and I learned how real Chinese handled their chopsticks. They put a little soy sauce on top of their rice, held the bowl up close to their lips, and shoveled the rice from bowl to mouth with the chopsticks rather than picking out grains in the tweezer motion one often sees in Chinese restaurants.

First we loaded aboard the bags of rice the Chinese had stacked in a little staging area near the pier. We had to make our way around an old woman who sat on the ground next to the bags, picking up kernels of rice one by one from among the pebbles and dirt. As we carried the bags toward the dock, some of them broke and rice fell between the crevices of the rocks. Then our ship and the other LCIs each loaded about 200 troops aboard with their arms, ammunition, clothing, and other personal gear. As soon as our ship left the dock and the area was clear, a crowd of Vietnamese swarmed over it on all fours, scratching for the few rice grains that had fallen between the rocks. This scene forced on our attention, as nothing else had, the tidal waves of human misery that modern warfare generates.

We headed toward the Liberty ships offshore in Henriette Pass, but fog on the way forced us to seek an anchorage. Our charts of the area were not of the usual high quality, and we moved among islands that jutted straight up out of the deep water, so that we sailed within a few yards of them and yet were unable to find a bottom shallow enough for our anchor cable. Finally, after considerable groping among the islands in the rain, fog, and growing darkness, we found a tiny harbor through Tye's expert study of the charts and managed to maneuver through its narrow opening to find shelter for the night. Next morning we proceeded to the SS *John McKay* and unloaded our troops and gear, then moved to Hon Dau Island anchorage, where LCVPs brought us another load of 350 Chinese troops and their gear. We carried these troops out and unloaded them, and our work was done. We tied up to an LST for the night, and next day returned to the small boat pier at Do Son.

Having completed in two days the assignment that had brought us all the way from the Philippines, we remained for another week at the Do Son pier along with the five other LCIs in our task force. Our officers took turns going to Haiphong on an Army bus, but I don't recall any enlisted men getting liberty. I stocked up on cigarettes and candy bars before leaving the ship, as these were our medium of exchange. Phil Rubin, the group medical officer, and I were the only ones from the 555 in a group of about twenty officers making the trip into Haiphong.

Fortunately, there were no Viet Minh roadblocks that day on our way to town. Our destination was a Haiphong hotel commandeered as an American officers' club, where we got a brief taste of how European colonial officials had lived abroad in the old days. I was assigned a large, luxurious, high-ceilinged room with an overhead fan and a large four-poster bed draped with mosquito netting. After a few minutes enjoying the unaccustomed spaciousness and soft bed, I went out to explore the city. In the street in front of the hotel, rickshas fought to be of service to us. I winced a little at the degrading prospect of a barefoot human being pulling me around in a ricksha, but obviously he needed the business and I needed his services. I was unfamiliar with the city, and if I wanted to go shopping or to the dance hall I had to engage a ricksha man who knew the way.

I took a tour of the city, through the worst conditions of poverty and starvation I have ever seen. We had already witnessed rural famine back at Do Son. Whenever we had thrown garbage over the ship's side, clusters of boat people descended on it to see what they could salvage. But at Do Son there were fish to supplement the scarce land food. Poverty there was nothing compared to the sterile poverty and famine of the city. Desperate beggars crowded around me every time I stopped to window-shop. Moved by the distress I saw in the beggars' faces, I gave away a few packs of cigarettes that they could trade for food. It quickly became evident that that was a mistake, as it only drew larger crowds that followed me everywhere I went. I suddenly realized that I was powerless and perhaps in danger in the sea of importunate faces and hands that clutched at me for attention. I was not frightened, because there was no anger in those faces, only desperation. I could not help being sympathetic to their plight, but the situation was getting out of hand, as I lacked any means to meet the magnitude of the need that surrounded me. I ordered my ricksha driver back to the hotel, and he slowly made way against the human tide.

Many causes had joined to create the poverty I witnessed. The Japanese here, as elsewhere in their "co-prosperity sphere," had systematically shipped home to Japan more rice than Indo-China could spare. The Vietnamese were half-starved all during the war. Then, in 1945 there was a poor harvest in the north and a good one in the south, but Allied bombing had destroyed the bridges connecting the two regions, so there was no way for supply and demand to rectify the imbalance. After the war was over, when American ships brought rice to the north to relieve the famine, it fell into the hands of corrupt Chinese generals, who sold it on the black market instead of giving it away, so that those who needed food the most had the least chance for it.

After nightfall Rubin and I went by ricksha to a dance hall controlled by the American military but staffed by Vietnamese and Eurasian hostesses, featuring a small orchestra that played barely recognizable American swing music. After dancing awhile, we picked up two attractive women and took them back to the hotel and to our beds. Perhaps I should have been more faithful to Sylvia or Diana or both, but after many months at sea I gave little thought to the ethics of my conduct. In an early stage of lovemaking, however, there was a knock on my door and Rubin's girl came in. The two Vietnamese women talked heatedly in a foreign tongue, and then my date explained indignantly that, immediately after having sex, Rubin had rudely kicked his girl out of the room so he could sleep alone. I tried to explain that I didn't approve of such conduct and wouldn't behave in that fashion, but my girl insisted on leaving with her friend immediately. In the midst of my frustration, my conscience reawakened but remained drowsy. I consoled myself by considering that I would have another chance in a few days.

Russell Tye was my companion in ribaldry a few days later, on my only other liberty in Haiphong. We went to the same hotel and the same nightclub as before. This time I found a stunningly beautiful and charming young girl. She had a face like a tropical flower, a lissome figure, and a complaisant manner. I whispered in her ear a phrase I had been practicing to get just the right accent and tone, both casual and correct: "Voulez vous coucher avec moi?" She nodded shyly, as though she was as new at such liaisons as I was, and gave me a little squeeze as we danced. I had to wonder, however, whether it was my irresistible charm or my relative wealth that made this conquest so easy. Tye, meanwhile, was facing major trouble. Just as he began to get acquainted with his dance partner, the Chinese general in charge of the region came into the dance hall with his entourage, and he fancied the same girl as Tye. A showdown ensued, and Tye, after considering his options, decided retreat was the prudent course. Reluctant to settle for a second choice, and doubtless feeling a revived loyalty to the girl he had left back home, Tye decided to abandon the chase and sleep alone that night.

Leaving Tye to fend for himself I took my girl back to the hotel room. I made love to her that night, but in a way that respected her dignity and accorded her due courtesy. That turned out to be not only the right course but the smart one. She responded well to that. Maybe she had expected rude treatment similar to Rubin's male chauvinist behavior a few days earlier and was agreeably surprised. I had few clues to her real feelings, of course, because she spoke little or no English and I spoke no Vietnamese and very little French. Her behavior, however, was responsive. We communicated perfectly in the sign language of caresses. Eventually we slept, but then at dawn we made love one last time before she put on her flowered sheath dress with the slit above the knee.

There had been no promise of money, and she made no request for it. She told me in French, in a combination of words and gestures I could understand, that what she really wanted was to go to America on my ship! I certainly hadn't anticipated that request. Obviously, she wanted to get as far as possible from the poverty and violence ahead in Vietnam. I told her as clearly and kindly as I could that what she asked was impossible, and after pleading desperately for a while she finally became reconciled to the circumstances. I insisted on loading her down with all the cigarettes I had brought, and walked out with her to the street to wave her out of sight in a ricksha. It was actually, from any rational perspective, a rather banal one-night stand, but in my own youthful, romantic state of mind it seemed like the good-bye scene in one of those Hollywood movies like *Casablanca*. Going back into the hotel, I roused Tye. We had a delicious breakfast of papayas and mangoes in the hotel dining room, then headed back to the ship. I had gone to Haiphong on a casual lark, but instead I got a close view and even a little experience of the pathos and tragedy of life among the victims of war.

Following orders I no longer remember, just before we left Vietnam we sailed north through the Bay of Along to the town of Hon Gay and spent three days there tied to the dock. One other LCI accompanied us, and our skipper was put in charge of the expedition. We sailed by deep channels past dozens of tiny islands rising straight out of the water, a seascape unlike anything else we had seen, as though the sea had engulfed a mountain chain.

Even before we tied up at the dock in Hon Gay, a vigorous trade in souvenirs began with small boats that gathered around our ship. Soon the friendly interchange turned hostile, however, and when we tied up at the dock an angry crowd of villagers threatened to storm the ship. They gesticulated and waved sticks and cudgels at us. Several of them tried to explain their complaints, but of course we couldn't understand their language, only that they had what they considered a grievance. The skipper sounded general quarters and had the gun crews train our 20-millimeter guns on the crowd, while I sought information from the crew as to the cause of the anger. I finally learned that several men had taken the cigarette packs out of the cartons and sold them separately, then stuffed the cartons with rag waste and traded them as though they contained cigarettes. The families in the bumboats, who had invested their savings in trade goods, had thus bargained away all they had for empty cigarette cartons. No wonder they were enraged! Finally the mayor of the town arrived, harangued the crowd, and dispersed it after we gave him cartons of cigarettes to distribute among the aggrieved parties.

We ourselves could not determine which complaints were legitimate or who the culprits were, but we strictly forbade any further scams of this kind. I was shocked that our men were totally lacking in shame or remorse. They apparently thought it didn't matter how we treated the people, since they were foreigners. Not all of the callousness was on our side, however. One Vietnamese family pulled alongside in a boat, and a child about two years old stood there naked and looking very cold. We threw over a sweater and pointed for the mother to put it on the child, and she did. The father then came over, took the garment away from the child, and put it on himself.

Phil Rubin, our medical officer, set up a one-man medical clinic in a tent ashore, and by the next morning a line stretched out of sight as people waited for treatment. Most of them were in the most endangered age groups, the very old and the very young. Rubin, who had behaved so badly in Haiphong, redeemed himself in my eyes by the long hours of care he devoted to the afflicted. He applied sulfa to open sores, thumped chests, salved sore eyes, and passed out pills by the handful. He used all the canned condensed milk we had on the ship, watering it down for the children and babies, many of whom had the distended abdomens and shrunken limbs of the starving. Before we left port he had used up all the medicine he had. When it was time to leave, though, he packed up his tent and stolidly turned his back on the long line of waiters, on a human need too vast for a single doctor to alleviate.

Meanwhile, Cotton Clark wandered through Hon Gay to the office of the coal company that was the main employer in the town. There he met the attractive young widow of a Frenchman who had operated the mine before the war and during the early stages of the war, when Indo-China was still controlled by the Vichy government. He had been killed by the Japanese, leaving his wife and two children stranded in the war-ravaged country. She was as desperate to get out of Vietnam as my night companion in Haiphong, and she begged Clark to smuggle her and her children aboard ship and take them to the first port we reached. Of course he couldn't do that, but he gave her his name and address. Two years later he heard from her in Paris. He wrote letters in her behalf to the American embassy in an effort to help her get a job there.

We returned to the anchorage at the mouth of the Red River, received there our first mail in more than a month, and on November 30 set out on the long route home.

THIRTEEN

Homeward Bound

We got underway from the coast of Vietnam on November 30 to re-join our LCI group in Subic Bay. At the breakneck pace of eight knots it took six days to get there. I described the voyage to Diana: "the sea was so rough it was like riding over a cobblestone road in a one-wheeled wagon. The rust on the bottom of the water tanks got stirred up from the bouncing, so our water supply was about the color of ice tea and tasted like the drippings from an old dirty dish rag. The cooks were sick, in fact everybody was, and the cupboard was as bare as a week-old hambone."

After a few days at Subic Bay without liberty, we got our orders to go to Guam in convoy with other LCIs. We took this to mean we were heading home, though no one directly said so. Our route took us south of Luzon through the central Philippines, where we maneuvered around many small islands. We passed through San Juanico Strait between Samar and Leyte, a waterway so narrow that it seemed like a river. We felt as though we could reach out and touch the thick jungle and the bamboo-and-grass huts lining its banks. Over a stretch of six-ty miles the strait was less than a mile wide, and in some places only about fifty yards wide, with a current as swift as a river, full of eddies. Several times our small ship was caught in whirlpools so strong we could only barely pull out of them. Entering Leyte Gulf, we struck out across the Philippine Sea toward the Marianas. The sea was rough, and every few hours some ship in the convoy broke down and forced all the others to slow their speed and wait. We had more trouble than a fleet of junk wagons. The other ships in the convoy were LCSes, built similarly to LCIs but larger and newer, and therefore less subject to breakdowns. The old four-striper in command of our convoy got so angry at the constant breakdowns of LCIs that he swore that he would not go any farther than the Marianas with them. Halfway across the Philippine Sea, the flagship notified us that our destination had been changed from Guam to Saipan, perhaps because Saipan had better repair facilities. We reached there after six days. Saipan was a volcanic island with a wild, hilly interior still alive with armed Japanese soldiers who refused to believe the war was over.

We spent two weeks at Saipan anchored offshore at Tanapag harbor, with no opportunity for liberty. I took a swim in the allegedly shark-infested waters, but sharks were not the sea creatures that bothered me. "There are quite a few jelly-fish that always seem to land on the tenderest areas of the epidermis," I wrote Diana. "I've reached the conclusion that of all the low names to call somebody, jelly-fish ranks lowest. I sure like to swim, though, on account of I was bawn and bred in the swimmin' hole. Maybe I'm 'half-toitle,' as one of the seamen said. I've never believed him, though, since he claimed he saw a woman give birth to twin puppies. One of the steward's mates claims he saw a goat give birth to a human child, 'Gawd strike me dead,' he said to one of the men. They argued about it for about two hours the other night."

While at Saipan we transferred about fifteen members of our crew to other duty, leaving us quite shorthanded for our voyage home. One of them went to the hospital for chronic seasickness and the others to LSTs that would remain in the western Pacific. Most of the transferees were "boots" just a few months out of the States whom we had picked up as replacements, but one of them had twenty-two months' duty aboard our ship and deserved to go home. Why he was chosen was never explained.

Ever since the end of the war I had been giving a lot of thought to my own future plans, and as we prepared to return home the future loomed larger and larger in my thoughts. Except for this brief sojourn in the Navy, most of my experience of life had been in school. While in college I had developed a keen appetite for the life of the mind. I thought I had a way with words and dreamed of being a writer. But what kind of writer? My college experience in journalism had been disillusioning, and I had no desire to become a hack news reporter. Writing fiction appealed to me, but so did the sort of nonfiction that went beyond reportage. I had been a political science major in college, but its approach seemed to me too reductionist, concerned too exclusively with man as the political animal. History, on the other hand, offered broader vistas, perspective, and a recourse to the deep pools of mankind's total experience. I decided to return to school and study history. At Saipan I wrote to a longtime family friend who had recently become the dean of the graduate school at Vanderbilt. "I've been planning for quite a while to go to Vanderbilt for my master's degree," I wrote Philip Davidson, "taking advantage of the provisions of the 'GI Bill of Rights.'" My wartime experiences had stimulated an interest in history as a more comprehensive field of study, but with unconscious irony I cast the die in favor of history under many illusions about my wartime experience as historic. I knew very little about history as a scholarly discipline or about the nature of scholarly research into the whys and wherefores of human experience. I tended to think of history instead as epical narrative or as a grand panorama painted on a broad canvas.

Christmas was not merry in Saipan. Now that the prospect of going home had been dangled before us, we were more homesick than festive. Right after the war ended, Christmas had become a pivotal date. We had expected to be home by Christmas. Maybe a better cook for our Christmas feast would have helped elevate our mood, but I doubt it. Clark and I and about half the crew finally got ashore for a short stroll on Christmas Day, but Tye and the other half were stranded aboard. It occurred to Tye that now was the time and occasion to uncork the fifth of bourbon he had kept in his abstemious way at the bottom of his drawer ever since we had left San Diego six months earlier. He passed the whiskey bottle among the crew in a gesture of defiance of "Navy Regs," but evidence of the crime disappeared in a short while.

On December 29 we headed toward San Diego by way of Eniwetok and Pearl Harbor. Reaching Eniwetok after six days at sea, we anchored there for a couple of days in the shadow of carriers and cruisers, then got underway again for a fourteen-day voyage to Hawaii. The voyage was lengthened by an unexpected incident at sea. At about the half-way mark, our flagship received a radio message to detach a ship, with a medical officer aboard, to rendezvous with a patrol ship far to our south and render medical assistance. We were dispatched as the only ship with a medical officer, to a rendezvous point about ten degrees north of the equator. The patrol ship had responsibility for traveling in a ten-mile circle for forty-five days at a stretch, and ours was the first ship they had seen for a month. We never learned why they need-ed to patrol the open ocean now that the war was over, but for what-ever reason they were there doing their duty. We transferred Lieuten-ant Rubin to the other ship. The patient had a shaving of steel, microscopic in size, lodged in his eyeball. Rubin decided to take him to Pearl Harbor rather than operate himself in choppy water, and we moved the patient to our ship with some difficulty by breeches buoy. Then we proceeded independently of the convoy to Pearl Harbor.

A coffee maker incident will illustrate the weather conditions we experienced on this routine voyage. Just before evening chow on Jan-uary 16, the ship rolled so sharply in the heavy sea that the coffee maker flipped out of its container and splashed boiling coffee on the legs and lower trunk of Harry Tourtillotte, our engineer. He shucked off his pants in record time and thus suffered only surface burns. Doc Rubin treated them with a boric acid ointment. We finally arrived at Pearl Harbor on January 20, three days after the other ships of the convoy.

"Today I have eaten a quart and ½ of ice cream," I wrote Diana from Pearl Harbor, "a whole cake, two papayas, half a pie, two soupbowls of radishes, a head of lettuce, several each of oranges, apples, grapefruits and sundry other appetizing bits, and still hungry enough to eat you if you were in reach." I might have gotten a bellyache on that diet, but never scurvy. In addition to the fresh food, another advantage of be-ing in Hawaii was that it was possible to reach the States by telephone, though not with very good connections. I couldn't call Sylvia, because she had just moved to a new apartment and I did not have the num-ber. I managed to reach Diana at college, but I could hear only a little of what she said and didn't know whether she could hear me. What I had hoped would be a welcome turned into a shouting match. I did hear one thing distinctly, though, that her brother was stationed on a destroyer based at Pearl. I thought it would ingratiate me with her and her family if I looked him up. When I finally located his ship he was standing watch, but we sat on an ammunition box and munched bologna sandwiches and potato chips while we talked. "I think he's mighty eager to get out of the Navy," I wrote his parents, "but he has a pleasant life aboard the DD, with plenty of time to read. His ship is going back into commission now that it is de-commissioned. I suppose he's already told you how thoroughly fouled up the de-commissioning organization is. We're sailing to San Diego this afternoon to run the gauntlet of de-commissioning ourselves, but I'm hoping for better luck."

Many months earlier, when I thought we were going to Shanghai or Hong Kong, I'd promised Diana to buy her an ebony statue there, but I gave up on the idea when we went to Vietnam instead. Now, suddenly, I had something close to what I had promised. "I've found it," I wrote. "It's not a little black god. But it's about the ugliest, most repulsive looking creature ever conjured up in a Chinese opium dream—a sort of Chinese Bacchus with a fat belly leaning on a staff and drinking from a wine bottle held over his tilted face. It's gilded, with a black stand. The steward's mate bought it when we were in Indo-China and was going to throw it away when I found it underneath his bunk at bed-check this morning and paid him a fantastic sum for it. It is fascinatingly ugly, a monstrosity."

During our stay in Pearl Harbor Russ Tye found that his brother, whom he had visited on the other side of Oahu on our outward journey, was still there and waiting his turn to go home. He had enough points for discharge and gave some thought to riding back to the States on our ship. We could have used him as a fourth bridge player to replace Phil Rubin, who left us at Pearl Harbor for reassignment. But the plan fell through when he could not get another officer to take his place.

Cotton Clark also ran into a close friend from back home who was waiting for a berth on a Liberty ship returning to the States. Clark tried to persuade him to get his orders changed and go back to the States on our ship, and at first he thought it a good idea. The next day, however, he came back and said, "I've had a change of heart. I think I'd better wait." He had asked a chief petty officer the fatal question, "Have you ever ridden an LCI?" and the reply was, "Hell, yes, I've ridden an LCI and don't you get near one." So Clark's best friend turned down his offer of a ride.

Pearl Harbor seemed to be my chance to get some badly needed dental work free before I would be mustered out of the service and have to pay for it myself. A year earlier, during the invasion of southern France, I had lost some fillings in my front teeth and had cracked others. After that, we were never in any suitable place long enough to get proper dental attention, except in San Diego, where I had other things on my mind. At Eniwetok, after a year of neglect had caught up with me, I developed a painful toothache. Sylvia noted that the smell of oil of cloves lingered on my letter paper. I went aboard a carrier that had briefly anchored in the atoll, seeking relief. After pulling an abscessed tooth, the dental officer took a long look at the rest of my mouth and decided I needed such major work that he couldn't handle it in the short time that we were in the same port. The matter drifted for several more months. Pearl Harbor, on the other hand, had the extensive facilities I needed, if only our time in port was long enough.

Navy dentists didn't coddle the patient as private dentists did. In the space of half an hour, my dentist at Pearl Harbor pulled four of my teeth, stuck a wad of cotton gauze in my mouth, and sent me on my way. He said I would not be at Pearl Harbor long enough for the bridge-work necessary to replace the missing teeth. I left the dentist's office looking perfectly all right on the outside but bleeding considerably on the inside. As soon as I stuck out my thumb to hitchhike back to my ship, a gorgeous nurse skidded her jeep to a stop and gave me a ride. Dreams of a brief romance immediately came to mind. Though my mouth was full of blood, saliva, and gauze, I kept it tightly shut. She seemed to like me and tried to make conversation, but I could only grunt and mumble. Finally, eager to take advantage of this passing opportunity, I leaned out of the jeep, spat a huge wad of blood-soaked gauze into the breeze, and turned to respond to her remarks. Though as a nurse she must have seen some bad sights, a horrified look came over her face at the sight of all that blood and spit. My hopes of a date sank immediately, and she put me out of her jeep at the first opportunity. I saw her shaking her head in disbelief as she drove away, and when I got back to my ship I took a long look in the mirror to try to understand what had driven her away. I saw a snaggletooth grinning back at me, and for many months after that I avoided mirrors whenever I could.

We had a smooth voyage from Pearl to San Diego in company with five other LCIs, but the nearer we got to the States the more homesick we became. We chafed at every delay. It was excruciating to have to tow our flagship for two days because of an engine breakdown. About a week out of San Diego, our ship's radio picked up a broadcast of Francis Craig's orchestra from Nashville, Tennessee. This was a band that used to play for dances at Vanderbilt, and at the sound our manly skipper melted down into a homesick little boy. He eventually recovered his air of command, however, and we sailed into San Diego on February 8. We would remain for the next three weeks. Tye and I would have alternate watch days, but our duties were nominal. School was out every other day.

As we approached the mainland, I wrestled with the dilemma I had created by my ardent pursuit of two women at once. Wartime had allowed that, but peacetime was bringing on a day of choice and retribution. I would soon have to choose between Sylvia and Diana, between a consummated adult relationship with an older woman—thirty-five seemed much older at twenty-three than it would later—and a more adolescent, more dreamed about than actual relationship with a girl my own age. I wanted them both, and if the war had continued for my convenience I could have been faithful to both in my fashion. Probably even before I reached the California shore, I was half-consciously and tentatively making up my mind to end my affair with Sylvia. It would free me to pursue the end of the rainbow with Diana. But I loved Sylvia too much to actually let her go, so I temporized and waited for some outside force to determine my fate. Besides, I had so much still to learn about love, and I wanted more time under her gentle tutelage to study love some more. I would delay making a final decision until the last possible moment, when perhaps the decision would be made for me.

At the first opportunity I hurried up to Los Angeles to be with Sylvia. We had written to each other almost daily since I had left there the previous spring, but letters were a poor substitute for sight and touch, and letters often missed their mark. In some ways we were awkward strangers again. We had much to rediscover and relearn and decide about each other, and about the tactile language of love, and it must be crowded into the next few weeks. Ars longa, vita brevis. When I reached Sylvia by telephone, I was disappointed to discover that she was sharing her apartment temporarily with a girlfriend at work who was recovering from a breakup with her boyfriend. The arrangement was temporary, but the same thing could be said about my time in port. This meant that Sylvia and I had no privacy, but fortunately she had acquired a car, and we drove all over Los Angeles, Hollywood, Beverly Hills, Long Beach, and Santa Monica seeing the sights and gazing at each other. Our evenings, however, we had to share with her friend. I noticed also a new streak of gray in Sylvia's hair, a little reminder of the difference in our ages. Nothing about my homecoming to Sylvia was the way I had romantically anticipated it.

After I had made several frustrating trips to Los Angeles, Sylvia and I felt an urgent need for time alone together, time to get reacquainted, to rekindle the fire, to decide whether we had a future together. Had I had already unilaterally decided, if only half-consciously? I do not know anymore after all this time. I doubt if I knew then exactly what I wanted or what I intended. But I did have a plan to deal with all these questions. On one of my trips along the coast I stopped at a hotel in Del Mar, a beach resort with a still not reopened racetrack near San Diego. Summoning up my boldest manner, I reserved a room for myself and "wife" who would be visiting me for a week. Del Mar would be close enough for me to report back to the ship during the daytime but to spend every evening with Sylvia. Sylvia took a week's vacation from her job to join me.

The week began almost as idyllically as our night the previous May in Capistrano. We made love, wandered along the chilly beach, and made love again. Every second day I would leave to take my day on watch aboard ship, and return that evening for two nights and a day with Sylvia. But the old magic had somehow disappeared. I was happy to be close to her again, but too busy and too tired from the travel back and forth and my light duties on the ship. But something other than tiredness was separating us. I was also in a quandary. I loved her, I loved her not, I loved her, I loved her not. She, on the other hand, had whole days on her hands while I was off at the ship. This turned out to be time to brood over my real and imagined slights and indecisions. Sometime, in the callous, unthinking way of youth, I must have dropped hints of my daisy-petal quandary: that I was too young for her (her translation: she was too old for me), that I couldn't marry her because I wanted to have children (her response: when did I ever ask you to marry me?), that I was uncertain about my postwar future (her thought: he is planning to leave me). Finally, one night, I said tersely after dinner that I was too tired to make love that night. This was the final straw. She burst into tears and cried inconsolably and accusingly all night, while I sat on the edge of the bed feeling numb and helpless. All I could do was repeat glumly that I had simply told the truth, that I was physically tired and would be all right the next day. It took me some time to realize that in one brief remark I had ripped the fabric of togetherness. She never again gave me her heart—or her body or lips— no matter how piteously I pleaded.

I didn't give up without a struggle. I did everything I could think of to overcome her resistance, but with a growing sense of hopelessness. After our week was up, I returned every night I could to her apartment in Los Angeles, staying all night, begging her at intervals to relent. Her friend had moved out, but that made no difference. In the end, I would lie awake on her sofa for a few hours every night while she slept on the bed to get ready for her workday ahead. I invited Tye to come up and meet her, but they took an instant dislike to each other. Sylvia insisted that I did not love her and not really want her, and I replied with increasing feebleness that I did so want her. I was sick at heart, but I felt desperately determined not to take no for an answer. Toward dawn each day I would leave to return to my ship. One night an old acquaintance called her for a date while I was there. He was a Mexican-American. She went downstairs and rode around in his car for hours while I lay sleeplessly awaiting her return, imagining all sorts of things about what they were doing. When she returned, she denied everything that I had imagined. I hoped that my last night with her would overcome her resolve to repel my advances, but she never relented. In the end it was *she* who made up *her* mind. We said in parting that we would remain friends even if we could not be lovers, but I knew in my heart that this was good-bye.

Our LCI set out again from San Diego on March 2, bound for the Canal Zone on the first leg of our journey back to the East Coast for the decommissioning of our ship. Our skipper was in tactical command of a little convoy consisting of two other ships. The first week was smooth sailing, and this calm gave me a chance to sort out my mixed feelings about Sylvia and the shameful botch I had made of my relationship with her. Sylvia had had more experience with the tough breaks of life than I, and she saw through to the rotten heart of my indecision. With the honesty I had always admired in her, she did not fool herself. She refused to tolerate a less than committed lover and accepted the hurt and heartache such a course entailed. Compared with her, I was emotionally still a babbling child. I hoped that by leaving I could banish my shameful conduct from memory and put an end to all reminders of it. However divided my mind had been earlier, I now decided unilaterally to make a complete break with her. I would simply run away. I never wrote to Sylvia again, and after about a month her letters to me also ceased. I was not yet mature enough for a real love affair with all of its consequences.

While I silently brooded over my bitter memories, our ship skirted Baja California and the main west coast of Mexico within sight of the shore. When we reached the Gulf of Tehuantepec early one morning, the wind increased rapidly until it whistled in the shrouds, and began to emit an unearthly howl. We heard that this wind was called *el viento del diablo*, the devil's breath, but we coined our own, more suggestive term: Tehuantepecker. We altered course to follow the coastline rather than cut directly across the gulf, but that did little good. We began the day opposite a lighthouse, and the wind and current were so fierce that, after pounding hell out of the waves all day, at nightfall we had traveled barely beyond that same lighthouse.

Clark concluded that we'd better find a sheltered anchorage and wait out the storm. He ordered the three ships into the little port of Salina

Cruz, which consisted of a breakwater, a dock, a few despondent banana trees, and several thousand Indian inhabitants. We anchored overnight in the lee of the mountains. Next morning, the storm having
abated somewhat, we discovered that by laying offshore a few miles,
sheltered somewhat by the mountains and the short expanse of water
allowed for waves to build up, we could move forward, pitching and
tossing toward our destination. The wind obliged us by gradually di-
minishing. The sea remained stirred up for several more days, but by
the time we reached the Bay of Panama the storm had become only a
memory. Hundreds of whales, about twelve to thirty feet long, wallowed in the water around us and greeted us with their waterspouts.
They seemed as contented and carefree as cows in a pasture. During
our last night in the Pacific we accidentally bumped into a whale, but
it apparently assumed that the blow was unintentional and did not
charge our ship in Moby Dick fashion.

Entering Balboa harbor early in the morning, we went immediately to the canal, passed through it entirely that day, and moored before
nightfall at a pier in Coco Solo, on the Atlantic side. We stayed at Coco
Solo for four days, and everyone on the ship had two liberty nights.
The second time around, however, the place seemed to have lost its
bizarre wartime character. The growing resentment of Panamanians
toward Americans was evident. Besides, getting home was the high
time that was now on our minds.

We got underway for the week-long journey to Charleston, South
Carolina, in company with other LCIs and one LSM, a ship that carried both troops and tanks and opened in the bow. It was about twice
the size of an LCI and wallowed like a tub in the water in the manner
of an LST. As we traveled along, we could not help noticing an unusual amount of jetsam floating in the water in the wake of the other ships.
We had to dodge from time to time to keep from fouling our screws.
The ships were scuttling as much as they could spare of their Title C
supplies, and we soon began to follow suit. Title C was a broad Navy
category of expendable marine supplies. All the ships were cleaning out
their supply lockers in wholesale fashion, anticipating that their decommissioning process would be simplified if they had a minimum of
Title C supplies on hand to account for. Heavy objects such as cans of

paint sank to the bottom of the ocean, but lighter items such as line floated for days. A tracker could follow our entire journey from Panama to South Carolina by the trail of Title C in our wake.

We reached Charleston on March 27 and this time did *not* go aground in the middle of the Cooper River. We assumed that we would each receive at least a week's leave as soon as we reached port, but that was not to be. Russell Tye, who had gotten only a three-day pass when we had been at Charleston a year earlier, was now given two weeks' leave to visit his family, apply for return to college, and plan his wedding later in the spring. I agreed to be best man at his wedding, assuming that by then I would be free of the service. Clark and I, however, and a cadre of the crew remained aboard for the decommissioning procedure.

Some LCIs remained in commission after the war as training ships for the Naval Reserves, even journeying far up navigable rivers to inland training centers such as Chicago and Cincinnati. Most LCIs, however, including ours, became part of the "mothball fleet." We had to dismount our 20-millimeter guns and transfer them and their ammunition ashore. All maps and charts and navigational instruments went to appropriate offices ashore, though I managed to seize as souvenirs some "top secret" charts and profile reconstructions of the Normandy coastline. We destroyed or turned in all codes and ciphers. We resisted the strong temptation to keep small arms and binoculars. Reluctantly, we gave up the ship's radio and its loudspeaker. We heard rumors that the radio would be smashed, in compliance with a wartime agreement between Philco and the government that none of its government-issue radios would be dumped on the postwar market. We had no way of knowing the truth about this, but it fitted our Depression Era suspicion of big business that carried over into the war period. We also expected a return to economic depression as soon as the war was over. Everyone in the country was surprised at the postwar boom that resulted from conversion to a peacetime economy and the beginning of the cold war.

While permanent equipment of the ship had to be transferred formally to the naval base ashore, even after we reached port expendable supplies continued to be dumped over the side to avoid having to list them on inventory. This practice on the part of most of the ships led to a local scandal. So much debris was soon floating in the water of the Cooper River that it became hazardous to ships moving in and out of the base. Surplus food was among the principal items of jetsam, and the Charleston newspapers had a field day reporting on the carcasses of beef floating down the river at a time when most civilians were starved for good beefsteak.

We were busy, but life did not consist entirely of work during the decommissioning process. It was April, and the Battery area of Charleston was in full bloom. As baseball season approached, Cotton Clark wandered off one day to watch the Charleston baseball club work out. They were a Class B club in the Southern League, managed by a man named Chick Autry. While watching in the bleachers, Cotton struck up a conversation with Autry, who remembered or was reminded that Cotton had once played baseball at Vanderbilt. "Cotton, how about trying out?" he asked. "I haven't had a glove on my hand for three years," Cotton replied. "I understand that," said Autry, "but we really do need a third baseman. It won't take you long to get in shape." So Cotton took a holiday from the Navy one afternoon, put on the Charleston baseball uniform and glove, and "fiddled around" at third base. Autry watched him awhile and then said, "Now, I want to hire you to play for us this summer." Cotton would be out of the Navy by then, of course. He said he would think about it, but he had already made plans to marry his college sweetheart in Nashville in July, and he also got to thinking about night rides on those broken-down buses between towns all over the Carolinas. Finally he said, "Chick, I don't think I'd better." Nevertheless, he was flattered by the offer, and never forgot it. After the war, Cotton would become a successful stockbroker in Nashville, but a part of him always regretted that he had not given a try to professional sports—or, better yet, coaching. He would have enjoyed coaching, with its opportunity for building character in young men. Each of us had to make our own painful adjustments to the new postwar world, and usually without much time for deliberation.

Having remained aboard as watch officer for the first two weeks at Charleston while Russell Tye went off on leave, I turned my duties over to Tye on April 11. On the following day, I began my separation from the service. All the personnel still attached to the ship at that point were billeted in government quarters ashore, and a continuous guard of two men was set up at the ship. The refrigeration unit and generators were secured, a final inventory was completed of all equipment remaining, and a truck loaded with the last of the ship's material pulled out for the naval storage depot. The main engines and generators acquired a coating of some sort of plastic. A decommissioning party passed its judgment on the ship's readiness for decommissioning, and finally on April 18 the tug *Josephine* came alongside. Casting off all lines from the dock, the ship moved under tow up the Wando River to its final resting place. By then the only officer still aboard was the skipper, Harold W. Clark, as LCI(L) 555 reached its mooring with other decommissioned LCIs. There was a funereal aspect of decommissioning that I have always been glad I missed. Both bow and stern anchors were dropped, each with thirty fathoms of cable, and the ship was securely tied to the other ships. While Cotton Clark saluted, the ship's ensign and commission pennant were lowered for the last time. The officers and men returned to the base aboard the tug. The ship was now no longer a naval vessel but merely the chattel property of the Sixth Naval District. I now know about the final week of the 555 only by reading the last entries in the ship's log preserved in the National Archives in Washington. By that time I had left the ship, left the Navy, and begun to grapple with postwar life.

FOURTEEN

The Past as Future

As I left the ship that had been my home for two formative, maturing years, I felt only a slight pang of separation. I did not understand yet how much the ordered, hierarchical social structure of the Navy had become a part of my inner being. Only when I had shucked off the uniform that symbolized a fixed status and fixed responsibilities did I realize how much I had come to depend on this outwardly imposed ordering of my life. Freedom had been such a rallying cry of the war years that I never realized how much of it I had surrendered in order to serve it. Freedom, now that it was mine to grasp, seemed less attractive than it had seemed as an abstraction. The Four Freedoms of wartime propaganda began to transmogrify into the four horsemen of the Apocalypse as one after another of my wartime illusions was shattered. My fear of freedom was not as intense as that of a convict released after years of incarceration, but it was in many ways similar. In the Navy I had been Somebody. Now I was Everyman. I would have to clothe myself in a new identity that was not "gratuitous issue."

Though mentally I was now a civilian, my severance from the Navy was far from total or clear-cut. The Navy placed me on inactive reserve as of the end of my accumulated leave, about a month and a half later. My term of active duty had been two years, ten months, and twenty-nine days. I would officially be in the Navy and would continue to draw my pay until the end of my terminal leave. After that, my only indication of continued readiness for active duty was to take one Navy correspondence course. That little was enough for the Navy in 1954 to offer me a promotion to full lieutenant, but my refusal to qualify for the promotion by taking a physical examination caused the Navy to realize that I was no longer interested.

My heart beat a little faster in both fear and eagerness as I faced the prospect of civilian life. It called for new clothes, new venues, new status. New status? Aye, there was the rub! Status was wrapped up in clothing. During my two years at sea I had grown from boyhood toward manhood. But this man I had become was a serviceman, accustomed to salutes not only from naval personnel but in another sense from the civilian world. Once stripped of the uniform that proclaimed to myself and to the world who I was, where would I be? I might be right back where I came from, a boy again, shy again, proud of my ability but petrified by the need to assert it. To say the least, I was ambivalent about plunging into the anonymous pool of civilian life. While outwardly I was rushing forward toward this new phase of my life, inwardly I was a swirling eddy of hesitation and self-doubt. My breakup with Sylvia was both a cause and a symptom of all my uncertainties.

I had had considerable time on the long voyage home to ponder about what I wanted to be and do in civilian life. First things first, I thought. Pushing thoughts of Sylvia to the back of my mind, I simultaneously brought Diana toward the forefront. I believed that I had a clear plan, to go to New York City, and as soon as possible thereafter to propose to Diana. She had graduated from college in December and had moved almost immediately to New York, finding a lowly, entry-level job in a famous advertising agency on Madison Avenue. Though I was still on the rebound from my relationship with Sylvia, I was now ready, at least in my Walter Mitty dreams, to sweep Diana off her feet by proposing marriage. It did not even occur to me that she might reject me, either for a career or for another man.

My second objective, to prepare myself for a civilian career, seemed equally attainable—until I actually attempted it. I had already decided, months earlier, that I would become a historian. I had even taken the decisive step of applying for a graduate fellowship in history. My plan was to get a master's degree at Vanderbilt and then make up my mind whether to stay there for a doctorate or move on to another institution or possibly another career field.

There were also many mundane decisions to make. Though I could still fit into my old civvies, I needed more stylish clothes if a-wooing I would go. I must have the double-breasted suit then coming into fashion. Before I could cut a dashing figure as a civilian, I would also require major dental work to improve my snaggletoothed smile. Though I had never had time for dentistry during my sea duty, I was determined to force the Navy to pay for my teeth, my only war wound, while I was still formally a serviceman on my six-week terminal leave. It came to me in a flash that I could combine my trip to New York to court Diana with an extended visit to the Brooklyn naval hospital for dental work.

My mind swirled with these plans, but first I needed to make a duty visit home, secure my father's help in buying my new wardrobe, and gather what other resources were needed for the plunge back into civilian life. My entire family, I found, was in transition to peacetime life. My brother Allen was stuck at the Army quartermaster depot in Wilmington, Delaware, unable to get a discharge because of the strategic importance of the Quartermaster Corps during the downsizing of the military, but he too had college plans under the GI Bill. Brother George (Buddy) had spent several months in the occupation of Germany but was now out of the service, living with his wife near Pennsylvania State University, where he would later finish college and graduate school in electronic engineering. My sister Stella had just graduated from the University of Georgia and was living at home awaiting admission to graduate school in Romance languages. Harriet, the youngest, was an undergraduate at the Georgia State College for Women in Milledgeville, majoring in child study with the expectation of working in my mother's nursery school. At this stage of our lives, with the prospect of aid from the GI Bill of Rights for the three boys, we were a school-going family. My father could never have put all five of us through college without the GI Bill, nor without the added family income from my mother's nursery school. It still continued, for despite the shutting down of most war industries, both parents in many families continued to work outside their homes and needed nursery schools to serve in loco parentis.

My father took charge of my outward adjustment to civilian life. He had always been a smart dresser, and as far as his means allowed had always kept abreast of the latest fashions. This was one trait that I did not inherit, but my father introduced me to his tailor, who quickly outfitted me with several suits tapered to fit my thirty-inch waist. I remember particularly well a brown, double-breasted tweed. It was not only in style but about as far from a Navy uniform as I could find.

My father also brought me up to date on local politics, and I registered in time to vote in the Democratic primary for the liberal woman incumbent in my congressional district, Helen Douglas Rankin. She had succeeded Robert Ramspeck, an excellent congressman who had resigned in anger when voters complained of his sponsoring a congressional pay raise during the war to keep in step with wartime inflation. Rankin was several shades more liberal than my father, but he greatly admired her personally and urged me to vote for her. I recall standing with my father in a line about a block long in front of the county courthouse in Decatur waiting to vote. There was an equally long separate line of persons of color, also waiting to vote. I remember expressing my disgust that the blacks had to stand in a separate line, while my father was outraged that blacks were even voting. These were the opening salvos on a subject about which my father and I would debate heatedly over the years and about which we would diverge ever more widely. Racial justice would become a central feature of my inevitable, quiet rebellion against my father. In this instance, however, we were both voting for the same candidate. She lost the nomination, then got many votes as a write-in candidate in the general election but lost.

As soon as possible I left home for New York. I stayed in the leading midtown hotels, the Astor, the McAlpin, and even the Waldorf-Astoria, one after another for a few days each. I moved frequently because, even though the war was over, hotel space in New York was still in great demand, and I could never get a room for an entire week. Also, I was undecided about just how long I would be in town. Because Diana had to work, I was left to my own devices to amuse myself all day. But around five o'clock I would be waiting at the entrance to her Madison Avenue office building to find her in the crowd that came rushing out of the elevators. We went out for drinks and dinner, to a show or a movie, or sometimes to an art gallery to select prints, mostly of French impressionists, to decorate her room. Then, sometime before midnight, I would escort her back to the apartment house for young women where her parents had insisted that she live. I wonder whether there are still such dormitories in the Big Apple today. I wondered even then, in that far-off innocent time, that there were such places. During my days, I explored Manhattan from end to end. I waited and waited for just the auspicious moment to spring my marriage proposal.

Some days I dabbled in research of a kind at the New York Public Library—the main building downtown, with the fat-assed lions guarding its entrance. I remember particularly one of the topics I explored, the riddle of Ayn Rand. During my idle hours aboard ship I had read Ayn Rand's *Fountainhead*, and, like many another impressionable youth of my generation I was captured by its narrative power and half-persuaded by its case for radical individualism. I found a cure of sorts in the New York Public Library. The antidote was supplied by Ayn Rand herself in the form of an unpublished play she had written in the thirties, a humorless anti-Communist rant. The existence of this play suggested that Ayn Rand's conservative social views in *The Fountainhead* were a priori rather than developed as a logical extension out of the plot of her book. Thus I was enabled to separate Rand's doctrines from their literary packaging and free myself from her web. This intellectual self-liberation was an important part of my growing up. In the future, no book would be my master, but rather my servant or my good companion.

Diana was suspiciously eager to see the inside of the posh Hotel Pierre, near Columbus Circle. I didn't quite understand why, but I agreed to take her there one day for lunch, which I figured would be more within my means than dinner. Its carpeted interior was very dark—we could barely see across the restaurant. In this gloaming, the looming waiter offered me what I presumed was the sugar bowl. I took a teaspoonful and dropped it in my coffee. The cup foamed and bubbled like a cauldron for about a minute. What I thought was sugar turned out to be saccharine. Even that long after the war was over, there was still a civilian sugar shortage, but as a serviceman I had little awareness of such things. I drank the coffee anyhow, with an air of bravado, while Diana giggled. It probably had enough saccharine to give cancer to a white rat my size.

Diana confessed eventually that the real reason she had dragged me to the Pierre was that my rival suitor was staying there. She probably hoped to catch a glimpse of him, or excite his jealousy, or simply wanted to study the atmosphere he lived in. In any case, her using me thus was unflattering. I had actually known about this young man several years earlier, and had suppressed the memory. I saw him once during a summer vacation at St. Simon's Island on the coast of Georgia, just before I went into the service. He was staying at the more posh resort on the other side of the island. He was a banker's son, with more money and maybe better looks than I. But maybe he was not as smart as I was, and totally lacked a sense of humor. He was smart enough or young enough to avoid wartime service and had just graduated from college. Diana and I did not see him at the Pierre, or at least I didn't, but a few days later Diana persuaded us both to attend a baseball game with her à trois, at Yankee Stadium. He and I were barely civil to each other, and I don't remember much about the game. I outwaited him. He left town after a few days, but the very fact of his existence brought my relationship with Diana to a crisis.

I thought the time had come to propose to Diana, though it probably was the worst time I could have chosen. I gave more thought to the choice of just the right setting of privacy and quiet, an ambience hard to find in noisy Manhattan. Finally, I thought I had a clue. I maneuvered Diana into a horsedrawn cab around Columbus Circle. There, with the gentle clop-clop of the horse's hooves as accompaniment, out of earshot of the cabbie outside, I pled my case as best I could. I thought I was quite persuasive, and I fully expected her acceptance. To my astonishment she turned me down. She was obviously amused by my offer, and said she was flattered. But she had come to New York to give a career a try, she said, and would not be ready to consider marriage for several years. I was devastated. My ego was already shaken by the insecurities of civilian life. It collapsed under the weight of this rejection. I felt like a fool. I had turned down Sylvia, who loved me, only to pursue this flirt! The parallels between my treatment of Sylvia and Diana's treatment of me did not even occur to me at the time, but they certainly do now.

I did my best to repair the damage. I made Diana promise not to marry anyone else for a while, least of all my rival, and I mustered all my talent for satire to point out the many ways in which my rival was unworthy. I said he would bore her to death. She agreed to think further about my proposal, but offered no grounds for hope. When I saw her again in Atlanta that summer, nothing had changed. She never married me, but on the other hand she never married my rival, either. There was some small satisfaction in that.

Meanwhile I found my way to the Brooklyn Navy Yard and presented the case for my bridgework. That did not work out any better than my marriage proposal. Maybe it was just hard for a snaggletooth to be persuasive. The Navy dentists evaded my demands by saying the work would take longer than my remaining terminal leave. In the end, I had to go to a private dentist in Atlanta that summer and pay for the work myself. Now that I was at the Navy Yard, however, I seized the opportunity to look up my high school friend June, whom I had not seen since I visited her in Elizabeth, New Jersey, while I was in midshipmen's school. I made a date with June for a night when Diana was busy, plied her with more drink than she was used to, and tried to find in her some solace for my disappointment with Diana. I was making out with her in the backseat of a taxi when she suddenly vomited all over the backseat. That certainly put the quietus on whatever my intentions were. We got out, gave the hacker a large tip to stop his grumbling, and hailed another taxi to get her back to her quarters. We parted forlornly, and that was the last time I ever saw her. I spent another frustrating evening with a woman I picked up at the Astor Bar. She turned out to be a lesbian who was using me to get into a certain nightclub to see her girlfriend. They would not have admitted her without an escort. When the two women began kissing each other behind my back, I figured out that I was the patsy, but I was drunk enough or naive enough to try to lure her away from the other woman. I was soon so drunk that I allowed a stand-up comedian in the night club to use me with my southern accent as the straight man in his act. The two girls and I left with another serviceman they had picked up, but somewhere along the way they dumped me on a street corner and went off as a threesome. It seemed to be my night to be abused and scorned.

As my money ran short, I moved from a hotel to a rooming house to stretch my limited means. I also entered a federal employment office seeking a job that would allow me to linger a while longer in New York. I had had little experience in job-hunting, but I soon discovered that the prospect of going up to a stranger and asking for a job paralyzed me. The interviewing officer declared me overqualified for any of the jobs he had available, and advised me to go back where I came from. My plans to return to college, he said, made me a poor prospect anyhow for a permanent job. It was clearly time for me to brush New York's dust from my heels. I couldn't make it there. Maybe not anywhere.

Saying good-bye to Diana, I left New York and high hopes behind and hitchhiked home to save money. On the way I visited both of my brothers, Allen in Wilmington and Buddy near Penn State. I journeyed on to Middlesboro, Kentucky, arriving in time to serve as best man in Russell Tye's wedding.

Finally I reached home with most of the summer yawning before me. My father found me a temporary job working for the U.S. Department of Agriculture. Every day for several weeks I traveled by train to Macon, a mill town about fifty miles south of Atlanta. A Macon flour mill had sold hundreds of carloads of flour to be shipped to Europe for distribution to war refugees by UNRRA, the United Nations relief agency. It was my job to take samples of flour in each carload for Department of Agriculture testing and approval. I would climb up in each freight car, select a flour sack at random, open it and scoop out enough flour to fill a large tin sample container, mark the car number on a tag, and lock the car with a metal government seal. This was dusty work for a white-collar man. By the end of the day more than my collar was white. I had about twenty-five samples in a large canvas bag slung over my shoulder, and flour on my clothes from head to foot. No matter how hard I slapped my my pants, I was still dusty from hair to shoe tops. I wore a tie to try to give a little class to my appearance, but when I returned to the passenger depot to board my train for home each day, the conductor threatened not to let me ride the train. Each day his manner grew more hostile. He did not want me to sit down in his seats. I stared him down and haughtily informed him that I was a federal agent and had a perfect right to board the train, but each day he cast doubt on whether I would get home that night. Divested as I was of my former rank and uniform, the civilian world seemed to me a bleak landscape of hazards and humiliations.

After my temporary job mercifully came to an end, I spent the remainder of the summer of 1946 in Decatur with my parents, moping about the house in desultory search of a goal or even a focus. I burned Diana's letters one afternoon in the trash incinerator in our backyard, but for some reason I kept all of Sylvia's letters. Sometime that summer I renewed a slow-motion correspondence with my English friend Kay. Weeks would pass between letters, and my heart was not in this warmed-over romance. My father was gone all day, deeply preoccupied with his own adjustments to postwar changes in his work, but my mother was there with her nursery school, in which she was assisted by another woman and occasionally by my sister Harriet, who was home for the summer from college. As the only male adult around the house, I attracted a large following among the nursery school children. The more indifferent I was to them, the more eagerly they followed my every move.

I found a few useful chores to do around the house. The wooden garage built over a ravine behind the house, which we had never used, finally collapsed and fell over the steep hill into the creek. Its granite facade also fell, and I used the stones to build and cement a granite wall about a foot and a half high across the end of the driveway, with a small spillway for the rainwater that coursed down the driveway. The nursery children took a keen interest in my work.

In the fall of 1946 I took the train to Nashville and entered graduate school at Vanderbilt University, with a fellowship in history to supplement my monthly stipend from the GI Bill of Rights. I moved into a large room in Wesley Hall, a rather ramshackle building directly across the street from the classroom buildings and wooded campus. Wesley Hall had formerly been a YMCA college. It had a gym and indoor pool and rooms for about seventy students on the fourth floor. I was delighted by the prospect of such an immediately available pool, and I began to swim laps and practice sprints on the very first day.

I had two roommates, Joe Martin and Bob Blevins, both also working on master's degrees. Joe was a few years older than I, an Army veteran of three years' combat in the European theater, rather thin and nervous, as though he had seen too much of the war. He was married, and left town about every second weekend to stay a while with his wife and son. He was something of a loner but otherwise congenial, and he was wise and generous with his car, an old prewar clunker that required water in its radiator from time to time.

Bob Blevins was about my age, twenty pounds overweight and rather pompous, too much a glad-hander to suit my taste, but on the whole a good companion until later, when we became rivals. After graduating from a small Pennsylvania college, he had spent the remainder of the war years in an essential civilian occupation, as a teacher in a one-room school in the Pennsylvania mountains. He majored in English, one of the stronger disciplines at Vanderbilt. Bob and I soon became regular dinner companions at the Peabody College cafeteria a couple of blocks up the road from our dormitory, where we hoped to meet the women students who predominated on that campus. Vanderbilt's student body was predominantly male, though there were a substantial number of women undergraduate and graduate students.

I enrolled in graduate classes and also worked as a teaching assistant in the American history survey course taught by Professor Frank Owsley, the history department star in both scholarship and teaching. In this new environment I had a severe attack of the shyness that had plagued me since the beginning of adolescence and was now exacerbated by my changed circumstances, when I doffed my uniform for civvies and became an insecure graduate student. I was now in an alien community in which I knew none of my cohorts and was at the mercy of my professors.

To make matters worse, the university itself was in the throes of complex changes, most of them for the good but accompanied by bitter quarreling between professors and administrators. The end of the war brought a large expansion of both undergraduates and graduate students under the impetus of the GI Bill of Rights. Big-time football also returned at the insistence of alumni and trustees, and over the protests of faculty. The Fugitives and Agrarians who had dominated the arts and humanities faculty at Vanderbilt in the 1930s had largely scattered to other institutions by the end of the war, but enough of them remained to quarrel with the efforts of the university administration to achieve a more urban outlook and a higher national academic standing.

When, about six months before my arrival, Chancellor O. C. Carmichael resigned to head the Carnegie Endowment for the Advancement of Teaching, a heated contest developed over his successor. Philip Davidson, dean of the Graduate School, was the faculty's choice for chancellor, but the trustees quickly vetoed that, apparently on the ground that he was soft on football and too liberal to suit their tastes. They chose instead C. Harvie Branscomb, dean of theology at Duke University, to lead the campus into the new era. Branscomb's leadership later faltered in the civil rights crisis of the 1960s, but for the moment he was a key figure in Vanderbilt's move from provincial to national university. He arrived about the same time I did.

Though Dean Davidson had been the faculty favorite during the chancellorship debate, he was now caught in the middle between chancellor and faculty and forced to execute sometimes unpopular decisions in an atmosphere of turmoil and suspicion. I was grateful for his sponsorship. Since I had not gone through the customary channels of selection as a history student on fellowship, however, I felt uncertain of the welcome of some of my history professors. Perhaps I imagined more faculty skepticism about me than actually existed.

Soon after my arrival at Vanderbilt, all of the entering M.A. students were required to take the Graduate Record Exam. I believe it was the first time this national examination was given, at least at Vanderbilt. My score on the history portion of the exam was mediocre, which was understandable for one who had not been an undergraduate history major, but my score on the verbal and quantitative sections was at the top of the class, and particularly high in the verbal category. This did not surprise me, since I had been at the top of my college freshman class on its placement examination. It did surprise my history professors, however, and they began to treat me with more respect. I partially overcame the impression my inarticulate shyness had created, and, with my self-confidence thus boosted, I began to come out of my shell and take more of a part in seminar discussions.

One of my courses was a historiography seminar taught by the head of the history department, William C. Binkley, who also edited the

Journal of Southern History. His method was oral discussion, and later seminar papers on the nineteenth-century master historians. My own report was on Justin Winsor, author of a multivolume *Narrative and Critical History of America*. Since I had not been an undergraduate history major, historiography was a foreign language to me. When called upon, I was literally tongue-tied, atremble and incoherent, in marked contrast to the glib students around me. In the end I squeezed out a B, largely on the strength of my written paper, but my memory of that seminar is of almost unmitigated embarrassment. Despite his relatively high standing as a historian, Binkley seemed to me pedantic and sarcastic, more a taskmaster than a teacher, and I obviously did not make a great impression on him.

Frank Owsley's seminar on the Old South, on the other hand, was more to my liking. It reflected his own jovial, shepherding spirit. I enjoyed my paper for him on an early southern agricultural reformer. Owsley was not a very demanding teacher, but his own example as a scholar inspired us to do our best to emulate him. He had recently pioneered in the use of the manuscript census for his book on the yeoman farmers of the Old South. Much of our seminar time was taken up by his stories and jokes, always witty but not always germane and sometimes taking the form of "darky" stories. Though I did not unqualifiedly approve of his teaching methods, when the time came I chose him as my thesis adviser.

Sometime in January, Professor Owsley accepted my proposal for an M.A. thesis on a member of Jackson's "kitchen cabinet," William B. Lewis, whose papers I managed to buy on microfilm from the Pierpont Morgan Library in New York, and supplemented with local sources at the Tennessee State Library and the Tennessee Historical Society. I do not recall much advice on my thesis, but that may have been because I simply went to work on my own, in the belief that writing was an individual matter.

Peabody College for Teachers was just across Hillsboro Road and up a block from Vanderbilt, and students from the two schools often ate in one another's cafeterias in order to broaden our circle of acquaintances. One evening, as my roommate Bob Blevins and I were on our way to the Peabody cafeteria in hope of meeting girls, we passed two

Peabody girls walking in the opposite direction, possibly headed to the Vanderbilt cafeteria but more probably to a steakhouse further along on Hillsboro Road. Bob knew them and spoke to them but speeded his walking pace, not bothering to introduce me. One of the two girls in particular caught my fancy, a rather tall brunette with long hair over her shoulders, a nice slim body, and beautiful hazel eyes. I couldn't understand why Bob so impatiently moved on toward Peabody cafeteria. A day or so later, when Bob and I were carrying our trays from the Peabody cafeteria line to a table, we saw the same pair of Peabody roommates again, but Bob pointedly ignored them and went on to another table. When the two girls finished their meal, however, they came over to our table for a chat, much to Bob's discomfort. The one I had had my eye on introduced herself. She was Sadie Morton, and her friend was Delaine Pierce, both from West Virginia. We offered to walk them back to their dormitory, but they told us that Delaine had some work to do in the Vanderbilt library. Just as they probably expected, I somehow got rid of Bob and turned up at the Vanderbilt library about the time they reached it via their dormitory room. Since I had stack privileges, I was able to speed up the retrieval of the books that Delaine needed, and thus got into her good graces. But it was Sadie I was really interested in, despite Bob's emphatic claim on her, and I sensed that she liked my understated humor better that Bob's loud bluster. She was a more serious conversationalist than Delaine, who was animated and sexy but somewhat scatterbrained. I secretly plotted to steal Sadie away from Bob somehow.

A few days later we ran into Sadie and Delaine again in the cafeteria, and they invited us to a dance given by their dormitory that weekend. We gave evasive answers, because we had already made plans to go to a dance at Ward-Belmont College, a sort of "finishing school" a few blocks past Peabody along Hillsboro Road. After we had spent about an hour at the Ward-Belmont dance, however, Bob and I both decided we would rather be at the Peabody dance. So we joined it already in full swing. Sadie and Delaine were there in their long dresses as hostesses of the dance. Bob made a beeline for Sadie and took her out on the dance floor. I asked Delaine to dance, but as soon as someone cut in on me, I found Sadie again and cut in. Bob probably noticed her beaming smile. I whirled Sadie around the floor with what I thought was Astaire-like grace, though she explained to me later that dancing was not my forte. In spite of that, however, I had the feeling she liked me, and we had such a good time together that we did not notice that Bob had given up and left the scene.

Somehow, over the course of the next weeks or months, I gradually maneuvered to move Delaine out of the picture and had Sadie all to myself. We met at the library, stage-whispering until others insisted on silence. We wandered around the steps of a replica of the Parthenon in a public park near the campuses, a relic of a Nashville commercial exposition many years earlier. We also spent much time at the movies, of course, where a certain kind of silent communication was the rule. Eventually I lured Sadie all the way to the Grand Ole Opry itself, in downtown Nashville at the great barn of Ryman Auditorium.

Though Bob had the earliest claim on Sadie's affections, it had never been a serious involvement until my own interest in her aroused his jealousy. He did not take kindly to my cutting him out, however, and could not even understand it, as he considered himself more of a ladies' man than my scrawny, unprepossessing self. About a month after the West Dormitory dance, Sadie and I were sharing a meal in one of the hole-in-the-wall eateries near the campus when someone put a nickel in the jukebox and it played "The Tennessee Waltz" over and over. It was then at its height as a popular song. We broke out in laughter as the lyrics sank into our consciousness. It was as if Bob had taken his sad tale of woe to a Nashville songwriter: "I was waltzing my darling to the Tennessee Waltz, when my best friend, he stole her away."

In November of 1946 I attended my first historical convention, the meeting of the Southern Historical Association at Birmingham. It was only about a hundred miles from Nashville, and five or six of us graduate students piled into someone's broken-down prewar automobile for the trip. I recall frequent stops as we went over the mountains to fill the steaming radiator. We checked into the ramshackle headquarters hotel and formed a part of the audience for the sessions. The Southern Historical Association had been founded only a few years before the war, and had been forced by gas rationing and dwindling active membership to miss annual meetings for several immediately preceding years. The 1946 meeting was attended by about a hundred members, and there were only eight sessions in addition to the presidential address. My most vivid memory of the convention was of a wild drinking party of male and female graduate students in our room that went on into the wee hours and of my painful hangover the next day.

Wandering through the hotel lobby, I also saw close up some of the great and near-great historians of the day. Professors Owsley and Binkley and Dean Davidson took prominent roles in the meeting and were the centers of conversational gatherings. We graduate students hung about on the fringes but tried to avoid attracting attention. Francis B. Simkins, with whose textbook, *The Old South and the New,* we were all acquainted, could be observed in the back of one of the baroque meeting rooms snoring loudly from time to time until poked in the ribs. Being but a lowly graduate student, I probably missed or misunderstood some of the highlights of the meeting.

Back at Vanderbilt, I took full advantage of having an indoor swimming pool in my dormitory building. I organized a Vanderbilt swimming team and persuaded the athletic department to appoint me as a player-coach. We competed against several local teams and even went as far as Knoxville to swim against the University of Tennessee. We lost, but not overwhelmingly, and I managed to win one of my races and tie another. Swimming was a part of my adolescence that I was reluctant to give up. I even persuaded Sadie to watch me from the bleachers in one of our local meets.

By the time of the Christmas break, Sadie and I had become such close companions that I invited myself to visit her and meet her family. After spending Christmas Day with my parents, I boarded the train for Cincinnati, took the C & O to Charleston, and rode an old, ramshackle bus on a dark and snowy night along the Kanawha River and up a long hollow to the mining town of Winifrede, where Sadie's father was the mine superintendent. When I asked the bus driver to let me out at her house, my visit to the boss's daughter became the main topic of whispered conversation among the miners on the bus. The driver let me out at the bottom of their driveway and pointed the way to the brightly lit house. As I approached the gate, the family dogs barked fiercely, one of them small and yippy, the other a huge brown dog with a throaty woof. Sadie's brother Jack came out to find out the source of the commotion and rescued me from the dogs. I met her father, mother, and what seemed an endless number of brothers and her older sister. She was the "baby" of the family. I don't know what Sadie's family thought of me—they didn't wear their feelings on their sleeves—but they were evidently impressed that I was smart enough to find my way to their secluded "holler" unaided. Sadie's description of me in her letters home had probably led them to wonder how I would look. She had written that I was broad-shouldered but thin, and with a tiny waist. Her mother later told me that from Sadie's description they had expected me to resemble a wasp.

The day after my arrival, Sadie's sister Mary entrusted her Edsel to my care and we drove into Charleston for a movie. There was snow and ice on the streets, and my most vivid memory of that drive was when Sadie directed me to turn the wrong way down a one-way street. After looking at my Georgia license and the car's Maryland registration, a policeman gently warned me when in a strange city to watch the other traffic and move in the same direction.

Returning to the Vanderbilt campus, I enrolled in a new set of classes, including a political science course from Denna Frank Fleming, a student of the League of Nations and later a pioneer revisionist historian of the cold war. Henry Lee Swint taught me United States social and intellectual history, but with a peculiarly southern focus. He heaped sarcasm on most of the views I expressed and did not seem to have any higher regard for me than I had for him or his course. I decided I should try to complete my M.A. program in a single year—that was still possible in those days—and look elsewhere for my doctoral training. I would seek a graduate program with a more national and cosmopolitan outlook, not realizing that Vanderbilt itself and its history department were moving in the same direction.

I applied for admission to Harvard and Columbia, both of which responded that they were swamped with applicants in the postwar educational boom stimulated by the GI Bill and could not admit me. At Johns Hopkins University, however, I made a special case for admission. Years before while I was an undergraduate at Emory, my classics professor was a great admirer of C. Vann Woodward, who had graduated from Emory, and he lent me his copy of Woodward's classic biography of Tom Watson, the Populist champion of equality in his earlier years and later a racial bigot. Woodward's ironic tone had appealed to me, and when I discovered that Woodward was teaching at Johns Hopkins I made the point that I hoped to study under his direction. That may have had nothing to do with their decision to admit me, but I have always felt that maybe it established my claim to clarity of purpose in my graduate study. Howsoever it may have come about, sometime in the spring of 1947 I heard from Johns Hopkins that I was admitted with a job as a teaching assistant. The pay would be meager, but when combined with my cache of war bonds and my GI Bill stipend it would support me—and perhaps another!—in rude comfort. It seemed to me that I could dimly see ahead a way out of my agony of postwar readjustment toward a career as a historian and teacher. The assistantship would be a test of whether anyone as tongue-tied as I could be an effective teacher.

During the winter and spring I began serious research on my M.A. thesis, in whatever time I could spare from my classes, my teaching assistantship (which turned out to be largely a matter of grading papers), my swimming team, and my courting of Sadie. It was a tall order, but in those days I had boundless energy. The microfilm of William B. Lewis's correspondence revealed him to be not a significant adviser of President Andrew Jackson but rather a White House factotum who ran the president's small errands both personal and political. He was in charge of ridding the White House of bedbugs, for example, and defended the president and his wife from slanders in the public press. The Lewis Papers were my principal source, but since Lewis had spent many years in Nashville before Jackson's presidency and returned there afterward, I sought to embellish my account with local sources.

My professors warned me in advance that the director of the Tennessee Historical Society and the chief librarian of the Tennessee State Library, whose buildings were only about a hundred yards apart, were not on speaking terms with one another. I decided on the strategy of completing all of my work with one of them before approaching the other, and never mentioning the other's name. Territorial claims and turf control loomed large in those days before professionalism took over in the historical societies and archives, and such fuss and feathers are not unknown even today. I had been forewarned sufficiently to watch my step in the minefields of local history, but even the most cautious researcher was in danger of being denied access to documents. I first approached the director of the historical society, a prissy little man in a rumpled suit who was suspicious of my credentials but accepted my letter from Professor Owsley as an indication of serious purpose. As I came to his office day after day he encouraged me to wade through countless collections that contained only a few orts of germane information, mostly footnote rather than text material. My presence day after day as the only researcher perhaps relieved his loneliness and gave meaning to his work, but it was of little help to me. Finally, I told him that I felt I had exhausted the resources of his holdings and made the mistake of saying that next day I would be going to the Tennessee State Library.

Next morning, as I arrived at the State Library just at opening time, my heart sank when I saw the director of the Historical Society headed in the same direction. As I approached the desk to make inquiries about certain collections I knew to be there, he rushed up, declared in a loud voice that nobody there knew what was in their holdings, and tried to place my orders for me. I finally had to ask him to leave, explaining as politely as I could that his presence was embarrassing me. He abandoned his proprietary claim on me and left in a huff, but the damage had been done. It did not help that the old battle-ax in charge, the widow of the previous librarian, came from the same county as my father and remembered him as the man who had demanded that her late husband return the copy of the Harlan family genealogy he had borrowed. I had heard of that ancient quarrel many times, but had hoped she might have forgotten. Not only the Librarian but all of her assistants seemed to consider me as an interloper, and only with great difficulty and forbearance was I able to coax them into letting me see their pertinent documents.

As I began to shape my notes into a coherent narrative of the career of a small-time politician I began to gain a sense of the nature of history. I had thought of history originally as epic narrative, filled with epic heroes. But there was nothing epic about William B. Lewis. He was a grubby little machine politician and social climber, using his closeness to the White House to arrange an upscale marriage for his daughter. An important element of history must always be the telling of salutary and cautionary tales, but history also affords opportunities for analysis of human experience and human character. History is thus akin to literature as a part of the humanities that help us understand ourselves. I can see now that my account of William B. Lewis lacked any depth of understanding of the politics and political culture of the Jacksonian era that might have come from immersion in the historical literature. I was, however, groping toward the understanding that informs social history, the understanding that history is about the people, not merely about leaders and impersonal social forces.

Though I wrestled with history by day, I wrestled with Sadie Morton by night. My roommate Joe Martin took pity on us young lovers and lent us his ancient car to drive to lovers' lanes in the outer suburbs of Nashville. Our favorite drive was out past Belle Meade mansion to Percy Warner Park. We spent hours there on spring nights gazing at the stars and exchanging confidences.

Sadie and I traveled mostly alone, but I also remember dances together at Peabody, double-dating with a childhood friend then living in Nashville, and going far out in the country to a party given by Cotton Clark, my former skipper, and his wife. Cotton was by now caught up in the milieu of the business world, and probably could not understand how the academic life could attract me, but he was as full of good humor and generosity as ever and made me feel at home in his alien environment, which we would describe today as "yuppy." On another occasion I accompanied Cotton to Cookeville, where he officiated at a college baseball game as the only way he could now "loosen up the ol' wing."

When the spring break came I persuaded Sadie to meet my parents. When my father asked her if she would like a martini, she first declined because she thought she should. I interrupted to say, "Of course, she would." She took the drink and sipped it like a trouper. I decided that anyone who could handle one of my father's ten-to-one martinis should be a member of the family. I proposed to Sadie at the next opportunity, the following night after a party with some old schoolmates on North Decatur Road. I was ready with elaborate arguments, but to my surprise she immediately accepted. It required another trip back home about a month later, however, to pick out the engagement ring with my father's help. He took me to one of his pawnbroker friends in downtown Atlanta, a man who had seen him through hard times during the depression years. It must have been a pretty good ring he sold me, for Sadie is still wearing it.

When the spring term ended, Sadie went home for the summer and I stayed on at Wesley Hall to write my thesis, my last requirement for the M.A. degree. When I finished it to my satisfaction, about midsummer, I mailed it off to Professor Owsley, who was teaching the summer session at the University of Maryland in College Park. After giving him about two weeks to read it, I took the train to Washington and rode the trolley to College Park. Professor Owsley and I sat on the ground under a beautiful old oak tree in front of Taliaferro Hall, only about a hundred yards from my present office where I am writing this memoir, and discussed my thesis. He seemed rather surprised that I had managed to write it without help, and may even have completely forgotten it. He was pleased with my lively writing style, however, and made only a few minor suggestions. He generously encouraged my future career despite the fact that I had chosen to move on to Johns Hopkins. In effect, he welcomed me into the historical fraternity. Then Owsley began to describe his own difficulties at the University of Maryland. The history department there was filled with Communists, he said in a conspiratorial whisper. I think the truth was that as a southern conservative free-thinking northern liberals sounded subversive to him.

Leaving my meeting with Professor Owsley feeling elated that he had thought so well of my thesis, I decided to test a bit of family lore passed on to me by my father, that my great-grandfather Thomas Jefferson Dorsett had been a founder in the 1850s of the Maryland Agricultural College that later became the University of Maryland. Sure enough, his name appeared on a bronze plaque at the Founders' Gate, as did that of his brother. The fact that there were about a hundred other names on the plaque somewhat diminished the honor. Years later when I had become a faculty member at the University of Maryland, a cousin gave me a copy of the shares of stock in the college my great-grandfather had bought in 1856. I could say to university administrators, if necessary, "You can't fire me, I'm a stockholder." Fortunately, I never had to put that to the test.

I made the necessary changes to my manuscript and took it to my second reader, Professor Binkley. He had no comment on the text, though I suspected that he thought it too colorful to be accurate, but he dryly pointed out some peccadilloes in the bibliography. I had, for example, rendered the publisher Macmillan as MacMillan. I dutifully corrected these errors and submitted the thesis for my degree. A year later, without asking my permission, the *Tennessee Historical Quarterly* published my entire thesis in two articles. I was now a published historian.

In the late summer Sadie and I made plans for our wedding on September 6, about a week before the academic year began at Johns Hopkins. We decided on a lawn wedding in her large, gently sloping yard, a perfect spot if it did not rain. A local Presbyterian minister performed the ceremony. My entire family, including my parents, two brothers and two sisters, and my uncle Louis, came to the wedding. My brother George served as best man, while Sadie's best friend since elementary school, Frances Ann Shrewsbury, was her matron of honor. My two sisters and her sister were among the bridesmaids and made it a very family affair. The Harlan family, needless to say, was vastly outnumbered by the Mortons and their extended kin from Virginia and West Virginia, but the two families mixed well with one another.

Well before the wedding, Sadie and I made plans for our honeymoon and our accommodations at Johns Hopkins. Using Vanderbilt history department stationery, I wrote to Big Meadows Lodge, a newly built luxury hotel on the Skyline Drive, to arrange for a week's lodging. We made a trip to Baltimore, where Sadie stayed with her sister, a faculty member in the Johns Hopkins School of Nursing. We leased a second-floor apartment about five blocks from the Johns Hopkins campus from two elderly ladies who lived downstairs. We couldn't have known in midsummer that when cold weather came these ladies would bundle up in shawls and turn the thermostat down to save fuel costs, while we froze upstairs.

As the wedding day approached, I stayed with my family at a Charleston hotel and commuted to the wedding rehearsal. It rained so hard the evening before the wedding that we had to stop the car on the side of the road to wait out the storm. On the big day, however, the sun came out. A crowd of Morton relatives arrived and piled up the wedding gifts. My sister Stella brought from her summer in Mexico a large bowl of beaten Mexican silver that is still our most distinctive wedding gift. The wedding was on a Saturday, and it seemed that every miner's family in town gathered on the railroad tracks across the creek or peered through the fence into the yard. The wedding was the big event in this little town. As my brother and I waited at the foot of the lawn, the bride rode by automobile from the house down the hillside. Her five-year-old nephew accompanied her, and for months afterward he described the occasion as "when Sadie and me got married."

Standing there on the lush summer grass, Sadie and I plighted our troth. We then moved to the house, met innumerable relatives and friends, cut the wedding cake, and made our escape in a gaudily decorated car with rocks rattling inside the hub caps. At the first sizable town to the east, we got a quick car wash and after that turned fewer heads. But somewhere along the way, when we stopped at a light, we were spotted by a garrulous friend of the family who probably spread the word about the direction we were heading. We had dinner at the General Lewis Hotel in Lewisburg, and headed toward Natural Bridge, Virginia, where we planned to spend the first night. Unfortunately, we took a shortcut, which soon ended in a dirt road and finally a ditch, while the rain of the night before returned with a vengeance. We were stuck in the ditch for an hour or so until rescued by friendly passersby, and finally reached the hotel at Natural Bridge in the wee hours and thoroughly soaked. What a way to begin a honeymoon. It has rained a lot in the forty-eight years since then, however, and we are still together.

After a late sleep and a brief look at Natural Bridge, we moved on to the Skyline Drive. A fog gathered on this winding mountaintop road so thick that we could only inch along, and had to get out of the car in order to read the road signs. When we reached the lodge, they were surprised to see a couple so young. I had used Vanderbilt stationery, and they had assumed that I was at least a middle-aged professor. They usually booked honeymoon couples at another, less expensive facility down the road. We insisted on the accommodations we had arranged, however, and did not care that almost everyone we saw that week was over fifty. We only had eyes for each other. The fog lifted, and we wandered through the trees, the meadows, and the waterfalls. After several days we had a brief surprise visit from Sadie's sister, brother, sister-in-law, and five-year-old nephew Peter. He asked over and over, "Where is your living room?"

After exploring the local caverns and becoming more intimately acquainted, we returned to West Virginia to gather our belongings. After dark that night all hell broke loose outside the house as the townspeople beat on pots and pans in an old-fashioned shivaree. They refused to leave until we passed out some stale cigars and fresher candy. Only then, according to the code of the hills, were we well and truly married. Next morning we headed for Baltimore and our new life.

Louis R. Harlan is University Distinguished Professor Emeritus at the University of Maryland, College Park. He is the author of *Booker T. Washington: The Making of a Black Leader 1856–1901* (1972), winner of the Bancroft Prize, and *Booker T. Washington: The Wizard of Tuskegee, 1901–1915* (1983), winner of the Bancroft, Beveridge, and Pulitzer prizes. With Raymond W. Smock, he edited *The Booker T. Washington Papers* (University of Illinois Press, 14 volumes, 1972–89) and has written other books in African American history. He has been president of the American Historical Association, the Organization of American Historians, and the Southern Historical Association.

LIBRARY
Kendal at
Lexington